EXPLORING PREHISTORIC IDENTITY IN EUROPE

OUR CONSTRUCT OR THEIRS?

Edited by

Victoria Ginn, Rebecca Enlander and Rebecca Crozier

Oxbow Books

Oxford & Philadelphia

Published in the United Kingdom in 2014 by
OXBOW BOOKS
10 Hythe Bridge Street, Oxford OX1 2EW

and in the United States by
OXBOW BOOKS
908 Darby Road, Havertown, PA 19083

Paperback Edition: ISBN 978-1-84217-813-3
Digital Edition: ISBN 978-1-84217-747-1

A CIP record for this book is available from the British Library

Library of Congress Cataloging-in-Publication Data

Exploring prehistoric identity in Europe : our construct or theirs? / edited by Victoria Ginn, Rebecca Enlander and Rebecca Crozier.
   pages cm.
 Includes bibliographical references.
 ISBN 978-1-84217-813-3
 1. Prehistoric peoples--Europe. 2. Anthropology, Prehistoric--Europe. 3. Social archaeology--Europe. 4. Europe--Antiquities. I. Ginn, Victoria (Victoria R.)
 GN803.E98 2014
 936--dc23
                    2013047762

Printed in the United Kingdom by Hobbs the Printers, Totton, Hampshire

For a complete list of Oxbow titles, please contact:

UNITED KINGDOM
Oxbow Books
Telephone (01865) 241249, Fax (01865) 794449
Email: oxbow@oxbowbooks.com
www.oxbowbooks.com

UNITED STATES OF AMERICA
Oxbow Books
Telephone (800) 791-9354, Fax (610) 853-9146
Email: queries@casemateacademic.com
www.casemateacademic.com/oxbow

Oxbow Books is part of the Casemate Group

Cover image: Rebecca Enlander
Colour images published with generous assistance from the Marc Fitch Fund

This volume is dedicated to
Professor James Mallory, the original Indiana Jones

CONTENTS

LIST OF CONTRIBUTORS

PROFESSOR JIM MALLORY
Professor (Emeritus), School of Geography, Archaeology & Palaeoecology, Queen's
University Belfast, Belfast, BT7 1NN
Email: (j.mallory@qub.ac.uk)

DR REBECCA ENLANDER
School of Geography, Archaeology & Palaeoecology, Queen's University Belfast, Belfast,
BT7 1NN
Email: (renlander01@qub.ac.uk)

DR VICTORIA GINN
School of Geography, Archaeology & Palaeoecology, Queen's University Belfast, Belfast,
BT7 1NN
Email: (vginn01@qub.ac.uk)

SAMANTHA REITER
ESR Researcher, Forging Identities Project. Department of Anthropology, Archaeology and
Linguistics, Aarhus University
Email: (samantha.reiter@dainst.de)

DR REBECCA CROZIER
Archaeological Studies Program, Albert Hall, Lakandula Street, University of the Philippines,
(Dilman Campus), Manila
Email: (ccrozier05@qub.ac.uk)

DR SAM WALSH
Archaeology, School of Forensic and Investigative Sciences, University of Central Lancashire,
Preston, Lancashire PR1 2HE
Email: (Swalshosteo@gmail.com)

DR CAROLINE MALONE
School of Geography, Archaeology & Palaeoecology, Queen's University Belfast, Belfast,
BT7 1NN
Email: (c.malone@qub.ac.uk)

DR KERRI CLEARY
Archaeological Consultant, Cork
Email: (Kerri.Cleary@gmail.com)

Dr Eoin Grogan
Sean-Ghaeilge, Room 20, Arts Building, National University of Ireland, Maynooth
Email: (eoin.grogan@nuim.ie)

Sara Boyle
School of Geography, Archaeology & Palaeoecology, Queen's University Belfast, Belfast,
BT7 1NN
Email: (sboyle15@qub.ac.uk)

Heide Wrobel Nørgaard
ESR Researcher, Forging Identities Project. Department of Anthropology, Archaeology and
Linguistics, Aarhus University
Email: (farkhw@hum.au.dk)

Dr Dirk Brandherm
School of Geography, Archaeology & Palaeoecology, Queen's University Belfast, Belfast,
BT7 1NN
Email: (d.brandherm@qub.ac.uk)

Michael MacDonagh
National Road's Authority, Ireland
Email: (mmacdonagh100@gmail.com)

Mark Sapwell
Division of Archaeology, University of Cambridge, Downing Street, Cambridge CB2 3DZ
Email: (mas218@cam.ac.uk)

Eimear Meegan
UCD John Hume Institute of Global Irish Studies, University College Dublin, Belfield, Dublin
4, Ireland
Email: (Eimear.meegan@ucdconnect.ie)

Professor Audrey Horning
School of Geography, Archaeology & Palaeoecology, Queen's University Belfast, Belfast,
BT7 1NN
Email: (a.horning@qub.ac.uk)

Cătălin Nicolae Popa
Division of Archaeology, University of Cambridge, Downing Street, Cambridge CB2 3DZ
Email: (cnp24@cam.ac.uk)

Nicole Taylor
Christian-Albrechts Universität zu Kiel, Institut für Ur- und Frühgeschichte (Raum 140B),
Olshaunsen Strasse 40, D-24118, Kiel, Deutschland
Email: (nicole.taylor@ufg.uni-kiel.de)

Dr T. L. Thurston
Associate Professor, Department of Anthropology, SUNY Buffalo, 380 MFAC, Ellicott
Complex, Buffalo, New York
Email: (tt27@buffalo.edu)

FOREWORD

Jim Mallory

This book began its journey with an idea for a symposium conceived by three post-graduate students within the Past Cultural Change research cluster at Queen's University Belfast, of which I was then the Director. The students wished to host an event which combined theory and practice within an archaeological framework. Having obtained funding from Queen's University Student-led Initiative, The Prehistoric Society and the Northern Ireland Environment and Heritage Agency it was possible to host a two-day event that was free for all attending delegates. Student bursaries were offered to encourage travel from across the water.

The principal aim of the symposium was to address the theme of identity within a prehistoric context. This fell under the remit of one of the Council for British Archaeology's research themes: 'Archaeology in the classroom and beyond: developing local and national identities' and one of the priorities of the Heritage Council, Ireland: 'Cultural identity, territory and boundaries'. The combination of an international keynote speaker and archaeologists from the private and non-academic sectors enabled the sharing of expertise. The symposium examined identity as a relational construct expressed through material culture, variations in domestic architectural styles, and the prolonged, intermittent use of particular spaces and places. A wide range of case studies, both temporally and spatially, enabled further exploration of these thought processes. It was then possible to tease out diachronic and geographic patterns in expressions of identity. The conference also examined how our own identities have had an impact upon archaeological interpretations, both historically and currently. This had a particular resonance as the conference was held in Belfast, where, although Ireland represents a distinct geographical continuum, the archaeology has not been unaffected by the political nuances of the island.

Over 60 delegates from Ireland, Britain, Europe, and America attended the symposium. The keynote speech, *'Travelling cultures' in theoretical and archaeological perspective*, was given by Professor Helle Vandkilde (Aarhus University), one of the main coordinators of the 'Forging Identities: the mobility of culture in Bronze Age Europe' research project. The guest closing speaker was Dr Joanna Brück (University College Dublin). Due to the success of the symposium it was decided to pursue the publication. Unfortunately, as with any such project, several of the speakers were unable to contribute due to other, pressurised commitments, including Professor Helle Vandkilde and Dr Joanna Brück, among others. However, this enabled the coordinators to offer a publication opportunity to those who had presented posters at the symposium. The publication moves beyond a simple regurgitation of the papers presented at the symposium and has developed into a cohesive and important contribution to the discussion of archaeological identities. Recognition goes to the three post-graduate editors who have produced the volume in such a timely fashion while pursuing their own research agendas.

ACKNOWLEDGEMENTS

The editors would firstly like to thank all our contributors to this volume. Thanks also must go to all the delegates who attended the *Interpreting Identity* conference and who made the weekend such a success. None of it would have been possible without the support and encouragement of Professor James Mallory and Head of the School of Geography, Archaeology and Palaeoecology: Professor Keith Bennett. Funding for the conference was generously given by The Prehistoric Society, Northern Ireland Environment Agency and the Queen's University Belfast Student-led Initiative. The coloured images in this volume have been kindly supported by the Marc Fitch Fund to whom we extend our gratitude. Finally, the constant encouragement of Dr Eoin Grogan, and the support and infectious enthusiasm of Dr Caroline Malone must also be acknowledged.

1

INTRODUCTION

Rebecca Enlander and Victoria Ginn

This introductory chapter consists of two parts. In Part I we begin to define what identity means to an archaeologist, and to consider the visibility of identity constructs within the archaeological record. In Part II we present a short case study in which we explore the creation and maintenance of identities within the Atlantic roundhouse tradition.

Part I: Locating identity

'The archaeological record is made up of, among other things, the direct and indirect results of countless individual actions' (Johnson 2004, 241). It can be questioned whether or not we can relate the results of these actions, i.e. the archaeological remains, to the intentions and identity of the people who carried them out. This chapter and the following chapters presented within this volume do not claim to re-address the legitimacy of exploring past identity. Rather, they explore tentatively the identity potential of various elements of the observed archaeological record, including domestic and ritual architecture, material culture, mortuary sites, and human remains. They succeed in providing a narrative for the identification and investigation of identity in the archaeological record, and the tangible facets of those identities that can be drawn out.

Definitions of identity

The term identity is defined as 'The quality or condition of being the same in substance, composition, nature, properties, or in particular qualities under consideration; absolute or essential sameness; oneness' (Oxford English Dictionary). It has been used most frequently in archaeological literature in reference to ethnic and cultural identity. Traditional perceptions of identity – made prominent by the writing of Childe and others – view it as a construct which is objective, and socially inherited. In this early history of archaeology, the identification and classification of organising principles of wider historical processes, or grand narratives, dominated the discipline through the establishment of distinct typologies and chronologies. Jones and Graves-Brown (1996, 1) emphasise that 'questions of identity often come to the fore at times of social and political change'. As such, it is unsurprising that an archaeological concern with the actions of individual humans and their identities is a relatively recent phenomenon which arose – in its European context – after the collapse of the Soviet Union and the associated political turmoil of the 1990s. It is only with post-processualist, thematic approaches to gender, age, ethnicity, status, and occupation that questions about the identity of our predecessors, as observed archaeologically, have truly come to the fore. There has ensued an increasing scepticism of the importance placed on objective, all-encompassing cultural definitions of identity. For instance, Jones stresses that group identity is multi-dimensional (1997; also Jones and Graves-Brown 1996, 5), while Díaz-Andreu and Lucy (2005) emphasis potentially subjective and multi-natured identities on an individual and collective scale.

Since the 1990s, the archaeological perception of 'embodied' and plural facets of identity such as gender, sexuality and age have seen increased emphasis. The publication of volumes including '*Engendering Archaeology: Women and Prehistory*' (Gero and Conkey 1992) and '*Invisible People and Processes: Writing Gender and Childhood into European Archaeology*' (Moore and Scott 1997) led to an acceptance that gender identities and sexual roles are not necessarily dualistic or universal, but are transformed and influenced during our lifecycles. Biological identity is arguably more tangible and has seen increased emphasis, but the identity metanarrative is often simply ignored; for example, 'identity' does not appear in the index of Whitley's edited 1998 volume *Reader in Archaeological Theory: Post-processual and cognitive approaches.*

The increasing unease with an identity which is applicable to prehistory, particularly to prehistoric individuals, may be intrinsically linked to the development of agency theory, and its, at times, liberal application of free-thinking agents to the ancient past. In agency theory, knowledgeable agents act with intentionality upon the world around them and with other agents; their actions are not limited by social structure. On the other hand, a person's individual actions are usually constrained by those of other individuals, and are thus, to some extent, the products of the community. Agents, therefore, may not always be 'free' and the impact of power relations needs to be considered. The possible overemphasis of the role of 'free' agents in past processes and events has, in part, been caused by the comparative neglect of themes like the identity of status rarely moving beyond the premise of exchange and power (Díaz-Andreu and Lucy 2005, 5; Meskell 2002, 284; although refer to Brück 2001 and Grogan, this volume). Challenges by Thomas (2008: in response to Knapp and van Dommelen 2008) to the ability of acknowledging autonomous individuals in prehistory for instance, warn that imposing central agents on the distant past plays to modern western constructs of free individuals, and is in danger of producing an 'ethnocentric distortion' of the past (see discussion in Knapp and van Dommelen 2008; also Thomas 2000 regarding the individual in Neolithic mortuary contexts).

However, post-structuralist models of agency are socially defined against a backdrop of particular historical situations whereby people act within the 'historically situated agency' of their circumstances (Robb 2010, 499). Agents operate in a landscape of socially mediated values, the terms of their own individual identities (or self-hood), and relationships and social exchanges with other agents and culture. Such a definition of socially constituted persons which combines self-perception, relational identification, as well as intentional and unintentional actions is not considered an intrusive persona by the current authors, whether identified at an individual, multiple or communal scale. Robb (*ibid.*) goes beyond the 'autonomous individual' and, just as identities can be multiple, contested and redefined during a person's life course, he proposes multiple and collective agencies. Individuals can participate in distinct forms of collective agency and will adopt and modulate their actions consciously and unconsciously to best fit any given situation. 'It follows that a key parameter of how people construct their agency...is their understanding of the relations with others; this is true whether these other entities are understood as individual persons or groups' (*ibid.*, 503–4).

Computer simulation, although not used within this volume, provides an exciting avenue for the exploration of the actions of individual agents based on biological or economic theory (Graham 2009; Graham 2006; Lake 2004). Explicitly concerned with individual actions, agent-based simulations help move the landscape beyond mere distribution maps. It is a theoretically attractive methodology due to the combination of individual agency and whole society modelling, but also one that frequently comes under criticism for not reflecting the potentially irrational behaviour, subjective choices and complex psychology exhibited by human beings.

Visibility of identity
As Robb's framework suggests (above), under appropriate circumstances and armed with a theoretically informed and appropriately rigorous methodology, the analysis of 'historically situated' identity constructs is not an impossible task. There are, of course, limitations which must be recognised. With regards to the application of cognitive approaches, Flannery and Marcus (1998, 46) warn that 'when almost no background knowledge is available... reconstruction can border on science fiction. That is when every figurine becomes a 'fertility goddess' and every misshapen boulder a 'cult stone'" and this rings just as true for identity. So how do archaeologists begin to attempt to recognise and analyse a concept that is constantly invented and reinvented, is multiple and contradictory, represents a continual process of narration, and is susceptible to elaboration and even fictitiousness?

The attribution of cultural identity to material remains has a long and well-established history. Observing similarities and distinctions within past material culture – whether diachronically, synchronically or geographically – is perhaps the most common approach, and has certainly been used frequently throughout this volume (see also Díaz-Andreu 1996; Hides 1996; Thurston *et al.* 2009). However, the relationship between material culture and identity is complex, especially with regards to the boundaries of ethnic difference (Jones 1997). While 'material and environmental conditions clearly have a role to play in creating the opportunities for similarities to develop... they explain nothing in themselves – it is the cultural and social world of individual communities that take on a recognisable character' (Henderson 2007, 302).

Individuals, groups and societies are not simply passive victims of their identities. Instead, they continuously articulate and elucidate self-conscious definitions of identity which fluctuate over time. Archaeologists often prefer to examine these identities, and their dynamic nature, through extant material culture. By constructing spatial patterns of local and non-local material, and by analysing diachronic alterations in that material archaeologists hope to construct an idea of the collective 'Self' and 'Other' (see *e.g.* Pérez and Odriozola 2009, 266). The assumption that archaeologists can analyse varying patterns in material culture to shed light on identity constructs has forged the long-prevailing notion of chronological identity. Recent large-scale, Bayesian-orientated research projects, such as those on the Mesolithic–Neolithic transition in Britain (Griffiths 2012; Whittle *et al.*

2011), warn against the enduring associations between chronological periods, material and identities, however. Spatially and temporally discrete distributions of material culture are themselves not a reflection of bounded groups. A one-to-one relationship between cultural identity and similarities or differences in material culture cannot be assumed. Instead, archaeologists should conceptualise identity as self-defining, and as actively communicated through processes of manipulation of both economic and political resources (Jones 2007, 113).

Political identities
The chronological association between questions concerning the identity of past people(s) and contemporary political, social or economic uncertainty was highlighted above (also Jones and Graves-Brown 1996, 1). Meskell notes that 'relationships with particular historical trajectories, nostalgia and commemoration, and... the forceful materiality of archaeological remains' were sparked during the major political restructuring and consequent upheavals seen in the Soviet Union. His comments occur in a general discussion of archaeological approaches to cultural identity in the twentieth century, and he warns more generally that 'cultural heritage has been deployed in quests for specific modernities, sometimes at the expense or erasure of others' (2002, 288). Commentators with politically fuelled agendas, such as those cases described by Meskell, often use the collective memory to lay claim to past life experiences and places of significance. This process is at the expense of more encompassing, cultural narratives which accommodate multiple identities and consensual histories, and is especially prevalent in colonial contexts (*ibid.*, 292). Specifically, nationalist archaeologies have seen the manipulation of ethnic identities for political gain, a theme which is discussed by Popa (this volume) in reference to Romanian identity constructs. However, it is precisely these archaeological landscapes that hold the potential to contribute to wider narratives of social memory and national identity: as archaeologists we are privy to the materiality of contested landscapes of the past (*ibid.*).

The identity of place
Identities have long been perceived as linked to and correlating with specific geographical locations. Spatial computational modelling is becoming increasingly popular as an analytical tool, especially with the widespread availability of the push-button Geographic Information System (GIS) capabilities. The use of a GIS can enable a new perspective into the spatial dimension of human culture, into the ways in which place-based community identities have been represented in spatial form in the landscape, and it can also facilitate the analysis of how identity was actively created and renegotiated. The particular archaeological nuance of a specific landscape helps to define its identity, or at least its sameness and/or otherness compared to different landscapes. Of course the identity of a landscape is also porous and mobile: 'What a geographical location means to any group of people changes as its history is told and retold, and the meaning is no more stable than identity itself, therefore, places are constituent parts, but also products, of identity' (Sokolove *et al.* 2002, 25).

There has also been a tacit acceptance of 'modern political boundaries as a framework for the analysis of the past' (Jones and Graves-Brown 1996, 12) which a GIS can both hinder and help to overcome. The current authors used a GIS to analyse Irish rock art and Bronze Age settlement patterns in Ireland as part of their respective research. Both authors anticipated that modern political boundaries would not be able to force the acceptance of specific analytical boundaries as the island of Ireland itself provided a convenient geographic entity for study. However, the border between Northern Ireland and the Republic of Ireland created immense difficulties in aligning differentially developed datasets (such as soils, rivers and watersheds) within the two countries.

Part II: Scales of identity

In the remainder of this chapter we will use the roundhouse tradition in Atlantic Scotland as a setting to explore the creation and maintenance of local and non-local identities.

In addition to extant material culture (as highlighted above), monumental architecture is perhaps the most enduring and readily accessible relic of past societies. Atlantic Scottish roundhouses, and particularly nucleated broch settlements of the Iron Age, embody some of the finest examples of prehistoric architectural engineering in Europe (see Figure 1.1). In this domestic arena the themes of architecturally defined space, spatial ordering and structured deposition are brought together in order to narrate the visibility of local and non-local identities. Social organisation in past societies is evident through actual architectural boundaries or, more subtly, through the separation of daily tasks which may leave distinct zonal remains. Such expressions can be used as a tool in the exploration of identity, specifically the identity of those that shaped, and were shaped by them. Socially mediated identity, constructed through the application of spatial ordering, is particularly demonstrable in Atlantic roundhouses.

Architecturally defined space
Atlantic roundhouses emerge *c*. 600 BC (Hedges 1987, 117), are characterised by their massive dry-stone walls, and represent a radical departure from the previously encountered cellular settlement types. Some examples are rather complex and have the addition of guard cells, intra-mural cells and stairs, and scarcement ledges. These complex roundhouses are generally isolated and essentially self-sufficient units in the Western Isles and Shetland, but can also be part of clustered village settlements in Orkney, such as Howe of Howe (Ballin Smith 1994). A broch is a specialised form of complex roundhouse, identified by a discernible upper floor. Central brochs were occasionally surrounded by roundhouses and complex roundhouses which formed a broch village.

These three types of domestic dwellings all share a specific architectural trait: the control of movement within their confines. Sally Foster (1989) applied access analysis – a technique based on Hillier and Hanson's 1984 *Gamma analysis* – to broch village architecture in Orkney and Caithness. She demonstrated how the builders might have deliberately designed ways in which movement into, and within these houses was controlled. This would have resulted in marked differences in how local and non-local residents of the area might have perceived the buildings. To an outsider, a central broch tower and a sea of tightly packed roofs of the surrounding buildings may have seemed intimidating. Movement through the village was often controlled by the creation of a narrow passage through the other structures, passing spaces in which strangers could not freely interact. This passage was frequently aligned with the entrance to the central broch tower, and would have acted as a marked transition from the outside world into the centre of the village. This passage also mirrored the entrance to the central broch itself: a tunnel-like passage which was probably marked

Figure 1.1: Mid Howe broch village, Rousay, Orkney. Remains of the low, passage entrance into the broch tower, taken from the broch interior with guard cell just visible (left), and detail of an outbuilding (foreground), looking towards the mainland (right) (Rebecca Enlander).

(Foster 1989, 232–3 and Armit 2003, 105. See also Figure 1.1). This restrictive architecture of broch formation embodies an explicit physical boundary, in effect creating a powerful distinction between inhabitants and outsiders.

Ultimately, it could be argued that broch architecture edified social distinctions between the inhabitants of the broch village and outsiders. This analysis of broch village settlement identifies a closed community which was segregated and even isolated from the world beyond. The nucleated settlements of the Middle Iron Age in Orkney are certainly characterised by rigid distinctions: any occupant would have been required to negotiate a series of spatial boundaries between people and activities on a daily basis (Barrett and Foster 1991, 49). Furthermore, as an expression of identity, the broch towers and their associated settlement are proclamations of those social group's values and self-qualities (Cunliffe 2001, 359).

Spatial ordering

In addition to the significant architecture of these dwellings there is also a notable spatial ordering which highlights an explicit relationship with ancestral remains, specifically Neolithic mortuary structures. A clear link is apparent between a number of Iron Age sites and earlier structures. These sites include the broch village at the Howe, Stromness, which demonstrates a recurring fascination with Neolithic mortuary architecture in the form of a chambered tomb (Hingley 1996, 238; MacKie 2002, 219). Iron Age settlements at Quanterness (Hingley 1996, 236) and Pierowall Quarry (MacKie 2002, 247) also demonstrate a strong link with chambered cairns. At the Calf of Eday a Neolithic cairn containing two chambers was physically linked to an Iron Age settlement complex, located 30m away, with a massively constructed linear dyke (Calder 1937). The chambered cairn of Mid Howe on Rousay had been modified in the Iron Age with the addition of several walls which protruded from the cairn and circled landward, before they dissipated. Less than 1km away, similar alterations took place to the chambered cairn at Rowiegar. Iron Age buildings were also constructed on the actual Neolithic cairn, and part of the chamber was re-used as an earth-house (Calder 1937; MacDonald 1946, 211, 218–220).

The presence of peculiar subterranean structures (termed wells, although their architecture is much more elaborate) found within Orcadian broch floors has often been attributed to water collection and storage. However, these wells may have been designed to represent earlier, Neolithic chambered structures. Probably the most elaborate of these wells is found in the internal broch floor at Gurness, Orkney. To construct it, the builders carved into the solid bedrock, and then inserted a dry-stone structure which encompassed typical broch-like features, including stairs and corbelled cells (Armit 2003, 108). The precise function of these wells remains unknown, but human excrement and faunal remains have been found in some examples, suggesting that they were occupied for not unsubstantial periods of time. That these features make use of the deepest elements of space within these complexes and that their entrances were often narrow and confined, again highlights the control of access. It is likely that access was restricted to members of specific groups within the community.

Wells do not occur at Howe, Pierowall and Quanterness for instance, but the inclusion of chambered tombs within settlements may have served a similar, ritual purpose (Armit 2003, 111). Furthermore, the deliberate situation of settlements among Neolithic remains discussed above, or more generally, within ancestral landscapes, could be argued to assist in the creation of wider boundaries between the past and present. Through the positioning of architecture, communities anchored themselves to the landscape, projecting an image of longevity and shared ancestral identity, and further highlighting the distinction between inhabitant and outsider. The act of dwelling, as signified through architectural space, conceptualised wider cosmological order which was expressed through the control of experience and encounter (see discussion in Enlander 2008).

Architecture then is a medium through which actual bodily movement can be constrained. In this way, through the individual body, relationships with other individuals and groups of society are constructed and reconciled. The spatial organisation of the settlements discussed here was deliberately created to amplify distinctions between the settlements' inhabitants and outsiders. Furthermore, the endurance of architecture, and the direct connectivity with the Neolithic chambered cairns, becomes emblematic of (past) social identity. It is through the routine processes of dwelling – including movement into and within that dwelling – that facets of identity are realised.

Combining the analysis of movement with artefact deposition, for instance, can further highlight the prevalence and importance of symbolic divisions of space. This is especially noticeable in the collision between structured deposition at boundaries and thresholds and the deposition of human remains.

Structured deposition
Cleary (this volume) discusses the role of human bone deposition in Bronze Age Ireland, and highlights the significance of such remains occurring at settlement entrances and thresholds. This phenomenon has a longer history and a wider geography than presented in this volume (see also Crozier, this volume). With regards to Atlantic Scotland, the structured deposition of human remains in settlements – not just in thresholds – represents the mainstay of the Iron Age burial record.

The remains were placed in a variety of locations and represent structured deposits associated with entrances, foundations, closures/abandonment, and middens. Analysis of these remains (Armit and Ginn 2007; Ginn 2005) revealed occasional instances of worked or modified (including perforations for suspension) human bone at Cnip (Lewis), Hillhead (Caithness), Hornish Point (South Uist), and Icegarth (Sanday). These were interpreted as demonstrating a ritual practice which was not a regionally isolated phenomenon. Suspension holes suggested the possibility of body part display, reinforced by the position of skulls from Rennibister (Ornkey) and Saverough (Orkney). Potential curation of human remains (for up to several centuries) evidenced at Dun Vulan (South Uist) is reminiscent of Late Bronze Age practices, as seen at Cladh Hallan (South Uist). These trends have a mixed message regarding the preservation of identity. The display and curation of individual parts of individual people suggests that such preservation was important. Yet within settlements, the fragmented bones of multiple individuals were frequently mixed and deposited together and this does not indicate a preoccupation with preserving personal identity.

The idea that the remains may have functioned as medicine, as *muti*, has been put forward (Armit and Ginn 2007). Certainly, the use of particular body parts to cure or prevent particular illnesses helps to explain the occurrence of disarticulated bones and the special treatment afforded to the overtly ill (as at Crosskirk). It may also reinforce the importance of the identity of particular body parts of specific individuals.

Overall, however, the specific identities of these individuals is unclear, and their remains may have derived from multiple contexts. 'Some may have been members of the 'in-group' whose remains were selectively retrieved from excarnation grounds for use in domestic rituals…Others may have been trophies taken from enemies…slaves or other low-status individuals, objectified and used for specific ritual purposes…' (Shapland and Armit 2012, 101–2; also see Armit 2011). If we regard these remains as collectively objectified then their identities as individuals might not be especially significant. The process of actual dismemberment, or selective re-use of particular remains, and their circulation and deposition, arguably transforms the physical body into something else. In many ways this transformation acts as a reminder of wider concepts of personal identity and integrity: the living change state and these stages are marked through specific performances and realisations. Through their incorporation into architectural contexts and associated encounters with the living, these remains form part of the wider social structure. Whether they evoke wider ancestral significance is however, unclear.

Afterthought

Identity constructs operate in a landscape of socially mediated values and within a network of relationships and social exchanges with individuals, groups and artefacts. People are identified through their understanding of relations with others, and will adopt and modulate their actions accordingly. Hierarchal identities, for instance, may be realised in certain contexts but may be much more fluid or muted in others. In an archaeological context, material culture and environments may create opportunities for similarities and differences to develop. Just as local identity was actively created and renegotiated, so too have local landscapes, spaces, and the historically visible past. With regards to relational identification, certain aspects of identity or identification are mediated in visual landscapes, while a range of more fluid, moderate identities may be realised in different arenas. It must always be borne in mind that 'identities are never completed, never finished' (Hall 1997, 47). At a group level, notions of self and other are perpetuated with the emphasis of cultural difference, assumed or otherwise. Place and connection with place is used as a means of legitimising identity. To re-state Sokolove (*et al.* 2002, 25): 'What a geographical location means to any group of people changes as its history is told and retold, and the meaning is no more stable than identity itself, therefore, places are constituent parts, but also products, of identity'.

References

Armit, I. (2003) *Towers in the North: the brochs of Scotland.* Stroud, Tempus Publishing.

Armit, I. (2011) Headhunting and social power in Iron Age Europe. In T. Moore and X. Armada (eds) *Atlantic Europe in the first millennium BC: crossing the divide*, 590–607. Oxford, Oxford University Press.

Armit, I. and Ginn, V. (2007) Beyond the grave: human remains from domestic contexts in Iron Age Atlantic Scotland. *Proceedings of the Prehistoric Society* 73, 113–34.

Ballin Smith, B. (ed.) (1994) *Howe: four millennia of Orkney prehistory*. Society of Antiquaries of Scotland Monograph Series No. 9. Edinburgh, Society of Antiquaries of Scotland.

Barrett, J. C. and Foster, S. (1991) Passing the time in Iron Age Scotland. In W. S. Hanson and E. A. Slater (eds) *Scottish archaeology: new perceptions,* 44–56. Aberdeen University Press.

Brück, J. (2001) Monuments, power and personhood in the British Neolithic. *Journal of the Royal Anthropological Institute* 7, 649–67.

Calder, C. (1937) A Neolithic double-chambered cairn of the stalled type and later structures on the Calf of Eday, Orkney. *Proceedings of the Society of Antiquaries of Scotland* 71, 115–54.

Cunliffe, B. (2001) *Facing the ocean: the Atlantic and its peoples 8000 BC – AD 1500.* Oxford, Oxford University Press.

Díaz-Andreu, M. (1996) Constructing identities through culture. The past in the forging of Europe. In P. Graves-Brown, S. Jones and C. Gamble (eds) *Cultural identity and archaeology: the construction of European communities*, 48–61. London, Routledge.

Díaz-Andreu, M. and Lucy, S. (2005) Introduction. In M. Diaz-Andreu, S. Lucy, S. Babic and D. Edwards (eds) *The archaeology of identity*, 1–12. London, Routledge.

Enlander, R. (2008) *Inherited ancestries: a case study of Neolithic locality associations on Iron Age Rousay.* Unpublished MA thesis, University of the Highlands and Islands.

Flannery, K. and Marcus, J. (1998) Cognitive Archaeology. In D. S. Whitley (ed.) *Reader in archaeological theory: post-processual and cognitive approaches*, 35–49. London, Routledge.

Foster, S. (1989) *Aspects of the Late Atlantic Iron Age.* Unpublished PhD thesis, Glasgow University.

Gero, J. M. and Conkey, M. W. (1992) *Engendering archaeology: women and prehistory.* Oxford, Wiley Blackwell.

Ginn, V. (2005) *The deposition of human remains derived from domestic contexts in Iron Age Atlantic Scotland.* Unpublished MA thesis, Queen's University Belfast.

Graham, S. (2006) Networks, agent-based models and the Antonine itineraries: implications for Roman archaeology. *Journal of Mediterranean Archaeology* 19(1), 45–64.

Graham, S. (2009) The space between: the geography of social networks in the Tiber Valley. In F. Coarelli and H. Patterson (eds) *Mercator Placidissimus The Tiber Valley in antiquity: new research in the upper and middle river valley*, 671–86. (Proceedings of the Conference held at the British School at Rome, 27–28 February 2004) Rome, British School at Rome.

Griffiths, S. (2012) 'Scatter matters: Bayesian statistical modelling and evidence for overlap between Late Mesolithic and Early Neolithic material culture in England', lecture given at Queen's University Belfast, 20 March 2012.

Hall, S. (1997) Old and new identities, old and new ethnicities. In A. D. King (ed.) *Culture, globalization and the world-system: contemporary conditions of the representation of identity*, 41–67. Minneapolis, University of Minnesota Press.

Hedges, J. W. (1987) *Bu, Gurness and the Brochs of Orkney*. British Archaeological Reports, British Series 163. Oxford, Archaeopress.

Henderson, J. C. (2007) *The Atlantic Iron Age: settlement and identity in the first millennium BC*. London, Routledge.

Hides, S. (1996) The genealogy of material culture and cultural identity. In P. Graves-Brown, S. Jones and C. Gamble (eds) *Cultural identity and archaeology: the construction of European communities*, 25–47. London, Routledge.

Hillier, B. and Hanson, J. (1984) *The social logic of space*. Cambridge University Press.

Hingley, R. (1996) Ancestors and identity in the later prehistoric of Atlantic Scotland: the reuse and reinvention of Neolithic monuments and material culture. *World Archaeology* 28(2), 231–44.

Johnson, M. (2004) Agency, structure and archaeological practice. In A. Gardner (ed.) *Agency uncovered: archaeological perspectives on social agency, power and being human*, 241–9. London, University College London Press.

Jones, S. and Graves-Brown, P. (1996) Introduction: archaeology and cultural identity in Europe. In P. Graves-Brown, S. Jones and C. Gamble (eds) *Cultural identity and archaeology: the construction of European communities*, 1–25. London, Routledge.

Jones, S. (1997) *The archaeology of ethnicity: constructing identities in the past and present*. London, Routledge.

Knapp, B. A. and van Dommelen, P. (2008) Past practices: rethinking individuals and agents in archaeology. *Cambridge Archaeological Journal* 18(1), 15–34.

Lake, M. W. (2004) Being in a simulacrum: electronic agency. In A. Gardner (ed.) *Agency uncovered: archaeological perspectives on social agency, power and being human*, 191–211. London, University College London Press.

MacDonald, G. (1946) *Twelfth report with an inventory of the Ancient Monuments of Orkney and Shetland*. Volume 2. Edinburgh, Royal Commission on the Ancient and Historical Monuments of Scotland.

MacKie, E. W. (2002) *The roundhouses, brochs and wheelhouses of Atlantic Scotland c. 700 BC – AD 500: Part I the Orkney and Shetland Isles*. British Archaeological Reports Series 342. Oxford, Archaeopress.

Meskell, L. (2002) The intersections of identity and politics in archaeology. *Annual Review of Anthropology* 31, 279–301.

Moore, H. and Scott, E. (1997) *Invisible people and processes: writing gender and childhood into European archaeology*. Leicester, Leicester University Press.

Pérez, V. H. and Odriozola, C. P. (2009) Landscape, identity and material culture in 'Tierra de Barros' (Badajoz, Spain) during the 3rd millennium BCE. In T. Thurston and R. B. Salisbury (eds) *Reimagining regional analyses: the archaeology of spatial and social dynamics*, 266–90. Newcastle, Cambridge Scholars Publishing.

Robb, J. (2010) Beyond agency. *World Archaeology* 42(4), 493–520.

Shapland, F. and Armit, I (2012) The useful dead: bodies as objects in Iron Age and Norse Atlantic Scotland. *European Journal of Archaeology* 15 (1), 98–116.

Sokolove, J., Fairfax, S. and Holland, B. (2002) Managing place and identity: the Marin coast Miwok experience. *Geographical Review* 92, 23–44.

Thomas, J. (2000) Death, identity and the body in Neolithic Britain. *Journal of the Royal Anthropological Institute* 6(4), 653–68.

Thomas, J. (2008) Comments on 'Past Practices: Rethinking Individuals and Agents in Archaeology' by A.B. Knapp and P. van Dommelen. *Cambridge Archaeological Journal* 18 (1), 26–8.

Thurston, T., Westphal, J. and Rosegaard Hansen, M. (2009) Imagining Danish prehistory through 50 years: methodological and paradigmatic transformations in regional and interregional archaeology. In T. Thurston and R. B. Salisbury (eds), *Reimagining regional analyses: the archaeology of spatial and social dynamics*, 67–98. Newcastle, Cambridge Scholars Publishing.

Whitley, D. S. (ed.) (1998) *Reader in archaeological theory: post-processual and cognitive approaches*. London, Routledge.

Whittle, A. Healy, F. and Bayliss, A. (eds) (2011) *Gathering time. Dating the Early Neolithic enclosures of southern Britain and Ireland*. Vols 1–2. Oxford, Oxbow.

Material culture of the dead

Introduction

Eileen Murphy

As archaeologists we constantly strive to learn more about the people of the past – where they lived, the nature of their diets and subsistence strategies, how the environment impacted on their health, what raw materials they exploited to make tools, how they communicated with one another – and many, many other aspects of daily lives. We would probably agree that we have a generally good understanding of such issues for people from a wide variety of periods across the globe – although there is always more to be learned from new discoveries and from the re-examination of material discovered long ago. There is much more to being human, however, than the practicalities of daily life. What was it that motivated the people of the past? How did they interact? What sorts of different identities did they have? We know that modern people can use a variety of tactics for developing complex identities for themselves and others as they negotiate their way through life. In his discussions of personhood and identity Chris Fowler has suggested that, while the concept of the individual is important in the modern world, this may not have been the case in prehistoric communities who were not exposed to 'a world of mass production, capitalism, internalized reflection, privatized concerns, and social technologies' which he considers to have fuelled individualisation at the expense of interaction with the wider community and nature (Fowler 2004, 3). Bearing these differences in mind is it possible for us – as people living in the modern world – to really gain a true understanding of prehistoric identity?

The mortuary environment, with its association with the tangible remains of the people of the past, seems an ideal place in which to search for evidence of identity. As such, this section comprises three chapters which focus on seeking identity within the material culture of the dead. The first chapter is a thought-provoking piece in which Reiter attempts to disentangle the meaning and complexities of the term 'identity'. She considers private (or individual) and public identity separately and this develops into the underlying thesis for her chapter – the concept of 'I'-dentity as opposed to 'Eye'-dentity. She proffers that 'I'-dentity refers to an individual's private identity whereas 'Eye'-dentity refers to the manner in which a person or group are perceived by another individual or group. This neat division is, of course, not straightforward and she discusses how both types of identity can influence one another. The remainder of the chapter is devoted to seeking 'Eye'-dentity within a mortuary context. It is obvious that the dead do not bury themselves and she argues this is an ideal place in which to search for 'Eye'-dentity. Using the effective analogy of portrait painting for 'Eye'-dentity, she poses the question – whose is the hand directing the paintbrush? This leads on to the issue of power – the discovery of high status burials, such as the 'princess of Vix' causes Reiter to conclude that we need to appreciate that 'Eye'-dentity was not a democratic ideal – either in the past or the present.

The remaining two chapters in this section have a different emphasis and both demonstrate how scientific information obtained from osteoarchaeological analyses can be effectively combined with an interrogation of the burial context for the purposes of gleaning information about identity. Crozier begins with a discussion of the difficulties involved with obtaining conventional osteological information from British Neolithic human remains due to the recovery of only small numbers of individuals from Neolithic tombs. This paucity of people has led to interpretations which mark them out as somehow special, and it has generally been concluded that those interred within megalithic tombs had a distinct identity to the majority of the population. Quanterness is one of a small number of Orcadian tombs previously considered to have contained unusually large assemblages of human remains relative to the volume of material retrieved from contemporary tombs. Crozier's taphonomic research on this material has demonstrated that in actuality the numbers of individuals represented in these Orcadian tombs are not too dissimilar to those found in other tombs elsewhere in Britain and Ireland. She discusses the problems of assuming that MNI values derived from disarticulated assemblages are an accurate reflection of the true volume of remains originally contained within the tombs. Employing information derived from ethnography, computer modelling, excavation accounts, and the state of weathering apparent on the bones she demonstrates that tomb assemblages are subject to substantial levels of decay and that this, as well as the sequential interment of bodies, is probably responsible for the small number of individuals represented in such environments. She ends by urging a complete re-interpretation of the individuals buried within Neolithic megalithic tombs – rather than representing people with a special identity who warranted an atypical burial – she suggests that the vast majority of the main populace was buried within a tomb.

Walsh asks if it is possible to access identity through the osteoarchaeological record and uses information derived from the Bronze Age round cairn of Hindlow, Derbyshire, to answer the question. She sets the scene by critiquing previous studies of Bronze Age identity which she suggests ignored archaeological data at the expense of osteological information and vice versa. Clearly an integrated approach is going to yield the most informative results and this is what she advocates. After describing the complex depositional sequence of burials at Hindlow she discusses possible explanations for what appears to have been the deliberate disturbance of earlier burials – was this done as a positive act of remembrance to reaffirm group and individual identity or, alternatively, were these older burials deliberately disturbed as a way of asserting a different identity? She concludes that the longevity of use of the barrow enabled it to have a connection to the community and that it was therefore a mnemonic of social identity over time.

These three chapters demonstrate the rich array of information pertaining to prehistoric identity that may be derived from the mortuary environment. They also remind us to be cautious, however, in how we approach burial evidence for this purpose – while it is a relatively straightforward process to extract scientific identifiers from a burial, such as age and sex, we need to remember that the living will also have imposed an identity on the dead. Furthermore, there is the potential for our interpretations of identity in the mortuary context to be flawed if they do not use an integrated approach or take care to ensure that the interpretations are based on solid osteoarchaeological foundations.

References

Fowler, C. (2004) *The archaeology of personhood*. London, Routledge.

2

IDENTITY LIES IN THE EYE OF THE BEHOLDER: A CONSIDERATION OF IDENTITY IN ARCHAEOLOGICAL CONTEXTS

Samantha S. Reiter

Introduction

Through an examination of identity in modern times, it is possible to explore the question of identity in archaeological contexts. Ancient in-grave identity is not a reflection of the social standing of the deceased so much as it is a vision of the positions that individuals were believed to have held *by the people who buried them*. In this way, cemetery identities are more inverse social casts than individual representations. This chapter investigates the creation of in-grave 'eye'-dentity as a new means to gain a handle on the archaeological investigation of identity.

Identity today

Modern identity is a complex knot of Gordian proportions. Type 'identity' into Google, and you get some 375 million hits – you have identity theft, Personal Identification Numbers, identity crises, and proof of identity. Identity, in the general parlance, is meant to indicate *who a person is,* and yet radio, television and innumerable magazines advertise and encourage people to create, discover, rediscover or even get to know the 'new,' 'old,' 'thinner,' 'sexier,' or even 'real' versions of themselves. The Oxford English Dictionary, on the other hand, presents identity as being a cold, hard, immutable fact:

> 'Identity. Noun (pl. identities). 1. the fact or being who or what a person or thing is. 2. the characteristics of determining this…'(Soanes 2003, 553).

In other words, identity today has come to indicate three things: the *fact* of who one is, the means of determining this, and the proof of the same. This circuitous overlap poses less of a problem to archaeologists, as it is the first two permutations of identity which are of chief concern.

Identity-as-state-of-being is not as clearly cut as our government-issued identity cards and the Oxford English Dictionary would have us believe. Identities can be nested, plural,

Table 2.1: A portrait of two Europeans (*The individuals whose descriptions are given here are known to the author; their names have been changed for the purposes of this chapter).

Example A: Erwan Huillier* is from the region of Brittany in northwest France. He grew up bilingually speaking both French and Breton. His fellow Frenchmen think of him not as French, but as *Breton*. Outside of that hexagonally shaped country, people consider him to be culturally French, although perhaps not of the beret-wearing, baguette-brandishing stereotype they had imagined. As a visitor to the United States of America, perhaps he is seen first as an European, and then only secondly allocated to any one specific country. Outside of the EU, everything from the obvious differences in his speech patterns to the cut of his sports coat mark him out as *other*.
Example B: Sophia Bernhardt* was born in Mexico to one German and one Mexican parent. Hence, she has dual citizenship for those two countries. She lives and works in Sweden, but was once married to an Italian, and therefore also has Italian citizenship. Although she considers herself to be racially *Latina*, Ms Bernhardt has lived in the EU far longer than in the New World, and considers her cultural ties to be greater to Europe as a whole than to any one specific nation state within the European Union.

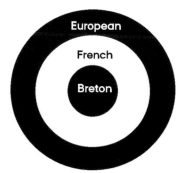

Figure 2.1: Graphic demonstration of the inclusive identity layers associated with Example A.

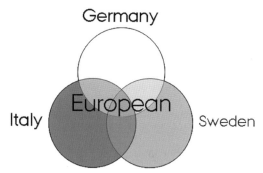

Figure 2.2: Graphic demonstration of the overlapping European identity layers associated with Example B.

and overlapping (Casella and Fowler 2005) (Table 2.1; Figures 2.1–2.2). One's identity-as-state-of-being is created both consciously (*i.e.* through the life course and choices of domicile as well as through 'identification' with any one country or group) and unconsciously (*i.e.* through place of birth). Identity is *not* inborn. It is constructed. Humans can 'play' identity in very specific, meaning-laden ways. The text produced by such games, to continue with the metaphor, is described by Tilley (1996, 7) as being 'blurred but indispensable', and it is to the deciphering of said text that our thoughts must now turn.

Identity in the past

According to the German wordsmith Karl Valentin, '*Fremd ist der Fremde nur in der Fremde*' (Valentin 2006: 'Strange is the only foreigner in a strange land'). Although his words confuse almost as much as they enlighten, he speaks an inherent truth about the way in which we define ourselves, both today and also in prehistory. Much like art being unable to exist in a vacuum, neither can individual identities exist independently of other people. People define and are defined by that which they are *not* (Simmel 1950, 30). Be you à *l'étranger* or *im Aussland,* you are literally in a strange place, outside of both comfort and ken. The similarity or dissimilarity of one's external environment to any individual's place of origin determines the popular perception of the identity of any one individual. To rephrase, a stranger is a stranger only in the homelands of people who are foreign to him. Hacking's idea that 'categories of people come into existence at the same time as kinds of people came into being to fit those categories' is an excellent archaeological illustration of the same concept (Hacking 1995, 247). One can only imagine that ideas of 'strangeness' must have been all the more starkly defined in historical periods.

Let us move on to that second denomination of identity, namely identity-as-characteristic for determining one's state of being. This form of identity is, to springboard from the above discussion, chiefly a question of perception and reception. Identity thus can be winnowed out into two disparate denominations: the private (or individual) and the public. These two modes are themselves the product of two different categorical phenomena which occur on the private/individual and public levels, respectively: identification and categorization (see Brubaker and Cooper 2000; Foucault 1991; Jenkins 1994). In this text, identification and categorization shall be understood as follows:

> *Identification:* First introduced by Freud as the process through which an infant internalises external persons through socialization (Freud 1923); identification here will be defined as an *inclusive* process which both originates from and is concerned with the self.
> *Categorization:* A process chiefly of *division*, but also of inclusion which originates – or is at least accepted and understood – on a public level, but is oriented towards the individual.

In terms of this chapter, these various identities are separated and defined differently. Henceforth, 'I'-dentity shall be understood to signify the understanding which the single individual maintains of himself. 'I'-dentity is a private identity, and would reflect the process of identification, if present. In philosophical and theoretical terms, this denomination is mostly closely akin to Bourdieu's *sens pratique*: that concomitantly cognitive and emotional comprehension that persons have of themselves and the social world with which they are surrounded (Bourdieu 1980). What I shall term 'eye'-dentity, by contrast, refers to the way – or ways – in which any one person or group is *perceived* by another person or group. This latter is a product of the phenomenon of categorization, and draws upon Jenkins' ideas about identity (Jenkins 1994).

The effect of 'I'-dentity on 'eye'-dentity

Whatever their prefix, before we move on to a discussion of the determination of the '-dentities' in archaeological contexts, we must first discuss their relationships to each other. The relationship between 'I'-dentity and 'eye'-dentity as private and public identities is, once again, a question of perception and reception. Any one person's 'eye-dentity' may or may not reflect the place he or she wished to fill in society, just as we are the products of the social worlds in which we live and attain maturity. Although he does not use the same terminology, Simon makes an apt observation about identity; that it is 'a social psychological mediator between input from and output in the social world' (Simon 2004, 2). In other words, Simon would argue that 'eye'-dentity and 'I'-dentity are not as independent of each other as would first appear. Recent scientific studies have discovered that first impressions are created in one tenth of a second (Willis and Todorov 2006); however, the sociological phenomena surrounding that brief, opinion-forming first interaction are highly complex. This synthesis of forces is akin to a push/pull effect. When an individual acts, he intentionally or unintentionally expresses himself. Following this, the people with whom he is surrounded will in turn be impressed in some way by him (Ichheiser 1949, 6–7). The convergence of what Icheiser refers to as 'expression' and 'impression' is discussed in Thomas' ideas about expectations of behaviour and the fulfilment of the same (quoted in Volkart 1951, 5). As the saying goes, you try to 'put your best foot forward' when meeting new people. One's 'I'-dentity – perception of the self and the definition of one's best characteristics – affects the opinions ('eye'-dentity) that others form of you.

This chain of influence flows in both directions. The Existentialist school would agree, as far as they see the limiting role of the expectations of the witness as a basic threat to individual freedom (Sartre 1976). Just as the individual can affect his 'eye'-dentity by means of presenting himself in a particular way, so too can his own self-perception be affected by society at large. To a certain extent, culture (here linked more to 'eye'-dentity and the public conception of the individual) provides the framework into which any one individual substantiates himself (Cohen 1994, 50). Bourdieu would argue the same: 'Habitus is the product of history which generates individual and collective practices in accordance with the schemas engendered by history' (Bourdieu 1977, 82). But Bourdieu goes too far in describing the omnipotence of the class or group over the individual; he effectively side-lines the forces of personal contradiction and contingency (Meskell 1999, 27). Possessions, dress, mannerisms, and social mores (or lack thereof) are the means that any one person has to create or affect the way in which he is perceived. These tools for the crafting of 'eye'-dentity have been referred to as 'technologies of the self' (Battaglia 1995, 4–5; Foucault 1984).

In his recent work, Fowler describes personhood as a constantly changing condition which is mutually constituted, attained and maintained by those relationships any person forms (Fowler 2004, 7). While at first glance his definition of personhood seems similar to 'eye'-dentity, that resemblance is superficial. 'Eye'-dentity differs from personhood in terms of intensity. Whereas personhood is held up by a force-neutral alignment of individual and society, 'eye'-dentity and 'I'-dentity are the subjects of ever-changing creation, imposition and – above all – negotiation between the various oppositional players involved.

All for one, but not one for all

'I'-dentity is so highly individualised that it is both unknown and unknowable for any person outside of the self. Eye'-dentity, however, as a group-defined identity as characteristic-of-state-of-being, is something which is of great usefulness within archaeological investigation, hence its presence as the main focus of this text.

It initially seems counter-intuitive to seek to trace the group-defined 'eye'-dentity of any one individual (or group), especially when this is done in the hopes that it might give clues to the past living reality of that person or persons. This sort of a conundrum is not unknown in archaeological circles, and closely mirrors that which is referred to as the 'osteological paradox' (Wood *et al.* 1992). In brief, the osteological paradox states that it is highly unlikely that one will be able to eke out an accurate testimony of the living reality of population by studying its dry bones, as the very fact of death removed the study material from the society one is seeking to observe. The unique character of mortuary ritual, however, is such that it is decidedly well-suited to the sort of cultural identity studies discussed here. Again, given that this chapter seeks to analyse chiefly 'eye'-dentity and not 'I'-dentity, burial contexts are an excellent ingress to the external thought processes surrounding and creating the social position of an individual or individuals within a living society (Hallam and Hockey 2001; Pollock 1983; Williams 2006; 2001). The funeral rite is dependent upon the selection and marking of a number of the social identities that have been associated *by the bereaved* with an individual in life (Binford 1971). As the great archaeological syllogism intones 'people do not bury themselves'. Therefore, it is understandable that the material goods buried with the dead 'are tangible incarnations of social relationships embodying the attitudes and behaviour of the past' (Beaudry *et al.* 1991, 150; see also Ang 1996, 145).

Tangible incarnations

In theory, it is one thing to argue for the construction of a group-constituted 'eye'-dentity and for the representation of said identity interpreted in the grave goods which accompany a given individual. But how can those assertions be applied and tested archaeologically? The best manner of investigating such a question is through a systematic investigation of contexts which express a high degree of difference. As William Carlos Williams wrote in 1927, 'there are no ideas but in things' (quoted Knowles 2009, 858). When conceptions of differences of age (see Sofaer 2000), sex (see Sørensen 1992), or region of origin (see Jockenhövel 1995; 1991; 1980; Wels-Weyrauch 1989) are expressed within the material culture associated with an individual, it is possible to investigate 'eye'-dentity in the past. To make an analogy with another one of those afore-mentioned 'technologies of the self' (Battaglia 1995, 4–5; Foucault 1984), if 'eye'-dentity were a portrait painting, the individual would be the subject, the grave the canvas, the grave goods the paint, and the group or community which orchestrated the funerary ritual the painter.

However, as is usually the case whenever a group of individuals engages in a single project, there must be a hierarchy of directive decision-making. To continue with the above analogy, if the group is analogous to the painter, whose is the hand that is directing the paintbrush? This last is a question of power. In order for any individual or group of individuals to wield power, their position must be accepted on some level by the greater populace, or else it will be overturned.

For example, in order for the so-called 'princess of Vix' to be interred with such care and rich grave goods, including the well-known and fabulously decorated *krater* (see Knüsel 2002), the deceased lady's position as a powerful person worthy of such a burial must have been at least passively acceded to by the funerary party. The chief point is to acknowledge that the creation of 'eye-dentity' in the past, as today, was not a democratic ideal. As is the case anywhere, 'the remains we recover are to be interpreted as creations by people in accordance with their representation of the natural and social world' (Miller and Tilley 1984, 2) with all of the inequalities and power plays therewith associated. Investigations of power in prehistory demonstrate that the concept was often indelibly linked with a foreign identity or even some concept of 'foreignness' in general (see Helms 1994; Sahlins 2008; Vandkilde 2007).

Conclusion

Academic study has washed up on the shores of the ontological island of identity, a place Ramachandran has greeted as 'the last frontier' (Ramachandran 2009). The metaphorical identity isle is, of course, not uninhabited – it is so heavily embroiled in the tangled webs of modern day politics that any assay onto its beaches, be it archaeological or not, must necessarily carry wider repercussions on the world diplomatic stage. Over a decade ago, Rossant wrote '[u]ltimately, Europe will rise or fall on this issue of identity' (Rossant 2000). The ongoing birth and omphaloskepsis of the European Union is such that the EU as a political body is particularly concerned with identity and what could be decried as 'the invention of tradition' (Hobsbawm and Ranger 1983, 1–14). Indeed, a few recent studies have alluded to the Bronze Age as the particular period in which a wider pan-European awareness first coalesced (see Earle and Kristiansen 2010; Kristiansen and Larsson 2005). Rowlands has argued that the existence or creation of a collective heritage acts as a safeguard against the fragmentation of society (Rowlands 1994, 128).

This is particularly important in Europe today in terms of the navigation between regional or national concerns and a wider pan-European-ness. The preservation of the past is part and parcel to political self-preservation (Hewison 1987, 45). Once the past has been secured, its presentation and interpretation can be made to serve whatever political ideology is in the possession of library and museum keys (see de Tocqueville 1986; 1973; Mead 1955; Métraux and Mead 2001). Truly, we have entered into the 'era of identities' (Halpern 2009, 12).

It is interesting to note that identity in the past has been a subject of much archaeological interest, making appearances at many international conferences as of late. Certainly, archaeological recognition of a sense of pan-European identity in prehistory would go a long way to shoring up an overarching sense of belonging to the EU in the 21st century. This last leaves us with the gaping maw of history (or prehistory, as it were) being created within the modern day…and an increased awareness of the uses (be they desired or no) to which our discipline is put.

Acknowledgements

The author is particularly thankful to her fellow Forging Identities project members, especially Helle Vandkilde and Tim Flohr Sørensen for their comments and suggestions on earlier versions of this chapter.

The research leading to these results has received funding from the European Union Seventh Framework Programme (FP7/2007–2013) under grant agreement number 212402.

References

Ang, I. (1996) *Living room wars: rethinking media audiences for a postmodern world*. London and New York, Routledge.

Battaglia, D. (1995) Problematizing the self: a thematic introduction. In D. Battaglia (ed.) *Rhetorics of self-making*, 1–15. Berkley, University of California Press.

Beaudry, M. C., Cook, L. J. and Mrozowski, S. A. (1991) Artifacts and active voices: material culture as social discourse. In R. H. McGuire and R. Paynter (eds) *The archaeology of inequality*, 150–75. Oxford, Basil Blackwell.

Binford, L. (1971) Mortuary practices, their study and potential. *Society of American Archaeology Memoir* 25, 6–29.

Bourdieu, P. (1977) *Outline of a theory of practice*. Cambridge, Cambridge University Press.

Bourdieu, P. (1980) *Le sens pratique*. Paris, Les Éditions de Minuit.

Brubaker, R. and Cooper, F. (2000) Beyond identity. *Theory and Society* 29, 147.

Casella, E. C. and Fowler, C. (eds) (2005) *The archaeology of plural and changing identities: beyond identification*. New York, Kluwer Academic.

Cohen, A. P. (1994) *Self consciousness: an alternative anthropology of identity*. London, Routledge.

de Tocqueville, A. (1973) *L'ancien régime et la révolution*. Paris, Éditions Flammarion. [originally published 1887].

de Tocqueville, A. (1986) *De la démocratie en Amérique*. Paris, Éditions Flammarion [originally published 1888].

Earle, T. and Kristiansen, K. (eds) (2010) *Organizing Bronze Age Societies*. Cambridge, Cambridge University Press.

Foucault, M. (1984) On the genealogy of ethics: an overview of work in progress. In P. Rabinow (ed.) *The Foucault reader*, 340–72. New York, Pantheon Books.

Foucault, M. (1991) Governmentality. In G. Burchell, C. Gordon and P. Miller (eds) *The Foucault effect: studies in governmentality*, 87–104. Chicago, Chicago University Press.

Fowler, C. (2004) *The archaeology of personhood: an anthropological approach*. Routledge, London and New York.

Freud, S. (1923) *The ego and the id: the standard edition of the complete psychological works of Sigmund Freud*. London, W. W. Norton and Co.

Hacking, I. (1995) Three parables. In R. B. Goodman (ed.) *Pragmatism: a reader*, 238–49. New York, Routledge.

Hallam, E. and Hockey, J. (2001) *Death, memory and material culture*. Oxford, Berg.

Halpern, C. (2009) L'Identité: hstoire d'un succès. In C. Halpern (ed.) *Identité(s): l'individu, le groupe, la société*, 7–14. Auxerre, Éditions Scienes Humaines.

Helms, M. W. (1994) Essay on objects: interpretations of distance made tangible. In S. B. Schwartz (ed.) *Implicit understandings: observing, reporting and reflecting on the encounters between Europeans and other peoples in the early modern era*, 355–77. Cambridge, Cambridge University Press.

Hewison, R. (1987) *The heritage industry*. London, Methuen.

Hobsbawm, E. J. and Ranger, T. (eds) (1983) *The invention of tradition*. Cambridge, Cambridge University Press.

Ichheiser, G. (1949) Misunderstandings in human relations. *The American Journal of Sociology* 15, 6–14.

Jenkins, R. (1994) Rethinking ethnicity: identity, categorization and power. *Ethnic and Racial Studies* 17, 197–223.

Jockenhövel, A. (1980) *Die Rasiermesser in Westeuropa*. Munich, Prähistorische Bronzefunde.

Jockenhövel, A. (1991) Räumliche Mobilität von Personen in der Mittleren Bronzezeit des westlichen Mitteleuropa. *Germania* 69, 49–62.

Jockenhövel, A. (1995) Zur Ausstattung von Frauen in Nordwestdeutschland und in der Deutschen Mittelgebirgszone Während der Spätbronzezeit und Älteren Eisenzeit. In Festschrift für Hermann Müller-Karpe zum 70. *Geburtstag*, 195–212. Bonn, Habelt.

Knowles, E. (ed.). (2009) *Oxford Dictionary of quotations*. Oxford, Oxford University Press.

Knüsel, C. J. (2002) More Circe than Cassandra: 1 the Princess of Vix in ritualised social context. *European Journal of Archaeology* 5, 275–308.

Kristiansen, K. and Larsson, T. B. (2005) *The rise of Bronze Age society: travels, transmissions and transformations*. Cambridge, Cambridge University Press.

Mead, M. (1955) *Soviet attitudes toward authority: an interdisciplinary approach to problems of Soviet Character*. London, Tavistock.

Meskell, L. (1999) *Archaeologies of social life*. Oxford, Blackwell Publishing.

Métraux, R. and Mead, M. (2001) *Themes in French culture: a preface to a study of French community*. New York and London, Berghahn Books.

Miller, D. and Tilley, C. (1984) Ideology, power and prehistory. In D. Miller and C. Tilley (eds) *Ideology, power and prehistory*, 1–15. Cambridge, Cambridge University Press.

Pollock, L. A. (1983) *Forgotten children: parent-child relations from 1500 to 1900*. Cambridge, Cambridge University Press.

Ramachandran, V. S. (2009) Self-awareness: the final frontier, *The Edge*. Available from: http://www.edge.org/3rd culture/rama 08index.html. [Accessed 16/03/2011].

Rossant, J. (2000) A common identity for Europe? You better believe it!, *Business Weekly*. Available from: http://www.businessweek.com/2000/00_47/b3708227.htm [Accessed 28/12/2010].

Rowlands, M. (1994) The politics of identity in archaeology. In G. C. Bond and A . Gilliam (eds) *Social construction of the past: representation as power*, 127–43. London and New York, Routledge.

Sahlins, M. (2008) The stranger-king or, elementary forms of the politics of life. *Indonesia and the Malay World* 36, 177–99.

Sartre, J. P. (1976) *L'être et le Néant: essai d'ontologie phénomonologique*. Paris, Gallimard.

Simmel, G. (1950) *The sociology of Georg Simmel*. New York, Free Press.

Simon, B. (2004) *Identity in modern society: a social psychological perspective*. Oxford, Blackwell Publishing.

Soanes, C. (ed.) (2003) The Oxford compact English dictionary. Oxford, Oxford University Press.

Sofaer, J. (2000) Rings of life: the rise of early metalwork in mediating the gendered life course. *World Archaeology* 31, 389–406.

Sørensen, M. (1992) Gender archaeology and Scandinavian Bronze Age studies. *Norwegian Archaeological Review* 25, 31–49.

Tilley, C. (ed.) (1996) *Citizenship, identity and social history*. Cambridge, Cambridge University Press.

Valentin, K. (2006) *Zitate*. Available from: http://www.karl-valentin.de/zitate/zitate.htm [Accessed 10/01/2011].

Vandkilde, H. (2007) *Culture and change in central European prehistory: 6th to 1st millennium BC*. Aarhus, Aarhus University Press.

Volkart, E. H. (ed.) (1951) *Social behaviour and personality: contributions of W. I. Thomas to theory and social research*. New York, Social Science Research Council.

Wels-Weyrauch, U. (1989) Mittelbronzezeitliche Frauentrachten in Süddeutschland. In (Collectif) *Dynamique du Bronze Moyen en Europe Occidentale Actes du 113e Congrès National des Sociétés Savantes*, 117–34. Strasbourg, Congrès National des Sociétés Savantes.

Williams, H. (2001) Death, memory and time: a consideration of the mortuary practices at Sutton Hoo. In C. Humphrey and W. M. Ormrod (eds) *Time in the medieval world*, 35–71. Woodbridge, Boydell.

Williams, H. (2006) *Death and memory in early medieval Britain*. Cambridge, Cambridge University Press.

Willis, J. and Todorov, A. (2006) First impressions: making up your mind after a 100-Ms exposure to a face. *Psychological Science* 17, 592–98.

Wood, J. W., Milner, G. R., Harpending, H. C. and Weiss, K. M. (1992) The osteological paradox: problems of inferring prehistoric health from skeletal samples. *Current Anthropology* 33, 343–59.

3

EXCEPTIONAL OR CONVENTIONAL? SOCIAL IDENTITY WITHIN THE CHAMBER TOMB OF QUANTERNESS, ORKNEY

Rebecca Crozier

Introduction

Human remains present us with the most intimate and tangible connection to our ancestors and, as such, they are one of the most emotive relics of our past. This connection to past societies has allowed human remains to become of great significance to archaeologists for reasons beyond their biological importance. Considered contextually with other physical remnants of our past, this evidence plays a pivotal role in our understanding of the complex relationship between our ancestors and the world in which they lived.

Identity, in osteoarchaeological terms, is traditionally focused upon demographic data: upon establishing population profiles founded on the assessment of age, sex and health. However, this important quantitative approach is hindered when applied to the British Neolithic period, due to the limited volumes of human remains (Smith and Brickley 2009, 148). Known assemblages generally comprise populations which have been counted in single figures, with the assemblage of 36 individuals found at West Kennet Long Barrow, Avebury, being one of the largest in mainland Britain (Bayliss *et al.* 2007, 86). In an accumulative study, Roberts and Cox (2003, 28) counted a total of 772 skeletons from 24 sites for the British Neolithic. The paucity of this resource is more apparent when contrasted with the thousands of skeletons identified from the Roman and medieval periods (*ibid.*). The small quantities of bone discovered within the majority of the Neolithic tombs are therefore regarded as disproportionate (Smith and Brickley 2009, 88). Indeed, the lack of osseous remains strongly indicates that the majority of the dead were subject to funerary practices – such as excarnation – which rendered them, ultimately, archaeologically invisible (Barrett 1988, 32; Fowler 2010, 15–6; Smith 2006, 684).

In light of the dearth of this material, the identity of the bodies contained within the surviving funerary assemblages is of particular interest, not only in terms of understanding social organisation, but also in the significance of the structures from which they were recovered. The underlying rationale behind the apparent minority practice of interment within a monument, most logically signals the presence of a distinctive identity. Factors connected to social status or lineages (Edmonds 1999, 61; Fowler 2010) are often advanced as explanations for such activity. These interpretations could be applied to individuals who are regarded as occupying an elevated position in society or, just as plausibly, a socially marginalised role, such as a shaman (Fowler 2010, 15). Evidence for violence, intimating a 'difficult death' (*ibid*.), has been identified on human remains in southern Britain (*e.g.* Knüsel 2006, 218–20; Schulting and Wysocki 2005). This evidence has generated the alternative hypothesis that it was the *manner* of death, rather than social status, which created the need for separation.

Strong similarities, both temporally and architecturally, have resulted in frequent comparisons between the megaliths of southern Britain and those found throughout Orkney in Scotland. The Orcadian tombs are also characterised by a general absence of human remains (Barber 2000, 185). It is perhaps, therefore, unsurprising that familiar hypotheses of high prestige individuals or the 'unacceptable dead' (Barber 2000, 187), are often advanced to identify the Orcadian bones. However, a recent re-analysis by the author of the human remains from the Orcadian tomb of Quanterness, Mainland, Orkney (Crozier 2012), has generated an alternative avenue of thought. Drawing on information contained in site reports, examples from the ethnographic record and osteological analysis, it is proposed that the identities of those within the Orcadian tombs may not be as 'special' as current interpretations invoke.

Orcadian tombs

Located at 59°N in the North Atlantic Ocean and consisting of approximately 70 islands and skerries, the archipelago of the Orkney Islands is separated from the north-east tip of the Scottish mainland by the Pentland Firth (Figure 3.1). Famous for its archaeological remains, the tombs of Neolithic Orkney in particular, are renowned for their stunning architecture. Their preservation and high degree of visibility within the landscape has piqued the interest of archaeologists and antiquarians for many years (see Davidson and Henshall 1989; Fraser 1983 for an overview).

In instances where remains have been discovered within these tombs, the assemblages typically comprise low volumes of bone (Table 3.1). However, three exceptions to this trend have been discovered. Excavated in 1972–74, the chamber tomb of Quanterness contained over 12,000 fragments of human bone (Renfrew 1979), the first time that an assemblage of this size had been discovered for the British Neolithic. A few years later, excavations by the landowner at Isbister, South Ronaldsay, recovered a human bone assemblage in excess of 16,000 fragments (Hedges 1983). Together these tombs contain a

Table 3.1: MNI for sites from Britain and Ireland (adapted from Smith and Brickley 2009, 88).

Site	Location	MNI
Isbister	**Orkney**	**85**
Quanterness	**Orkney**	**59**
West Kennet	England	36
Fussell's Lodge	England	34
Hazleton North	England	33
Parc le Breos Cwm	Wales	31
Ascott-under-Wychwood	England	21
West Tump	England	18
Boles Barrow	England	15
Burn Ground	England	15
Wayland's Smithy	England	15
Quoyness	**Orkney**	**13**
Point of Cott	**Orkney**	**9**
Pierowall Quarry	Orkney	8
Lanhill	England	7
Adlestrop	England	6
Haddenham	England	5

Figure 3.1: Location map of Orkney and sites mentioned in the text (Ordnance Survey* & Historic Scotland†).

significant proportion of the human remains archive for the whole of Britain, and were calculated to represent 157 individuals (Chesterman 1979, 99) and 341 individuals (Chesterman 1983, 79), respectively. More recently, a large volume of human bone was also discovered from the tomb at Banks, South Ronaldsay (Lee 2011), intimating that a significant number of individuals may have been associated with this tomb. Such quantities of bone not only differentiate these particular structures from other Orcadian tombs, but also from megaliths across the rest of Britain.

Despite the volume of archive material from Quanterness and Isbister, their potential remained largely untapped, receiving little attention until recently (see Lawrence 2006). Quanterness itself has not been subject to a thorough re-analysis, despite advances in osteological research, since the original study by Chesterman (1979). The reluctance to re-assess this material reflects not only the formidable amount of bone, but also the highly fragmentary and 'chaotic' condition of the remains (Renfrew 1979, 52). However, recent developments in taphonomic analysis inferred that this large assemblage had the potential to yield new information. In particular, the volume of human remains and the high standard of excavation at the tomb of Quanterness established this assemblage as a prime candidate for re-examination by the author.

Quanterness

In the 1970s, Colin Renfrew sought an appropriate site from which to acquire samples for radiocarbon dating (1979, 45). The chambered cairn of Quanterness, situated on the mainland of Orkney in the parish of Kirkwall, was first explored in *c.* 1805 by the Reverend George Barry (1805). From Barry's accounts, it was apparent to Renfrew that much of the cairn and its contents had suffered only minimal disturbance, making Quanterness the best candidate for excavation (Figure 3.2). In addition to obtaining dating material, the ensuing fieldwork programme (1972–4) also aimed to locate undisturbed burial deposits to clarify the mortuary processes (Renfrew 1979, 46). Approximately 80% of the main chamber and one of the six side cells (ZF) were excavated (Renfrew 1979, 162).

The human remains were found in a predominantly disarticulated, highly fragmented and chaotic state (Chesterman 1979). Examples of articulated individuals were identified within a cist cut into the floor of the main chamber (Pit A), and a pit cut into the top of the main bone spread (Pit C in the main chamber), though these remains were exceptional instances among the mass of fragmentary bones (refer to Figure 3.2). Chesterman (1979, 99) determined that the assemblage was composed of 85 adults, 35 teenagers, 26 children, and 10 infants. The data led Renfrew (1979, 162) to propose that here, at last, was evidence that had previously proven elusive throughout Britain: the presence of an entire Neolithic community. Furthermore, the identification of 32 males and 27 females intimated that there had been no exclusion from the tomb on the grounds of sex. The only identifiable bias was in the total absence of babies under eight months of age (Chesterman 1979, 99), an absence thought to signal a differential mortuary treatment for this age group (Renfrew 1979, 162). In fact, this absence of babies within the assemblage has contributed, in conjunction with the large volume of bone, to Quanterness being regarded as 'atypical' to other megalithic tombs (Richards 1988, 50).

In a subsequent appraisal of the Orcadian Neolithic population, Barber (2000, 185)

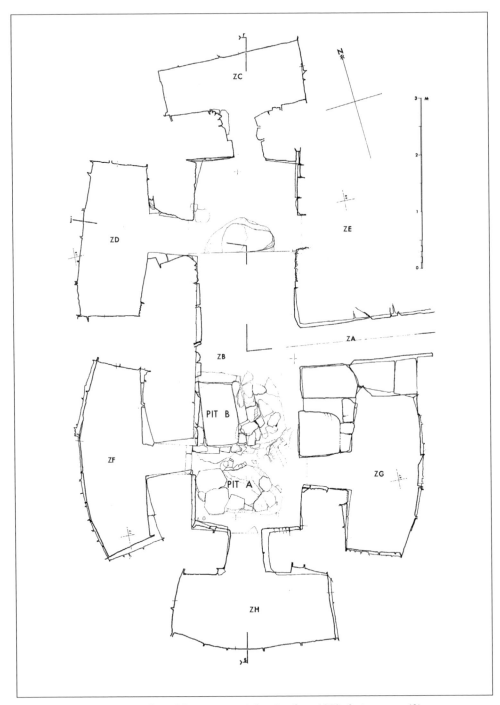

Figure 3.2: Plan of Quanterness (after Renfrew 1979, facing page 62).

questioned the assertion that the large volumes of bone from Quanterness and Isbister might represent entire communities. Barber (*ibid.*) contends that even if each of the 80 known Orcadian tombs contained around 340 people (as at Isbister), this would mean only 50 to 84 individuals of all ages on each island which, he argues, is not sufficient to sustain a 'viable population'. It is therefore argued that the Orcadian Neolithic, despite the greater richness in its human remains, still suffers from an absence of evidence for the main populace.

One of the difficulties with Renfrew's observation, and Barber's subsequent criticism, is that both hypotheses incorporate the numbers of individuals present as an absolute reflection of the quantity originally interred. In both instances an inherent assumption has been made: not only is there no excavation bias, but over the course of thousands of years, no other extrinsic factors may have affected the character of the final assemblage. The significance of this observation will be discussed in more detail later in this chapter.

Rethinking the numbers

From inspection of the original report, it was evident that the rationale employed by Chesterman to calculate the Minimum Number of Individuals (MNI) for Quanterness could have produced an over estimation (Schulting *et al.* 2010, 5). Therefore, one of the key aims in undertaking a re-assessment of the Quanterness remains was to verify the number of individuals actually represented. The analysis has led to a significant re-calculation of the original figure from 157, down to just 59 individuals (Crozier 2012). This may seem like a dramatic reduction, but a similarly pronounced diminution was recently reported for Isbister, from 341 (Chesterman 1983, 77), to 85 individuals (Lawrence 2006, 55).

The revised Quanterness MNI would appear to support Barber, and challenge Renfrew's original assumption that the osseous material represents a 'whole population'. The plausibility of such a hypothesis is further challenged by recent dating evidence. A new set of 20 AMS radiocarbon dates indicate deposition of human remains between 3510–3220 cal BC and 2850–2790 cal BC (95.4% probability) (Schulting *et al.* 2010), confirming a long period of use lasting between *350 and 720 years*. Therefore, when considering the new, substantially lower MNI, and the prolonged duration of tomb use, it may initially be suggested that Quanterness actually conforms to the hypothesis that a limited proportion of the population were interred within Neolithic megalithic tombs, as observed for the other British and Irish tombs (Smith and Brickley 2009). Naturally, this hypothesis assumes the MNI accurately portrays the number originally deposited within the structure.

As previously stated, the original figure of 157 individuals, in tandem with the absence of babies under eight months, earned Quanterness the mantle of 'atypical'. Re-analysis has not only revised the numbers of individuals represented by the remains, it has also resulted in the identification of at least two neonates (age 0–1 month). The very small size of bones from this age group most reasonably accounts for their omission from the original analysis. This observation undermines the previous assumption that babies were subject to different mortuary treatment, rather, they had been unidentified during the original analysis. Although the nature of the Quanterness assemblage precludes a satisfactory assessment of the demographic profile, and it was not possible to support Chesterman's original assessment, all age categories were identified. It was possible to further identify both males and females within the assemblage. Therefore the current evidence, as it stands, does not indicate any bias or 'special' selection for interment on biological grounds.

In order to further contextualise the Quanterness data, the assemblages from Point of Cott (Barber 1997), Cuween Hill (Charleson 1902) and Quoyness (Farrer 1870) were also re-examined (Figure 3.1). Investigation confirmed that these collections represent much smaller numbers of individuals (Table 3.1), ostensibly demonstrating little affinity with the large numbers from Quanterness. How might this discrepancy be rationalised? Accounts of disturbed deposits and decaying bone contained in the relevant excavation reports not only provide some explanation for these lower figures, but intimate caution is needed in our acceptance of the MNI as definitive.

At Quoyness, a MNI of 13 was calculated (Crozier 2012). Of particular interest in the original report is Farrer's (1870, 399) description of a stratum of bone, 0.4 m thick, that had been too decayed to lift. While it is impossible to be sure if this osseous material was all human, it clearly implies that the original volume of bone deposited in Quoyness was much greater than that which has survived for analysis today. For Point of Cott the MNI of nine represents a somewhat reduced figure from the original estimate. This, in part, is due to a number of fragments not being available at the time of re-analysis. Barber (1997, 68) states that soil samples taken from inside this chamber revealed very high levels of phosphate, which could indicate residue from human bone following decomposition (although this could feasibly be animal as well). Here, again, is an indication that the volume of bone, and therefore the MNI, was originally greater than has survived to the present. The excavation reports for Cuween Hill also infer greater volumes of bone within the tombs than was actually recovered. Charleson (1902, 733) observed up to eight individuals during excavation, however, three of these were from skulls that 'crumbled away when touched'. A similar observation of highly decayed bone, unsuitable for detailed inquiry, was also made at Quanterness (Chesterman 1979, 97).

Evidence within the reports clearly supports a hypothesis that the bone assemblages within these tombs have suffered an appreciable level of decay. Therefore, the MNI figures cannot reflect the true volume of bone originally contained within the tombs. Nevertheless, it is possible that while the final numbers recovered by archaeologists have been affected by 'normal' levels of decay, the variation in MNI between sites is real. That is to say, some tombs may have held greater numbers of individuals than others.

While the other assemblages included in this study have comparatively low MNI values, other Orcadian sites have been found to contain more substantial quantities of bone. For example, at Midhowe on Rousay, 25 individuals were identified (Callander and Grant 1934, 330). A second-hand description of Korkquoy, an 'immense chambered tomb' on Westray, describes skeletons lying in 'tiers', some apparently crouched, amounting to 60 or 70 individuals (Davidson and Henshall 1989, 141). Frustratingly, these remains are now lost, preventing verification. Although osteological analysis is in the preliminary stages, initial reports indicate that the recently discovered human remains at Banks Tomb in South Ronaldsay (Lee 2011) represent similar volumes of bone to those found at Quanterness and Isbister.

Issues of decay have been highlighted by Beckett and Robb (2009, 67) who argue that low numbers of individuals do not necessarily imply that only select sections of a population were buried in tombs. Using a computer simulated model, they argue that,

regardless of whether 100 or 1000
people were originally buried in their
'virtual tomb', the MNI never exceeds
100, and often converges upon far
fewer. The model assumes a practice
involving the sequential interment of
bodies, with new additions largely
destroying the burials already present.
This hypothesis would certainly go
some way to explaining the relatively
low numbers from all the sites across
Britain and Ireland.

Another form of bone degradation
(decay) is known as 'weathering'.
Weathering refers to macroscopic
surface changes observed on bone
that has been exposed on the ground
surface. The gradual degradation of
skeletal elements has been observed
to occur in a defined sequence, first
outlined by Behrensmeyer (1978). The
taphonomic re-analysis demonstrated
that all of the site assemblages under
investigation illustrated a range
of weathering stages (Figure 3.3).
However, an absence of advanced
levels of weathering (*i.e.* the bone is
splintered, fragile and/or easily falls
away when touched) is possibly due
to the friable nature of bone at these

*Figure 3.3: Crania from Cuween Hill displaying
differential weathering stages (Rebecca Crozier).*

advanced levels. In these advanced cases, the bone would be significantly degraded, creating
difficulties during excavation and at the post-excavation stage (Janaway *et al.* 2001, 201;
204), which may account for poor representation. The presence of a variation in weathering
lends credence to the original accounts from Quanterness that described the discovery of bone
in a broad variety of conditions. Furthermore, the range of decay identified in the reports
and in the taphonomic study, supports a hypothesis of sequential interment.

The review of the MNI figures demonstrates that Chesterman's original calculations over-
emphasised the numbers of bodies within a few Orcadian tombs. While the numbers are
still relatively large, they are no longer as vastly divergent from many of the other Orcadian
tombs as previously thought. Although the MNI data, in isolation, suggests that internment
in the tombs was a highly selective process, taphonomic analysis of the assemblage has
generated a more complex picture, illustrating an appreciable degree of bone degradation.
The extent of decay and weathering means that the recorded assemblages are unlikely to
present an accurate reflection of the true intensity of use of the megalithic structures in
Orkney. Undoubtedly, decay over time is not the only factor in need of consideration.

Ethnographic parallels

New methods of accounting for the perceived under-representation of individuals may be gleaned from the ethnographic literature. The close association of the Merina tombs of Madagascar with the ancestors (Bloch 1971) has previously been used to draw analogies for the interpretation of Stonehenge (Parker Pearson 1999; Parker Pearson and Ramilisonina 1998). Graeber's (1995) observations of the specific funerary practices, known as 'Famadihana', associated with the Merina tombs, is presented here to provide another perspective to help interpret the low numbers of individuals recovered from the tombs.

Famadihana refers to rituals held for the purpose of transferring a body from a temporary grave to its ancestral tomb, or from one tomb to another, or to remove the bodies temporarily for the purposes of wrapping them in new silk shrouds. During famadihana, Graeber (1995, 263) observed that the bodies are intentionally subjected to a great deal of rough handling: 'they are made to dance with living partners, pulled and tugged, wrapped and bound with extreme force, and then dragged into a still more tumultuous dance before being returned to their shelves'. In this way, after just 20 years and several famadihana rituals, there is little left to identify the remains as having been of human form. Furthermore, new tombs are continually being constructed as older tombs are emptied and abandoned (*ibid.*, 262). Of particular relevance for understanding low numbers of individuals within the Neolithic tombs of Orkney, is Graeber's (*ibid.*, 263) observation that despite each tomb being in use for at least a century, he was continually surprised by how few bodies the tombs contained. Graeber attributes this phenomenon partly to the building of new tombs, which led to the removal of ancestors from older tombs for placement in the new, but primarily resulting from the habit of the consolidation of bodies as part of the famadihana rites.

This example illustrates that despite longevity of use, and use by the entire population, the remains within these Merina tombs are not indicative of the true numbers of people placed within their confines. The employment of similar practices, involving the clearing out and relocation of bodies, could reasonably explain the empty tombs in Orkney. This ethnographic observation would also go some way to supporting Beckett and Robb's (2009, 67) hypothesis that low numbers do not necessarily indicate that a select proportion of the population were interred.

A new way of thinking

As suggested at the beginning of this chapter, the majority of the British Neolithic population is missing, evidently disposed of in an archaeologically invisible way. The individuals recovered from many of the megalithic tombs are, therefore, considered to have been a special and select few. This hypothesis is founded on the low volumes of recovered remains, in tandem with their placement within such enigmatic and permanent structures. The criteria suggested to warrant inclusion within the tombs range from shamans and community leaders, to those suffering 'difficult deaths', such as suicide or accident (Fowler 2010; Leach 2008).

In light of new evidence from this study, an alternative perspective, in terms of the Orcadian Neolithic, is suggested. This new hypothesis requires a fundamental shift in perspective, wherein the existing interpretation, founded on absolute recovery, is inverted. It has been suggested that the assemblages described here represent a fraction of the original volume of remains placed within the tombs, with taphonomic analysis indicating much of the bone has decayed over time. It is therefore considered entirely plausible that most of the population had been placed within the tombs. This premise is reinforced by the range of ages identified within the assemblage, which includes young children and infants. Descriptions of bone, rendered unrecoverable by decay in the site reports and evidence for variations in weathering underlines the need for caution in assuming the MNI accurately indicates the numbers placed within the tombs.

In accepting this hypothesis, it can be concluded that those individuals interred within the tomb had not been 'specially' selected for inclusion. If the general populace were entombed within these monuments it would have a profound effect upon our conceptualisation of their identity, shifting our perception of what constitutes 'special'. Indeed, the question now concerns the fate not of the main populace, but of those individuals that were socially taboo, or excluded, on the grounds of disease, mode of death, crime and disability, or social status. Were some individuals accorded a variation in treatment at all? Evidently, not all individuals were placed in similar structures, and this hypothesis has implications for the small numbers of human remains found on other, non-megalithic Orcadian sites. At Knap of Howar, Papa Westray, a fragment of human skull was located in the 'domestic' deposits within the house structure (MacDonald 1946, 183). An isolated deposit within the Knoll of Skulzie, Westray, was composed of a large number of human skulls associated with two polished stone axes (Richards 1988, 50). The mound from which these remains originate is thought to be a broch (Mackie 2002, 247), although there is no definitive evidence at present. At the Neolithic village of Skara Brae, a contracted burial from Hut 1 was considered intrusive, but the burial of two adult females beneath the walls of House 7 was considered to be a foundation deposit for the walls of the hut (Childe 1931, 139–42). Other human bones were found in the corner of Passage A (Hut 1), and associated with animal bone (*ibid.*, 140).

The frequency of human remains in these types of non-funerary contexts accounts for a small proportion of the osseous material from the Orcadian Neolithic, however, their presence should perhaps be considered more significant than previously thought (see Cleary, this volume, for an appraisal of such remains in a Bronze Age, Irish context). If such depositions were intentional and therefore a conscious act, this phenomenon would have implications for the perception that tombs bound and constrained the relics of the dead. Thus, any action involving the movement of remains around the landscape could be imbued with an even more powerful significance. While these 'alternative' deposits of human bone do occur in Orkney, they are less common than those reported from England, such as at Hambledon Hill (McKinley 2008, 504–5).

Conclusions

The overall aim of this chapter has been to encourage a greater consideration of what may have been lost from the archaeological record, and how it may bias our interpretations. It is important to recognise that the condition of human remains within the Orcadian tombs, at the point of excavation, equates to the final stage in a complex sequence of taphonomic events (Thomas 2000, 658). By fixating on MNI figures as definitive and absolute, the identification of those within tombs as 'special' becomes our own construct. Certainly within the Orcadian monuments, the possibility exists that those within the structures were not necessarily distinct from the rest of the population. Evidently, the remains of the majority of the Neolithic population are missing from Orkney, but this is argued to be the result of normal decay, possibly enhanced by activities akin to those illustrated in the ethnographical example given here. Rather than asking, 'where are the bodies buried?' (Barber 2000, 185), perhaps the question should be, 'were some people accorded differential burial treatment at all?'

Acknowledgements

This chapter is based on work carried out as part of the author's PhD project. I would therefore like to thank my supervisor, Eileen Murphy, for her support and enthusiasm throughout. Particular thanks go to Alison Sheridan (National Museum of Scotland) for kindly granting generous access to the human remains from Quanterness and Quoyness. Thanks must also be extended to the late Anne Brundle, for allowing access to the assemblages from Pierowall Quarry and Point of Cott. I am also very grateful to my colleagues, Victoria Ginn and Rebecca Enlander, for reading and commenting on earlier drafts.

References

Barber, J. (ed.) (1997) *The excavation of a stalled cairn at the Point of Cott, Westray, Orkney*. Scotland, The Scottish Trust for Archaeological Research.

Barber, J. (2000) Death in Orkney: a rare event. In A. Ritchie (ed.) *Neolithic Orkney in its European context*, 185–8. Cambridge, McDonald Institute for Archaeological Research.

Barrett, J. C. (1988) The living, the dead and the ancestors: Neolithic and Early Bronze Age mortuary practices. In J. C. Barrett and I. A. Kinnes (eds) *The archaeology of context in the Neolithic and Bronze Age: recent trends*, 30–41. Sheffield, Department of Archaeology, University of Sheffield.

Barry, G. (1805) *History of the Orkney Islands*. Edinburgh.

Beckett, J. and Robb, J. (2009) Neolithic burial taphonomy, ritual, and interpretation in Britain and Ireland: a review. In R. Gowland and C. J. Knüsel (eds) *Social archaeology of funerary remains*, 57–72. Oxford, Oxbow.

Bayliss, A., Whittle, A., and Wysocki, M. (2007) Talking about my generation: the date of the West Kennet Long Barrow. *Cambridge Archaeological Journal* 17, 85–101.

Behrensmeyer, A. K. (1978) Taphonomic and ecologic information from bone weathering. *Palaeobiology* 4, 150–62.

Bloch, M. (1971) *Placing the dead: tombs, ancestral villages, and kinship organisation in Madagascar*. London, Seminar.

Callander, G. J. and Grant, W. G. (1934) A long stalled chambered cairn or mausoleum (Rousay Type) near Midhowe, Rousay, Orkney. *Proceedings of the Society of the Antiquaries of Scotland* 68, 320–52.

Charleson, M. M. (1902) Notice of a chambered cairn in the parish of Firth, Orkney. *Proceedings of the Society of Antiquaries of Scotland* 36, 733–38.

Chesterman, J. T. (1979) Investigation of the human bones from Quanterness. In C. Renfrew (ed.) *Investigations in Orkney*, 97–107. London, The Society of Antiquaries of London.

Chesterman, J. T. (1983) The human skeletal remains. In J. W. Hedges (ed.) *Isbister: a chambered tomb in Orkney*, 73–132. British Archaeological Reports, British Series. Oxford, Archaeopress.

Childe, V. G. (1931) *Skara Brae: a pictish village in Orkney*. London, Kegan Paul, Trench, Trubner & Co., Ltd.

Crozier, R. (2012) *A taphonomic approach to the re-analysis of the human remains from the Neolithic chamber tomb of Quanterness, Orkney*. Belfast, Queen's University Belfast, unpublished PhD thesis.

Davidson, J. L. and Henshall, A. S. (1989) *The chambered cairns of Orkney*. Edinburgh, Edinburgh University Press.

Edmonds, M. (1999) *Ancestral geographies of the Neolithic*. London and New York, Routledge.

Farrer, J. (1870) Note of excavations in Sanday, one of the North Isles of Orkney. *Proceedings of the Society of Antiquaries of Scotland* 7, 398–401.

Fowler, C. (2010) Pattern and diversity in the Early Neolithic. Mortuary practices of Britain and Ireland: contextualising the treatment of the dead. *Documenta Praehistorica* 41, 1–22.

Fraser, D. (1983) *Land and society in Neolithic Orkney*. British Archaeological Reports, British Series. Oxford, Archaeopress.

Graeber, D. (1995) Dancing with corpses reconsidered: an interpretation of famadihana (in Arivonimamo, Madagascar). *American Ethnologist* 22, 258–78.

Hedges, J. W. (1983) *Isbister: a chambered tomb in Orkney*. British Archaeological Reports, British Series. Oxford, Archaeopress.

Janaway, R. C., Wilson, A. S., Caffell, A. C., and Roberts, C. A. (2001) Human skeletal collections: the responsibilities of project managers, physical anthropologists and conservators, and the need for standardized condition assessment. In E. Wiliams *Human remains: conservation, retrieval and analysis: proceedings of a conference held in Williamsburg, VA, Nov 7–11th 1999*, 199–208. British Archaeological Reports, International Series Volume 934. Oxford, Archaeopress.

Knüsel, C. (2006) The arrowhead injury to individual B2. In D. Benson and A. Whittle *Building memories: the Neolithic Cotswold long barrow at Ascott-under-Wychwood, Oxfordshire*, 218–20. Oxford, Oxbow.

Lawrence, D. (2006) Neolithic mortuary practice in Orkney. *Proceedings of the Society of Antiquaries of Scotland* 136, 47–60.

Leach, S. (2008) Odd one out? Earlier Neolithic deposition of human remains in caves and rock shelters in the Yorkshire Dales. In E. Murphy (ed.) *Deviant burial in the archaeological record*, 35–56. Oxford, Oxbow.

Lee, D. (2011) Banks chambered tomb, South Ronaldsay. *Orkney Data Structure Report*. Unpublished report.

MacDonald, G. (1946) *Twelfth report with an inventory of the Ancient Monuments of Orkney and Shetland*. Volume 2. Edinburgh, Royal Commission on the Ancient and Historical Monuments of Scotland.

Mackie, E. W. (2002) *The roundhouses, brochs and wheelhouses of Atlantic Scotland c. 700 BC– AD 500: architecture and material culture. Part 1 – the Orkney and Shetland Isles*. British Archaeological Reports, British Series Volume 342. Oxford, Archaeopress.

McKinley, J. I. (2008) Human remains. In R. Mercer and F. Healey (eds) *Hambledon Hill, Dorset, England: excavations and survey of a Neolithic monument complex and its surrounding landscape*. London, English Heritage Archaeological Report.

Parker Pearson, M. and Ramilisonina, R. (1998) Stonehenge for the ancestors: the stones pass on the message. *Antiquity* 72, 308–26.

Renfrew, C. (1979) *Investigations in Orkney*. London, The Society of Antiquaries of London.

Richards, C. (1988) Altered images: a re-examination of Neolithic mortuary practices in Orkney. In J. C. Barrett and I. A. Kinnes (eds) *The archaeology of context in the Neolithic and Bronze Age: recent trends*, 42–56. Sheffield, Department of Archaeology, University of Sheffield.

Roberts, C. A. and Cox, M. (2003) *Health and disease in Britain: from prehistory to the present day*. Stroud, Sutton Publishing Limited.

Schulting, R. J., Sheridan, A., Crozier, R., and Murphy, E. (2010) Revisiting Quanterness: new AMS dates and stable isotope data from an Orcadian chamber tomb. *Proceedings of the Society of Antiquaries of Scotland* 140, 1–50.

Schulting, R. J. and Wysocki, M. (2005) 'In this chambered tumulus were found cleft skulls...': an assessment of the evidence for cranial trauma in the British Neolithic. *Proceedings of the Prehistoric Society* 71, 107–38.

Smith, M. (2006) Bones chewed by canids as evidence for human excarnation: a British case study. *Antiquity* 80, 671–85.

Smith, M. and Brickley, M. (2009) *People of the long barrows: life, death and burial in the Earlier Neolithic*. Stroud, The History Press.

Thomas, J. (2000) Death, identity and the body in Neolithic Britain. *Journal of the Royal Anthropological Institute* 6, 653–68.

4

IS IT POSSIBLE TO ACCESS IDENTITY THROUGH THE OSTEOARCHAEOLOGICAL RECORD? HINDLOW: A BRONZE AGE CASE STUDY

Sam Walsh

Introduction

Different forms of identity have often been understood in terms of binary oppositions. Within archaeology this can be seen in studies which attempt to differentiate between identities using similarity and difference. This is particularly noticeable in studies of burial sequences within round barrows (Last 1998; Mizoguchi 1993) where later burials over time are thought to be referencing earlier burials which were used as a symbolic resource. This is inferred from the similarities or differences in aspects of the mortuary process such as position, direction of the body and grave-goods. A case study of a British Bronze Age mortuary site is used to question how we might examine aspects of identity through burial process and osteology.

Background

Previous discussions of identity in archaeology have usually been derived from artefacts, at times bypassing the human remains to discuss the grave-goods without relating them to the deceased (Brück 2004; Healy and Harding 2004; Jones 2002; Shennan 1975). The archaeological study of identity (especially within Bronze Age literature) has often been centred on the status of the dead, usually inferred from the number and rarity of artefacts. In contrast, osteological studies have been based on biological indications of physiological stress to indicate status and so on. Such indications include cribra orbitalia, stature, periostitis, enamel hypoplasia, and other palaeopathological evidence which can be very informative to our understanding the lives of past peoples. For example, cribra orbitalia is an area of porosity which occurs in the roof of the orbit and may indicate a mineral deficiency or metabolic disorder (Walker *et al.* 2009). Enamel hypoplasia occurs when there is interruption to the development of the tooth enamel (which can be seen as a defect on the tooth) for example due to infection, birth trauma or low birth weight (Waldron 2009, 244). These kinds of indications of health are important as they can tell us about episodes of ill-health during the life-course.

Osteological studies have focused on finding aspects of identity which are 'statistically significant' (*e.g.* Robb *et al.* 2001). Overall, empty demographic data or individual case studies are meaningless without discussion of the deceased within the mortuary context. Both these approaches, while useful and interesting, fail singly as these forms of evidence are often interpreted out of context.

Examining aspects of identity through burial process and osteology

Different forms of identity have often been understood in binary opposites, for example, agency vs structure, the individual vs the social, and the 'Self' vs the 'Other'. These things are defined by their opposites and lead to a very black and white view which cannot explain uncertainty or change (Hockey and James 2003, 13). Within archaeology this can be seen in studies which attempt to differentiate between identities, using similarity and difference. This is particularly noticeable in studies of burial sequences within round barrows (Last 1998; Mizoguchi 1993) where later burials over time are thought to be referencing earlier burials; this is inferred from the similarities in aspects of the mortuary process such as position and direction of the body. Within social theory, Jenkins (1996, 4) and Hockey and James (2003, 13) criticise this structured duality as a 'snap-shot' of something which is really a process, working on many levels of thoughts or actions. Jenkins (1996) suggests creating a synthesis between the two opposites, understanding identity as a process of being or becoming so a person's identities are never final. This means that identity can be understood as a process of events which occur over the life-course.

Osteologically visible processes could include age and the life-course and events which affect the body, such as illness, trauma and certain activities. Archaeologically visible identity processes may include the mortuary process, gender roles and status, while osteologically visible identity processes could be argued to represent the deceased in a biological sense.

Archaeologically visible processes may be said to be more obviously representative of the mourners and perhaps their relationships with the dead, as they are the active participants in the mortuary rite (Parker Pearson 1999). However, Sørensen (2009, 111) has discussed how the dead can affect the behaviour of the living and in this way manipulate the mourners and have power over the mortuary rite; the bereaved are 'moved to move' (Sheets-Johnstone 1999, 275).

There are numerous choices which can be made throughout the burial process: most notable of these is the choice of inhumation or cremation. Choices which are considered in this study are the layering of burials and mound phases and the disturbance of earlier burials. These burial choices may then be linked with osteological aspects of the deceased such as age, sex and disease.

Hindlow round cairn, Derbyshire

Hindlow, an Early Bronze Age round cairn in Derbyshire (National Grid Reference SK836917), was first investigated by Bateman in 1845 and in the 1950s a recue excavation was carried out by Ashbee and Ashbee (1981), who discovered the burials of around 21

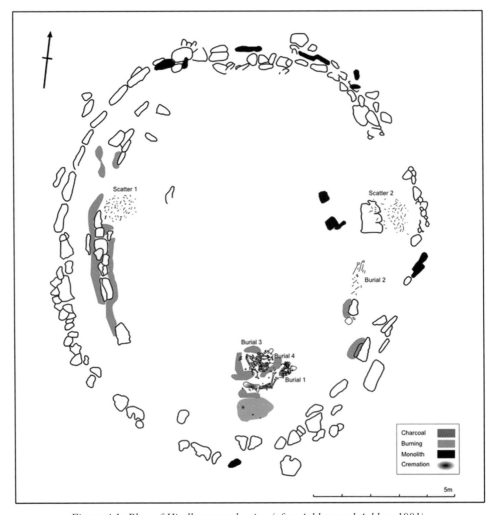

Figure 4.1: Plan of Hindlow round cairn (after Ashbee and Ashbee 1981).

individuals. Four of these were articulated and in stratified sequences with earlier disturbed burials (see Figure 4.1). The human remains have recently been analysed for Minimum Number of Individuals, age, sex, palaeopathology, and life histories by Walsh (2013) as part of PhD research. The results of this analysis, together with the re-evaluation of the Ashbees' report, have raised chronological issues concerning both the sequence at Hindlow and the relationships between burials.

Previous reliance on the model of primary burials followed by secondary burials seems to be problematic as this idea developed from the activities of antiquarians (Bateman 1848; Greenwell and Rolleston 1877) and has been incorporated into more recent research (Barrett 1990; Mizoguchi 1993). The idea of primary/secondary burial often does not agree with the evidence or explain the more complex phases of burials at various sites, for example

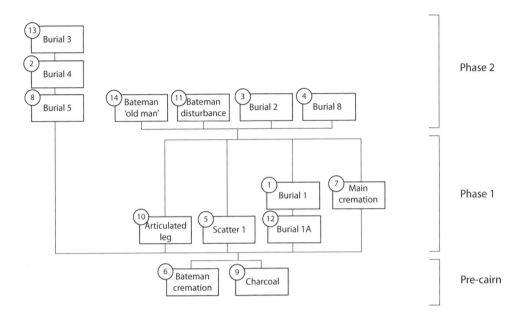

○ Radiocarbon sample

Figure 4.2: Model of phases at Hindlow round cairn.

at Deeping St Nicholas (French 1994) and Barrow Hills (Barclay and Halpin 1998). The sequence at Hindlow also seems to contradict this model as Bateman never found a central, primary burial, and it is possible that there was in fact no primary burial in the centre of this barrow. It is therefore apparent that there are other sites where the sequence is not 'typical'.

The human remains from Hindlow were represented by at least seven adult males, five neonatal infants and at least four adult females, although these were earlier in the sequence and more fragmented. All age groups were represented in the assemblage. Palaeopathological evidence included indications of osteoarthritis and joint degeneration of the spine, which together probably indicate strenuous activity, probably farming. Other indications of disease included linear enamel hypoplasia, periostitis, osteoporosis, and mandibular abscess.

Pre-cairn activity is evidenced by a possible early cremation, discovered near the centre of the cairn by Bateman. The initial cairn was associated with two areas of burial: one of which included the remains of two juveniles, which were found among the loose stones at the base of the cairn and on the ground surface (Ashbee and Ashbee 1981, 15).

Also early in the sequence was Burial 1A (a juvenile aged *c.* 10 years old) which was under Burial 1 (an adult male, aged 20–30 years old). Burial 1 had indications of infection on his skull, was laid with his legs slightly flexed and at his feet was a cremation. This cremation, accompanied with a bronze awl, probably represented the remains of a woman and it is unknown whether it was deposited before or after Burial 1 (see Figure 4.2).

Associated with the second phase of cairn construction was Burial 2 which was laid onto the larger stones of the primary cairn, only *c*.15cm below the turf in the southeast quadrant. Underneath the legs of Burial 2 were the remains of an infant. Also associated with this phase was a second bone scatter which included the remains of an adult (Burial 8), an adolescent and an infant. The inhumations which were found by Bateman were apparently near the surface and were perhaps stratigraphically comparable with Burial 2.

Burial 3, a man aged 35–50, was laid in a flexed position, facing the opposite way as Burial 4 and it seems possible that Burials 3 and 4 were deposited together.

At Hindlow, Burials 1, 3 and 4 were deposited in a way which disturbed earlier bodies. It is possible that this was done on purpose. In some Bronze Age studies it has been shown that certain graves were marked, perhaps in order to avoid or return to them, as part of protracted burial rites (Woodward 2002, 25). The continued deposition of bodies in the main burial area seems to show knowledge of the placement of these burials. It may be possible that this area was left open for some time. The returning to, and disturbance of, earlier burials may indicate a need to connect the older deceased with the more recently deceased which could be argued to be positive or negative. A positive connection could be interpreted as an affirmation of belonging to a particular social group. The negative alternative would perhaps be the purposeful destruction of the older remains, which are replaced with preferred bodies for whatever social or political reason.

Conclusion

At Hindlow the living seem to have returned to one area and disturbed earlier burials with later ones. This could indicate remembrance of the earliest dead in a positive way, to re-affirm group and individual identity. Alternatively, the oldest burials may have been purposefully disturbed as a way of asserting a different identity. This may be made visible from the sequence and practice of barrow burial and construction and osteological indications of life history. These ideas could be interpreted with barrow building as a visible construction of group identity. The community identified with each other through their relationship with the barrow (Holtorf 1998). The people who used Hindlow as a burial site, related their group to the barrow, it was a fixed place in their landscape. As a place for the dead the barrow formed a history – known or mythological – which could be referred to as a place of influence, where the dead could be revered, manipulated or avoided. The monument remains apart from daily life, but has longevity which enables a community connection so the site is returned to; the cairn becomes a mnemonic of social identity through time.

Post-script

Of the *c*. 21 individuals within the Hindlow assemblage a sample from each of the main contexts was radiocarbon dated (Table 4.1) using OxCal v4.1.7 (Bronk Ramsey 2009). This included three of the articulated individuals, two of the cremated individuals and three scattered individuals. Initial radiocarbon results indicate that the earliest use of the site was during the Neolithic, further burials then occurred throughout the Bronze Age. The main difference to the original hypothesised sequence was the lateness of Burial 4 which had been

Table 4.1: Radiocarbon dates of a number of burials from Hindlow round cairn.

OXA	Sample number	Burial	Dates	Cal BC (95.4%)
25385	6	Bateman cremation	4244±32BP	2915–2703
25384	5	Scatter 1	3783±32BP	2335–2057
25380	1	Burial 1	3682±32BP	2193–1963
25383	4	Burial 8	3617±32BP	2119–1890
25382	3	Burial 2	3565±31BP	2022–1777
25386	7	Main cremation	3564±33BP	2022–1776
25387	8	Burial 5	3523±32BP	1936–1753
25381	2	Burial 4	3312±30BP	1681–1518

thought by the Ashbee's to be among the earliest burials. These results will be published in full at a later date (Walsh *et al.* in prep).

Acknowledgements

Many thanks to Dr Rick Peterson and Dr Mick Wysocki (UCLan) for advice, Martha Lawrence at Buxton Museum for access to the Hindlow assemblage, and Professor Tom Higham (RLAHA) for advice and the NERC for radiocarbon funds. Also, many thanks to Rebecca Crozier, Victoria Ginn and Rebecca Enlander for organising both the conference which this chapter came from and for encouraging me to contribute to this publication.

References

Ashbee, A. and Ashbee, R. (1981) A cairn on Hindlow, Derbyshire: excavations, 1953. *Derbyshire Archaeological Journal* 101, 9–41.
Bateman, T. (1848) *Vestiges of the antiquities of Derbyshire*. Derbyshire, Scarthin Books.
Barclay, A. and Halpin, C. (1998) *Excavations at Barrow Hills, Radley, Oxfordshire, Vol. 1, the Neolithic and Bronze Age monument complex*. Oxford, Oxford University Press.
Barrett, J. (1990) The monumentality of death: the character of Early Bronze Age mortuary mounds in Southern Britain. *World Archaeology* 22 (2), 179–89.
Bronk Ramsey, C. (2009) Bayesian analysis of radiocarbon dates. *Radiocarbon* 51(1), 337–60.
Brück, J. (2004) Material metaphors: the relational construction of identity in Early Bronze Age burials in Ireland and Britain. *Journal of Social Archaeology* 4, 307–33.
French, C. A. (1994) *Excavation of the deeping St Nicholas barrow complex, South Lincolnshire*. Lincolnshire Archaeology and Heritage Reports Series. Lincolnshire, Heritage Trust of Lincolnshire.
Greenwell, W. and Rolleston, R. (1877) *British barrows: a record of the examination of sepulchral mounds in various parts of England*. Gloucestershire, Clarendon Press.
Healy, F. and Harding, J. (2004) Reading a burial: the legacy of Overton Hill. In A. Gibson and A. Sheridan (eds) *From sickles to circles. Britain and Ireland at the time of Stonehenge*, 176–93. Stroud, Tempus.
Hockey, J. and James, A. (2003) *Social identities across the life-course*. Basingstoke, Palgrave Macmillan.
Holtorf, C. (1998) The life-histories of megaliths in Mecklenburg-Vorpommern (Germany). *World Archaeology* 30 (1), 23–38.
Jones, A. (2002) A biography of colour: colour, material histories and personhood in the Early Bronze Age of Britain and Ireland. In A. Jones and G. MacGregor (eds) *Colouring the past*, 159–74. Oxford, Berg.
Jenkins, R. (1996) *Social identity*. London, Routledge.
Last, J. (1998) Books of life: biography and memory in a Bronze Age barrow. *Oxford Journal of Archaeology* 17(1), 43–53.

Mizoguchi, K. (1993) Time in the reproduction of mortuary practices. *World Archaeology* 25, 223–35.

Parker Pearson, M. (1999) *The archaeology of death and burial.* Stroud, Sutton.

Robb, J., Bigazzi, R., Lazzarini, L., Scarsini, C. and Sonego, F. (2001) Social 'status' and biological 'status': a comparison of grave goods and skeletal indicators from Pontecagnano. *American Journal of Physical Anthropology* 115 (3), 213–22.

Sheets-Johnstone, M. (1999) Emotion and movement. A beginning empirical-phenomenological analysis of their relationship. *Journal of Consciousness Studies* 6, 259–77.

Shennan, S. (1975) The social organization at BrANč. *Antiquity* 49, 279–88.

Sørensen, T. F. (2009) The presence of the dead: cemeteries, cremation and the staging of non-place. *Journal of Social Archaeology* 9(1), 110–35.

Waldron, T. (2009) *Palaeopathology.* Cambridge, Cambridge University Press.

Walker, P. L., Bathurst, R. R., Richman, R., Gjerdrum, T., and Andrushko, V. A. (2009) The causes of porotic hyperostosis and cribra orbitalia: a reappraisal of the iron-deficiency-anemia hypothesis. *American Journal of Physical Anthropology* 139, 109–25.

Walsh, S. (2013) *Identity as process: an archaeological and osteological study of Early Bronze Age burials in northern England.* Unpublished PhD thesis. Preston, University of Central Lancaster.

Walsh, S. Peterson, R. and Wysock, M. (in prep) Chronology and identity: comparative dating of four Bronze Age burial sites in Northern England.

Woodward, A. (2002) *British Barrows: a matter of life and death.* Stroud, Tempus.

Material culture of the living

Introduction

Caroline Malone

This section includes chapters that focus on extracting identity from the material record of the prehistoric past. The theme of identity in archaeology has become a quest for many scholars, but as such has sometimes become muddled with the more fundamental role of archaeology as a discipline, which surely is to understand the emergence and evolution of ancient societies from material evidence. Identity in archaeology, however one wishes to describe the concept, is all about distinguishing difference between forms of evidence that contain material and behavioural elements. These range from the very obviously man-made objects that are expressive vehicles of cultural and personal creativity, to the more diffused yet cultural constructions of living spaces, burial practices, food, farming, and manipulation of the wider landscape. Without the luxury of written records, cultural names or known individuals, prehistoric identity takes on a much more challenging aspect than does the quest for identities in later archaeology. Instead, we are reliant on scraps of surviving material and cultural patterning, that might or might not have been significant in the societies that made the material in the first place. Clearly methodological rigour and systematic study are important components that prehistoric archaeologists have to embrace in their quest to put identities of any value on the material they study.

The five writers in this section each examine how material remains – the very stuff of archaeology – have allowed exploration of different social expressions of identity. Nørgaard examines the role of the metalsmith through the processes of making objects, and brings her own personal and practical experience to the discussion. The fragments, residues, processing waste, and other components are examined, things that often are overlooked in the typical archaeological approach. Yet, as argued in the chapter, the specific practices of marking, making, decorating, and finishing metal objects holds valuable insights into the person who made them. Indeed, the very identity of the object is a reflection of its maker.

Cleary examines how human remains are manipulated within the social context of settlements in the Bronze Age. Her assessment explains how certain body parts were seemingly selected and then placed in what appear to be significant places in the domestic sphere. Many examples seem to demonstrate the strong intentionality of practices that imply human remains were considered as much a 'material' object as other made things. Though at some remove, bones are natural components of dismembered persons, and thus 'identities'. Very often the arrangement of body parts, of animal bones, skulls and curious deposits proclaim symbolic and perhaps metaphoric meaning that may prove to be culturally very specific, and thus a marker of identity in a particular community.

Bronze Age Ireland is once again the case-study area of Chapter 6, wherein Grogan examines two aspects of identity: that of the individual display of status, and the forging and maintenance of collective belonging. Grogan concentrates on shared experience and history, created through the construction and use of monuments within the wider structured landscape, from the small-scale burnt mounds possibly used for periodic feasting and localised structured deposition, to the larger endeavours that the creation of hillforts represent. Through his analyses of the province of Munster, Grogan emphasises the use of specific artefact types, notably the weapons and gold ornaments of the warrior elite, in the construction and maintenance of not only regionally structured identity, but also of status-related identity.

Houses are one of the most culturally significant foci of cultural construction, containing as they do, household, family and social identities woven into their fabric and form. Ginn's chapter examines how roundhouses of the Bronze Age encapsulate and symbolise living space of a community. Enriched by remarkable newly excavated evidence from County Londonderry and other sites across Ireland, Ginn is able to show how different component parts of the 'house' have been variously used in symbolic ways, such as manipulations to the entrance, the façade, the placement of objects, pots, hearths, and the like. Indeed, the study brings out many of the features that have become apparent in ritual archaeology, where transition between different spaces is marked by thresholds and entrances. Numerous models have been proposed to explain and explore the domestic house, but here is a soundly based example that takes the reader through the door and over the threshold into a world of distinctive Bronze Age identity.

Boyle examines pottery as a vehicle for exploring ancient Malta's early people. She presents a dynamic picture of changing stylistic identity discernible from the decorative changes in prehistoric pottery. These changes variously chart the external relationship of the Maltese islanders with the world beyond Malta and perhaps also the fluid sense of island identity. The chapter explores how pottery study is often central to interpretation of archaeological identities, an enduring register of style, pattern, form, and fabric that reflected identities and activities over time. Indeed, the perpetual question posed by archaeological pottery is how far it can be seen as indicative of wider cultural identity, change and interaction.

Collectively these essays provide us with an interesting insight into how current scholars are trying to refocus study on the more mundane aspects of prehistoric societies, the houses, the crafts, the pottery and the bodies, in their quest to explore ancient societies. For the Bronze Age especially, where continental traditions have put heavy emphasis on typology and sequence, it is refreshing to see exploration of material culture as a vehicle to investigate alternative evidence and interpretation.

HUMAN BONE AS MATERIAL CULTURE OF THE LIVING: A SOURCE OF IDENTITY IN THE IRISH MIDDLE–LATE BRONZE AGE?

Kerri Cleary

Introduction

The use of human remains as a tool by which to aid our understanding of who our predecessors were is at the very core of archaeology. Within Britain and Ireland, however, it is only in the last fifteen years that osteological research and traditional material-culture-based interpretative approaches have been intertwined in order to contribute to an understanding of social life and identity (*e.g.* Fowler 2004; Ingold 1998; Sofaer 2006). Although the term 'osteo-archaeology' has only been in use since the late 1960s (Moller-Christensen 1973, 411) the inter-relationship between the study of human biology and archaeology long pre-dates this, with the examination of human bones 'the province of scholars with medical backgrounds some of whom became interested in the past' (Sofaer 2006, 6). This practice created and continually reinforced a division between those who specialised in the biological body and those who developed interpretative archaeology. This chapter aims to integrate both approaches by exploring osteological data recorded from Middle–Late Bronze Age settlement sites in Ireland in order to explore the possibility that some human bone was purposefully treated like other forms of material culture through incorporation into structured deposits that may have been linked to the creation and maintenance of social identity.

Brück's (1995) study of the British Later Bronze Age led her to suggest that in various settlement contexts human remains were used as a metaphor and that these deposits were the result of either ritual actions or rubbish disposal, with the two activities not necessarily mutually exclusive. An examination of Middle Bronze Age settlements in southern England, although revealing little evidence for the use of human remains, did emphasise the range of other material culture, including animal bones, quern stones and pottery, utilised in 'odd' deposits, whereby items were deliberately placed in the ground to mark specific points in space and time (Brück 1999a, 152–5). These deposits, along with refuse disposal, are argued to be subtypes of structured deposition, in that 'people's culturally determined attitudes to refuse and its components govern how and where it is deposited' (Brück 2008, 649). In examining the occurrence of human remains on settlement sites it was therefore crucial to explore both the context of the deposits and the condition of the bone. The context into which human remains are placed is an integral part of the 'burial' process and within settlements, space may, for example, have been used to symbolise social relations and mark discontinuity in relationships between groups (Hingley 1984, 24). Settlements are the locations where many of the activities associated with the social and material reproduction of life take place. It is therefore not difficult to visualise a close link between settlements and 'rituals' or social procedures associated with maintaining the living community. By marking particular points in space and time they could express concepts of identity and commemorate a variety of social events.

The condition of the human remains is also extremely important when attempting to interpret the acts of deposition: the selections made, from age and sex to single, multiple or partial interments, and whether it was cremated or non-burnt, all represent choices that were most likely integrated into the 'ritual process'. The selection practice and pre-depositional treatment may be intrinsic to the symbolic importance of the material deposited and the message it is designed to portray. The biography that the human remains accumulated before deposition may also have been a significant factor in their selection, for example, if they were incorporated into a network of social exchanges or taken from a meaningful location/burial site. The latter is particularly important when one considers the possibility that human bone may have been curated before final deposition, perhaps even taken from older monuments. The re-use of Neolithic monuments for the interment of Bronze Age burials is well attested to in the archaeological record (Eogan 2004, 56; Grogan 2004; Waddell 1990). It is possible, however, that the process could also have been reversed, with human bone taken from these tombs and deposited at settlement sites. If so, perhaps this was a way of creating a link to the ancestors or simply as a recognised source of bone, a material perhaps acknowledged as necessary for inclusion into structured deposits.

A programme of radiocarbon dating the human bone would, however, be required to address this question and currently the only example dated is from Chancellorsland, County Tipperary (see below), which returned a date of 1530–1386 cal. BC[1] (3180±40 BP; GrA-5297), in-line with the Middle Bronze Age date for the occupation of the site (Doody 2008, 627). At other sites either the bone has not been considered for radiocarbon dating, or it had insufficient collagen levels, as was the case with the two human crania from Stamullin, County Meath (see below) (Ní Lionáin 2008, 2:70). Our role as archaeologists is to therefore scientifically record context and condition, while also integrating a more social exploration of the possible significance behind these deposits and recognising the potential diversity across various cultural situations. When the Irish Middle–Late Bronze Age settlement sites were examined in this way by the author (Cleary 2007; 2006) some interesting patterns began to emerge, particularly in relation to what are generally termed 'foundation' and 'closing' deposits, two of the more archaeologically recognisable methods of ceremonially or symbolically marking the passage of time or a significant location. In relation to the latter, an emphasis on points of transition, such as boundaries and thresholds, was observed and these acts of deposition could have been carried out at critical points or significant events in the lifecycle of the structure or the settlement as a whole, as well as within the lives of the individual inhabitants, such as births, 'marriages', deaths and other rites of passage (Brück 1999a, 154).

Overall, combined with the context of recovery, the condition of the human remains can suggest that they are more than simply discarded. 'While poor preservation of often fragile human bones can explain some of the human bone deposits found on settlements, there are also many examples of deliberate deposition of partial skeletons ... even fragments of fragments are utilised' (Chapman 2000, 6–7). In order to interpret if a true relationship exists between a deposit and the settlement's lifecycle it is therefore necessary to consider the implications of site formation processes, particularly when trying to clarify contemporaneity and structured actions. Throughout their life histories and even post-abandonment, entire sites interact with and are affected by their surroundings, through both cultural and non-cultural or environmental processes (see Schiffer 1987). Specifically relevant to interpreting the material culture uncovered during excavations of settlement sites is an understanding of how structures deteriorate and negative features, such as ditches and pits, infill. Understanding these formation processes can help archaeologists identify if human involvement is evident, be it deliberate deconstruction in the form of burning, or dismantling structural timbers prior to decay, or the intentional backfilling of a ditch or pit. In interpreting these formation events one must be cautious, recognising the limits that can be imposed by on-site recording and sampling strategies but also accepting the possibilities that recurring patterns and 'unusual' deposits can offer a window into past behaviour, particularly when one considers that 'many of the supposedly diagnostic properties of ritual practice are shared by secular action' (Brück 1999b, 315).

Moments in time: 'foundation' and 'closing' deposits

Deposits that can be interpreted as distinctly relating to the foundation/beginning and the closing/cessation of a particular human action may also have been intertwined with concerns about expressions of identity, both of the individual and the collective, but also in reference to wider social relations. They also tend to represent the persistent use of liminal contexts, such as boundaries and thresholds, which reflect a conscious use of space that can perhaps be interpreted as places of separation (see below).

The tradition of foundation deposits or sacrifices is particularly well-known through both archaeological and ethnographic research (see Merrifield 1987; Waterson 1990, 122–3). According to the *Encylopædia of Religion and Ethics* the ceremonies undertaken on the erection of foundations can be '… roughly divided into those whose object is: (a) to scare away evil spirits and destroy spells; (b) to conciliate the local spirits; (c) to provide a new tutelary power' (Hastings 1981, 111). It is notable that all of these reasons are based upon the belief in a human spirit or a form of life after death, a concept deeply intertwined with religion. This is an overarching assumption by many archaeologists and although a 'spiritual' dimension would seem to have been important to humanity since at least the Upper Palaeolithic, 'the shortcomings of 'religion' as a descriptive term are all too apparent', particularly in projecting modern parallels back in time (Insoll 2004, 5, 32).

In her examination of Iron Age foundation deposits, Green (2001, 166) also reiterated this belief that the incorporation of human remains into a building during its construction is 'arguably linked with gaining approval from the supernatural powers, perhaps in particular those on whose territory the building was raised'. However, she went further and inferred that the concerns of the living were equally important by suggesting that these deposits were also '…magically endowing the structure, and its builders, with good luck, prosperity and longevity'. This is just one example of multiple studies across time periods and geographical areas where the purpose of foundation deposits is debated, with other scholars linking them to concerns with maintaining fertility and subsistence. This is particularly applicable when incorporating objects such as quern stones, grain and pottery, or as a way of marking the structure as a dedicatory object for the life of the inhabitants (see Brück 1999a; 1995; Cleary 2007; Hill 1995). What then of the significance of utilising human remains in these contexts? Can they be interpreted as reflecting social relations and concepts of identity?

The rite of termination or 'closing' deposits is also a familiar concept in settlement archaeology and can explain somewhat unusual or deliberately structured deposits in the backfilling of ditches and pits, sometimes dug into the occupation layers of a structure's interior as a way of marking the end of its use life. Some ethnographic studies have illustrated the close relationship between the 'death' of a house and that of its occupants and the related need to perform rites appeasing the 'spirit' of the house or emphasising social continuity and rebuilding (see Waterson 1990, 132–5). Among the Iriama of Tanzania the house may be physically dismantled and the parts associated with livestock and grain returned to different sides of the family; elsewhere the corpse itself may be divided up, in some cases the blood goes to the mother's kin, the bone to the father's (Barley 1995, 102). The concept of managing or controlling 'death pollution' to successfully maintain a prosperous and fertile community is also widely attested to in the ethnographic material, particularly if the deceased had died in the house. Closing deposits may therefore mark this type of significant moment in a settlement's lifecycle, whereby a structure or an entire site has to be decommissioned or abandoned and/or there is a substantial shift in social relations and the related group identity.

On the edge and in the earth

Many deposits can be linked to liminal areas, such as boundaries and thresholds, which may reflect a need to define or mark out these points of transition as a way of reinforcing identity. In structures the locations chosen are often associated with entranceways. As places routinely encountered by moving from the outside to the inside, and vice versa, they would have provided a suitable platform from which to reinforce community identity, perhaps by strengthening the link between the inhabitants and the ancestors and by emphasising the separation between different social groups (Brück 1995, 259). The latter may also have been achieved by focusing on the larger boundaries created when a settlement space is defined through the construction of an enclosure, for example, the digging of a ditch or building of a palisade. This would have been a significant point in the lifecycle of a settlement and accordingly these boundaries and points of boundary transition were often chosen for structured deposition, perhaps symbolically 'distinguishing between insiders and outsiders, between those who could claim kinship and those who could not' (Brück 2008, 649). Another dimension to these deposits appears to be the process by which they were actually deposited, whereby 'their placement in features – cut by people – and penetrating the ground' meant that they were 'physically etched onto settlement space' (Hill 1995, 111). These acts of chthonic deposition may also have been deemed necessary to ensure continued sustainability through food and other resources derived from the earth.

Head first: skull deposits

As evident on Late Bronze Age settlement sites in Britain (Brück 1995) skull fragments are

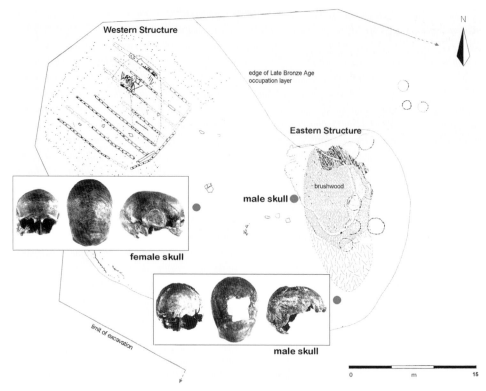

Figure 5.1: Ballinderry 2, County Offaly (after Hencken 1942, plates II, VII and VIII).

the most frequent category of human remains recovered and this continued into the Iron Age, with a general emphasis on the skull and leg (Armit and Ginn 2007, 123; Hill 1995, 13). This pattern was also detected for the Irish Bronze Age settlement sites, where there was a clear preference for skull fragments and long bones, including the pelvic region (Cleary 2006, 31). The particularly poignant symbolism of skulls is frequently addressed in archaeological and anthropological literature, for example, Brück (1995, 256–7) suggests that skull fragments may have been 'chosen for use because of their symbolic connotations...perhaps as seat of the intellect or soul', while Barley (1995, 158–9) describes the Dowayo ritual of mixing skulls 'to mark the transition from individual deceased to collective ancestor' at which point 'the living reassert their own individuality'. Biological and evolutionary anthropologists have also argued that an intact skull with large eye sockets displays a degree of neoteny, a trait visually appealing to humans and one that may have reinforced the skulls suitability as a symbolic vessel (see Bogin 1988). A skull may therefore have been recognisable as an appropriate ancestral relic that could be retained and venerated in a variety of contexts outside the mortuary domain in order to ensure the maintenance of society as a whole.

The three skulls, two male and one female, recovered from the base of the 'black layer' beneath the Late Bronze Age wooden structures at Ballinderry 2, County Offaly (Figure 5.1), is a well-known example and long regarded as a 'foundation sacrifice or some such

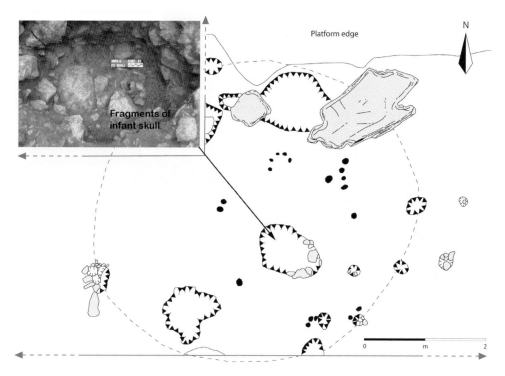

Figure 5.2: Knockadoon, Lough Gur, County Limerick (after R. M. Cleary 1995, fig. 13 and plate IV).

ritual deposit' (Hencken 1942, 17; O'Sullivan 1998, 81). Significantly, the frontal bone or face was absent from all three skulls; it had been cut off the female and one of the males from the top of the nasal ridge, while the second male consisted of only the top half of the skull and the brow ridges, cut from the skull after death (Howells 1942, 17–20; Newman 1997, 99). This 'de-facing' of the skulls is particularly intriguing as it might suggest that individual identity was deliberately removed, perhaps indicating that the concerns of the collective community were the focus of these deposits. A shift in personal identity to identity constructed with reference to the household group has been identified in Britain from the Middle Bronze Age onwards through a shift in the focus of deposition. Objects previously deposited with the dead were placed in ditches enclosing the settlement space and cremations in the mortuary realm were accompanied by what would be recognised as domestic pottery once used for cooking and storing food (see Barrett 1989, 124).

Deposits of partial skulls similar to those at Ballinderry have been recorded at other sites. The upper part of a cranium was recovered from the western edge of a Late Bronze Age occupation layer at Moynagh Lough, County Meath (Bradley 1997, 52), and a fragment of the right parietal bone of an adult skull came from a layer of occupation material that appeared to pre-date the Middle–Late Bronze Age structure at Site H, Lough Gur, County Limerick (Ó Ríordáin 1954, 429). A mid-19th-century reference to the Late Bronze Age lake settlement

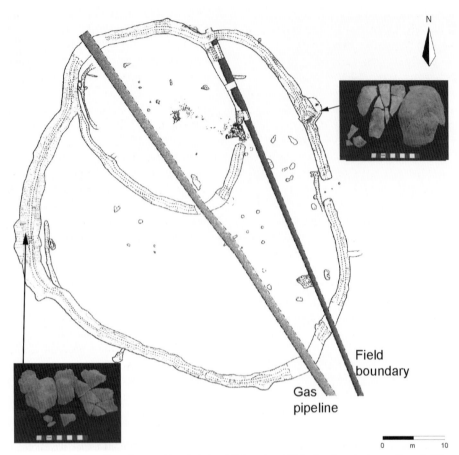

Figure 5.3: Stamullin, County Meath (after Ní Lionáin 2008, fig. 7 and plates 68 and 69).

at Clonfinlough, County Offaly, indicated that some human remains were recovered from alternate 'layers of black earth and burned clay and marl' beneath a 'closely-laid pavement', including at least 'one skull, and portions of some more were got on the exterior edge' (Kelly 1850–53, 210). Similarly, twenty-three fragments of an infant cranium, minus the face, were recovered from the basal fill of a pit, roughly centrally placed within the Late Bronze Age oval structure on Knockadoon, Lough Gur, County Limerick (Figure 5.2; Cleary 1995, 40–41; Ó Donnabháin 1995, 60). The deposition of the skull fragment was part of the infilling of the pit, but it is unclear if this pit was contemporary with the occupation of the structure or if it perhaps represented a foundation or closing deposit related to the occupation.

In another example relating to infilling, two human partial calvaria (skull cap) fragments were recovered from the fills of the outer ditch at the Late Bronze Age site of Stamullin, County Meath (Figure 5.3). One fragment from the base of the main fill on the northeastern side of the ditch was placed with the internal cranial surface facing upwards and in the vicinity of animal bone, including two abutting cattle skulls; the second fragment was from the lower fill on the western side of the ditch, similarly positioned with the internal surface upwards and directly above a small flint chunk (Ní Lionáin 2008, 1:38, 1:43; 2007). The former was deposited 9m north of the eastern entrance where the ditch had clearly been widened and the sides gently stepped, perhaps representing an access point for deposition. While the fragment was within a deposit that sealed a metalled surface, further occupation material contained in the overlying fills suggests that the skull may have marked a particular point in the lifecycle of the settlement as opposed to its abandonment (Ní Lionáin 2008, 1:50; 2:89). The fragments appeared to belong to two different adult individuals and that from the northeastern side of the enclosure was tentatively suggested to have been male (Fibiger 2008, 2:51).

Two skull fragments were similarly recovered from the basal fill of the inner ditch at the Middle Bronze Age site of Chancellorsland, County Tipperary, in a location close to the eastern entranceway associated with both phases of the outer ditch (Figure 5.4; Doody 2008, fig. 2.5.1:4). Unfortunately, it was not possible to definitively ascertain whether the two fragments, one from the frontal bone and one from the right parietal, came from the same individual, although they were similar in texture. It is suggested they probably represent a young, mature adult aged between the late teens and early twenties (Power 2008, 331). Two skull fragments were also recovered from a layer of 'dark soil and general habitation refuse' intermixed with the wall tumble from a Late Bronze Age enclosing feature on Knockadoon, Lough Gur, County Limerick (Cleary 2003, 124). One was a non-burnt fragment of the parietal bone from an adult skull and the other was a cremated skull fragment, possibly human and from a young adult (Barra Ó Donnabháin pers. comm.). The context of these bone fragments is again difficult to interpret. They may originally have been incorporated into the wall fill as occupation material during construction, as the sherds of pottery, stone tools and animal bone recovered from the fill of the upstanding sections were interpreted. Alternatively, they may have been deposited among the stones when the wall collapsed and went out of use, representing 'habitation debris' that may have 'accumulated as a result of people squatting in the shelter of the wall' (Cleary 2003, 124). Despite the difficulty of understanding the formation history of this context, the incorporation of both burnt and non-burnt skull fragments could tentatively be suggested as representing a deliberate selection for inclusion in the same deposit, perhaps relating to the opposing states of the body pre- and post-exposure to fire and the overall processes of transformation associated with death.

Significantly, burnt mound sites, which can be interpreted as more temporary or seasonal loci of occupation, perhaps even outliers to the more permanent settlements already mentioned, also have associations with human bone during the Middle–Late Bronze Age. At Cragbrien, County Clare, a skull fragment and part of the facial bone, probably from an adult male, was incorporated into an upper deposit of burnt stone, possibly associated with a trough that lay outside the wayleave (Hull 2007, 202). A human skull fragment was also recovered from the upper fill of a trough at Belan, County Kildare (Tobin 2007). The Belan skull was interpreted by the excavator as not contemporary with the trough but, given the other evidence, perhaps this should be re-examined. At Inchagreenoge, County Limerick, the complete skull of a young adult male had been deposited against the edge of a spring in a thin peat deposit above a spread of burnt stone associated with a Middle Bronze Age trough; the skull was subsequently covered by a layer of large non-burnt stones that capped or sealed the spring (Taylor 2007, 281–2). This has echoes of the skull fragment recovered from the King's Stables, a Late Bronze Age 'ritual pool' near the site of Haughey's Fort, County

Kerri Cleary

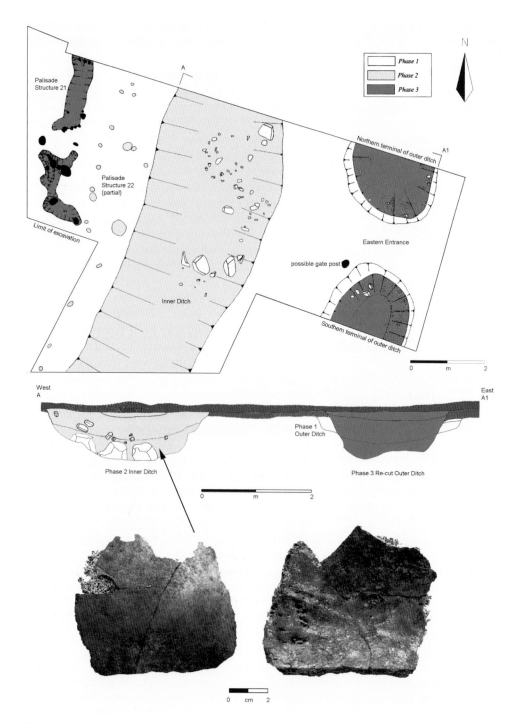

Figure 5.4: Chancellorsland, County Tipperary (after Doody 2008, figs 2.5.1:2 and 4 and plate 2.5.6:1).

Armagh (Lynn 2003, 54). This consisted of the facial portion, excluding the mandible, of a young adult male that appeared to have been cut from the rest of the skull (Delaney 1977, 61) and may, due to its poor state of preservation, have been taken from another context for re-deposition at this site. The occurrence of just the facial area of the skull in this type of context, an artificial pool with a ritual or ceremonial function, offers an interesting contrary to many of the examples from secular sites, whereby the faces were deliberately removed or related fragments were notably absent from inclusion in the deposits.

Fragmentation through fire

The process of fragmenting the body as a secondary burial practice has already been discussed in relation to the selection of particular parts of the skull, or rather the deliberate exclusion of others. It can be argued that a similar action of separation or fragmentation was achieved through the exposure of bodies or bones to intense heat. This burning could be equated with the 'killing' of artefacts associated with the deceased, sometimes interpreted as an act of purification in order to avoid death pollution (Parker Pearson 1999, 26), similar to the burning or dismantling of structures on the death of an owner (see Waterson 1990, 135). The act of cremation, whether as a primary or secondary burial practice, would have facilitated extensive fragmentation of the body and therefore probably a strong symbol for separation of the deceased from the living and the related loss of individuality. The possibility of additional fragmentation through intentional manual crushing and pounding should also be explored for these deposits, but this is a difficult process to convincingly determine (see Geber 2009, 227–30) and therefore needs to be tentatively suggested as another phase in a multi-stage mortuary treatment.

The recurring pattern of cremated/burnt bone recovered from Middle–Late Bronze Age settlements, specifically the structural elements of houses, suggests that selection and deliberate action was most likely in play. These deposits often focused on entrance or threshold areas, which as both liminal in nature, but also as places continuously traversed, would have 'acted as a means of creating and defining the social group that inhabited the settlement' (Brück 1999a, 154). Notably, the bone from many of these contexts could not be positively identified as human or still awaits osteoarchaeological analysis; while the fact that it may be animal bone cannot be excluded, equally nor can the possibility that it was human. This inability to distinguish most often relates to the sample size and level of fragmentation: 'the most easily identified fragments are mainly derived from the skull bones and teeth. ... Post-cranial bones, on the other hand, can be very difficult to identify to element if they have become heavily fragmented' (Geber 2009, 218). As discussed above, this could relate to natural taphonomic factors or deliberate secondary burial practices, such as crushing and selectivity. Significantly, the importance of differentiating between animal and human bone may not be important in these contexts where there are 'basic parallels between the treatment of human remains and animal remains in similar deposits' (Hill 1995, 105; also Cleary 2007). At Clonard/Folkstown Great, County Dublin (Figure 5.5), cremated or heavily charred bone was recovered from the two outer postholes in the southeast facing porch-like entrance of a truncated Middle Bronze Age structure, one of which also contained a small porcellanite axehead lying flat on the base of the posthole (Byrnes 2002, 8–9; Grogan *et al.* 2007, 116). Similarly at Caltragh, County Sligo (Figure 5.5), burnt bone from an entrance

Kerri Cleary

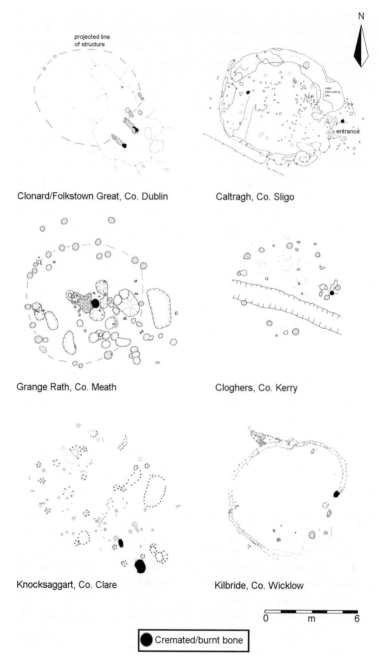

Clonard/Folkstown Great, Co. Dublin   Caltragh, Co. Sligo

Grange Rath, Co. Meath   Cloghers, Co. Kerry

Knocksaggart, Co. Clare   Kilbride, Co. Wicklow

● Cremated/burnt bone

Figure 5.5: Deposits of cremated/burnt bone at Clonard/Folkstown Great, County Dublin (after Grogan et al. 2007, fig. II.36); Caltragh, County Sligo (after Danaher 2007, fig. 5.5); Grange Rath, County Meath (after O'Hara 2004, fig. 6); Structure A, Cloghers, County Kerry (after Kiely and Dunne 2005, fig. 9); Structure B, Knocksaggart, County Clare (after Hanley 2001, fig. 18) and Kilbride, County Wicklow (after Breen and Kelleher 1998, fig. 3).

posthole and an internal structural posthole of the Middle Bronze Age Structure 1 were 'not further identifiable' (Piezonka 2004, 16), while at Grange Rath, County Meath (Figure 5.5), an internal structural posthole, roughly centrally located within the Late Bronze Age structure, contained forty two fragments of unidentifiable burnt bone (O'Hara 2004, 9; 33).

Of those sites where positive identification of human bone was possible, the liminality of the entranceways was again a focal point. At the Middle–Late Bronze Age site of Cloghers, County Kerry (Figure 5.5) cremated bone came from twenty-four contexts across the site; the majority was not diagnostic to species, but those identified as 'possibly human include long bones, hand/foot bones, vertebra, rib, scapula and skull' (Power n.d.; also Kiely and Dunne 2005, 53). All, except a possibly adolescent scapula fragment, are 'mature and consequently belong to individual(s) aged at least in the late teens, including a rib fragment and two long-bone fragments from a structural posthole at the probable entrance to Structure A' (Power n.d.). At Knocksaggart, County Clare[2] (Figure 5.5), cremated bone interpreted as 'possible token burials' was recovered from two postholes on the western side of the southeast-facing entranceway of Structure B (Hanley 2001, 34–40). At Kilbride, County Wicklow[3] (Figure 5.5), fragments representing an adult were lying vertically against the wall of an internal posthole that may have been structural, while further fragments came from a posthole at the end of the slot-trench, possibly marking a truncated entranceway (Breen and Kelleher 1998, 4; Lynch 1998). Notably, the bone from Kilbride was in a fragmentary condition, 'leading the osteoarchaeologist to suggest the possibility of pounding or grinding' (Lynch 1998). Overall, it is possible that these 'burnt offerings' are another element to the social practice of fragmenting objects through deliberate breakage, manipulation or significantly, exposure to fire. Chapman (2000, 139) has elaborated on this idea, suggesting a practice of enchainment through fragmentation, whereby a social relationship can be established or maintained through the exchange of parts of individuals' bodies. This practice would certainly lend itself to the interpretation of these structured deposits as marking significant points in the lifecycle of a settlement, with the inclusion of human bone as just one element of the material culture employed in these symbolic acts.

Discussion

In the Middle–Late Bronze Age the recurrence of human bones in contexts outside the mortuary realm suggests that these remains were imbued with a more complex meaning that transcends presupposed concepts of ritual and non-ritual (see Brück 1999b). Human bone was treated in a similar way to other forms of material culture by incorporation into structured deposits that marked important transitions in the lifecycles of sites, such as foundation and abandonment ceremonies, but also important spatial locations, specifically thresholds and boundaries. This concept of bodies and body parts as objects or material statements does not of course preclude them from retaining social meaning, indeed as Hallam *et al.* (1999, ix) state, 'the biologically deceased can retain an influential social presence in the lives of others'. By utilising human bone as a form of material culture the living could use it as 'an important symbolic resource, articulating not only concepts of identity but also notions of temporality and transformation' (Brück 2008, 649–50). During their lifecycles these Bronze Age societies would have undergone numerous 'rites of passage' (see van Gennep 1960); times when the community was brought together and social relations were created and maintained. The incorporation of human remains into these rites can therefore be interpreted as a medium through which this communal identity was reinforced. Perhaps the selections made also incorporated reference to differences between the recently deceased and the long dead as representing the various states of death and rebirth or 'the removal of one identity and emergence of another' (Fowler 2004, 80).

This argument towards a group rather than individual identity can also be examined by exploring both the contexts of recovery and the conditions in which the human bone was deposited. The recurring use of liminal locations, specifically entranceways and enclosures, would suggest these structured deposits denote points where and when social identity required reinforcing. As the boundaries of a structure or a settlement, or the place most frequently encountered and crossed, these locations would have been suitable arenas for a display of communal identity and where social roles and relationships could be defined and strengthened by using the dichotomy of inside and outside. The selection of different forms of human remains should also be explored. For example, where non-burnt bones were utilised, the reduction of flesh through excarnation would have been a strong symbol for the separation of the deceased from the living, and consequently an important transformation of the individual body into the material culture of the collective. Furthermore, the manipulation of some of the skulls involved 'de-facing' them by cutting away the facial portions, while the majority consisted of only fragments of the upper part of the cranium, again without the more recognisable eye sockets and nasal cavity. This selective fragmentation could represent a deliberate transformation of the bone from representing an individual, into an object to embody the larger social unit. A similar process could be argued for fragmentation through cremation, and the recurring use of only a 'token' deposit of bone in these contexts suggests that they may have burnt only selected bones for use as a symbolic representation, or perhaps collected or received a sample of bone from elsewhere. Overall, the inclusion of what appear to be illustrative samples of human bone implies that they were treated more like material culture of the living than revered ancestors; 'it was ideologically acceptable to fragment and disperse a human body, suggesting that, unlike the modern Western individual, the person may not have been considered a unified and transcendental whole' (Brück 2006, 309).

Overall, the incorporation of human bone into secular contexts during the Middle–Late Bronze Age in Ireland suggests that these burnt and non-burnt remains were utilised as another type of object through which social relations and group identity could be expressed. Their recurring inclusion in specific locations indicate that human bone, along with other material remains such as quern stones, pottery, metalwork, animal bone, and charred grain (Cleary 2007), was used to mark significant points in time and space that related to rites of passage within the society's lifecycle. The high level of fragmentation also appears to have been fundamental in the selection process, perhaps relating to the dissolution of the individual in order to emphasise the community identity and the practice of circulating and curating parts of the dead for inclusion in a variety of contexts relating to the creation and maintenance of the social relations and identity of the living.

Acknowledgements

I would like to thank several people. Dr Barra Ó Donnabháin, for his guidance both as supervisor of my MA dissertation, which forms the background for this research, and for assistance with various aspects of this chapter. Dr Joanna Brück for useful discussion at the Interpreting Identity conference. Rose M. Cleary for access to the Lough Gur bone and general discussions about the Lough Gur sites. The numerous archaeologists and archaeological companies who gave me access to unpublished data, especially Thaddeus Breen; Emmett Byrnes; Ken Hanley; Jacinta Kiely; Clíodhna Ní Lionáin and Rob O'Hara. James O'Driscoll for his work on the Lough Gur illustration. The conference organisers and monograph editors, their patience and hard work is greatly appreciated.

Notes

1   Calibrated to 2 sigma in OxCal 4.1
2   Knocksaggart and Kilbride remain undated but are morphologically consistent with Bronze Age structures; however, the similarities between Middle–Late Bronze Age and known Early and Developed Iron Age structures, such as Ballinaspig More 5, County Cork (Danaher 2002), Carrickmines Great, County Dublin (Ó Drisceoil 2007) and Killoran 16, County Tipperary (Murray 2005, 296–7), are also acknowledged.
3   Early Bronze Age pottery was recovered from the site but it was weathered and interpreted as residual (Brindley 1998).

References

Armit, I. and Ginn, V. (2007) Beyond the grave: human remains from domestic contexts in Iron Age Atlantic Scotland. *Proceedings of the Prehistoric Society* 73, 113–34.
Barley, N. (1995) *Dancing on the grave, encounters with death*. London, Abacus.
Barrett, J. C. (1989) Time and tradition: the rituals of everyday life. In H. Nordström and A. Knape (eds) *Bronze Age studies – transactions of the British-Scandinavian colloquim in Stockholm, May 10–11, 1985*, 113–26. Stockholm, Statens Historiska Museum.
Bogin, B. (1988) *Patterns of human growth*. New York, Cambridge University Press.
Brindley, A. (1998) Appendix I: pottery report. In T. Breen and H. Kelleher *Archaeological excavation, Bronze Age remains, Arklow By-pass, Kilbride Td, Co. Wicklow*. Unpublished excavation report, Valerie J. Keeley Ltd.
Bradley, J. (1997) Archaeological excavations at Moynagh Lough, Co. Meath 1995–96. *Ríocht na Midhe* 9(3), 50–61.
Breen, T. and Kelleher, H. (1998) *Archaeological excavation, Bronze Age remains, Arklow By-pass, Kilbride Td, Co. Wicklow*. Unpublished excavation report, Valerie J. Keeley Ltd.
Brück, J. (1995) A place for the dead: the role of human remains in Late Bronze Age Britain. *Proceedings of the Prehistoric Society* 61, 245–77.
Brück, J. (1999a) Houses, lifecycles and deposition on Middle Bronze Age settlements in southern England. *Proceedings of the Prehistoric Society* 65, 145–66.
Brück, J. (1999b) Ritual and rationality: some problems of interpretation in European archaeology. *European Journal of Archaeology* 2(3), 313–44.
Brück, J. (2006) Fragmentation, personhood and the social construction of technology in Middle and Late Bronze Age Britain. *Cambridge Archaeological Journal* 16(3), 297–315.

Brück, J. (2008) A comparison of Chancellorsland Site A with contemporary settlements in Southern England. In M. Doody (ed.) *The Ballyhoura Hills Project, Discovery Programme Monograph No. 7*, 642–52. Bray, Wordwell Ltd.

Byrnes, E. (2002) *Gas Pipeline to the West, Section 6: Clonard or Folkstown Great, Co. Dublin*. Unpublished excavation report, Margaret Gowen & Co. Ltd.

Chapman, J. (2000) *Fragmentation in archaeology: people, places and broken objects in the prehistory of south eastern Europe*. London, Routledge.

Cleary, K. (2006) Skeletons in the closet: the deposition of human remains on Irish Bronze Age settlements. *Journal of Irish Archaeology* 14, 23–42.

Cleary, K. (2007) *Irish Bronze Age settlements: spatial organisation and the deposition of material culture*. Unpublished PhD Thesis, University College Cork.

Cleary, R. M. (1995) Later Bronze Age settlement and prehistoric burials, Lough Gur, Co. Limerick. *Proceedings of the Royal Irish Academy* 95C, 1–92.

Cleary, R. M. (2003) Enclosed Late Bronze Age habitation site and boundary wall at Lough Gur, Co. Limerick. *Proceedings of the Royal Irish Academy* 103C, 97–189.

Danaher, E. (2002) *Ballinaspig More 5, Co. Cork*; 02E1033 (part 4). National Roads Authority Archaeological Database. http://archaeology.nra.ie/Home/ViewResult/b72fa4f3-61cf-45e2-8846-89edf97b0929. [Accessed January 2012].

Delaney, M. (1977) Appendix 3: report on the human skull fragments. In C. J. Lynn, Trial excavations at the King's Stables, Tray Townland, County Armagh. *Ulster Journal of Archaeology* 40, 59–61.

Doody, M. (2008) *The Ballyhoura Hills Project, Discovery Programme Monograph No. 7*. Bray, Wordwell Ltd.

Eogan, J. (2004) The construction of funerary monuments in the Irish Early Bronze Age: a review of the evidence. In H. Roche, E. Grogan, J. Bradley, J. Coles and B. Raftery (eds), *From megaliths to metals: essays in honour of George Eogan*, 56–60. Oxford, Oxbow Books.

Fibiger, L. (2008) Report on the human skeletal remains from Stamullin, Co. Meath. In C. Ní Lionáin, Volume 2: *Final excavation report, site of hotel development, Stamullin, Co. Meath*, 48–55. Unpublished excavation report, Arch-Tech Ltd.

Fowler, C. (2004) *The archaeology of personhood: an anthropological approach*. London, Routledge.

Geber, J. (2009) The human remains. In M. McQuade, B. Molloy and C. Moriarty (eds) *In the shadow of the Galtees: archaeological excavations along the N8 Cashel to Mitchelstown Road Scheme*, 209–40. National Road's Authority Scheme Monographs 4. The National Roads Authority, Dublin.

Green, M. A. (2001) *Dying for the gods: human sacrifice in Iron Age & Roman Europe*. Gloucestershire, Tempus.

Grogan, E. (2004) Middle Bronze Age burial traditions in Ireland. In H. Roche, E. Grogan, J. Bradley, J. Coles and B. Raftery (eds), *From megaliths to metals: essays in honour of George Eogan*, 61–71. Oxford, Oxbow Books.

Grogan, E., O'Donnell, L. and Johnston, P. (2007) *The Bronze Age landscapes of the Pipeline to the West: an integrated archaeological and environmental assessment*. Bray, Wordwell Ltd.

Hallam, E., Hockey, J. and Howarth, G. (1999) *Beyond the body: death and social identity*. London, Routledge.

Hanley, K. (2001) *A stratigraphic report on the archaeological excavation at Site AR85/86 Knocksaggart, Co. Clare*. Unpublished excavation report, Valerie J. Keeley Ltd.

Hastings, J. (ed.) (1981) *Encyclopædia of religion and ethics, Volume VI*. Edinburgh, Clark.

Hencken, H. O'N. (1942) Ballinderry Crannóg No. 2. *Proceedings of the Royal Irish Academy* 47C, 1–76.

Hill, J. D. (1995) *Ritual and rubbish in the Iron Age of Wessex: a study of the formation of a specific archaeological record*. British Archaeological Reports, British Series 242. Oxford, Archaeopress.

Hingley, R. (1984) The archaeology of settlement and the social significance of space. *Scottish Archaeological Review* 3(1), 22–31.

Howells, W. W. (1942) Human remains from Ballinderry II. In H. O'N. Hencken, Ballinderry Crannóg No. 2. *Proceedings of the Royal Irish Academy* 47C, 17–20.

Hull, G. (2007) 153. Cragbrien. In E. Grogan, L. O'Donnell and P. Johnston (eds) *The Bronze Age landscapes of the Pipeline to the West: an integrated archaeological and environmental assessment*, 202–3. Bray, Wordwell Ltd.

Ingold, T. (1998) From complementarity to obviation: on dissolving the boundaries between social and biological anthropology, archaeology and psychology. *Zeitschrift für Ethnologie* 123, 21–52.

Insoll, T. (2004) *Archaeology, ritual, religion*. London, Routledge.
Kelly, D. H. (1850–53) Account of an artificial island, and certain antiquities recently discovered near Strokestown, County Roscommon. *Proceedings of the Royal Irish Academy* 1(5), 208–14.
Kiely, J. and Dunne, L. (2005) Recent archaeological excavations in the Tralee Area. In M. Connolly (ed.) *Past kingdoms: recent archaeological research, survey and excavation in County Kerry*, 40–64. Tralee, The Heritage Council and Kerry County Council.
Lynch, P. (1998) Appendix III: cremated bone report. In T. Breen and H. Kelleher, *Archaeological excavation, Bronze Age remains, Arklow By-pass, Kilbride Td, Co. Wicklow*, 16. Unpublished excavation report, Valerie J. Keeley Ltd.
Lynn, C. (2003) *Navan Fort: archaeology and myth*. Bray, Wordwell Ltd.
Merrifield, R. (1987) *The archaeology of ritual and magic*. London, Batsford Ltd.
Moller-Christensen, V. (1973) Osteo-archaeology as a medico-historical auxiliary science. *Medical History* 17(4), 411–8.
Murray, C. (2005) Killoran 16. In M. Gowan, J. Ó Néill and M. Phillips (eds) *The Lisheen Mine Archaeological Project 1996–8*, 296–8. Bray, Wordwell Ltd.
Newman, C. (1997) Ballinderry Crannóg No. 2, Co. Offaly: the later Bronze Age. *Journal of Irish Archaeology* 8, 91–100.
Ní Lionáin, C. (2007) Life, death and food production in Bronze Age Ireland: recent excavations at Stamullin, Co. Meath. *Archaeology Ireland* 21(2), 18–21.
Ní Lionáin, C. (2008) (Vols 1 and 2). *Final excavation report, site of hotel development, Stamullin, Co. Meath*. Unpublished excavation report, Arch-Tech Ltd.
Ó Donnabháin, B. (1995) Appendix II: the human remains. In R. M. Cleary, Later Bronze Age settlement and prehistoric burials, Lough Gur, Co. Limerick. *Proceedings of the Royal Irish Academy* 95C, 59–63.
Ó Drisceoil, C. (2007) Life and death in the Iron Age at Carrickmines Great, County Dublin. *Journal of the Royal Society of Antiquaries of Ireland* 137, 5–28.
O'Hara, R. (2004) *Grange Rath, Colp West, Co. Meath*. Unpublished report, Archaeological Consultancy Services Ltd.
Ó Ríordáin, S. P. (1954) Lough Gur excavations: Neolithic and Bronze Age houses on Knockadoon. *Proceedings of the Royal Irish Academy* 56C, 297–459.
O'Sullivan, A. (1998) *The archaeology of lake settlement in Ireland, Discovery Programme Monograph 4*. Dublin, Royal Irish Academy.
Parker Pearson, M. (1999) *The Archaeology of death and burial*. Stroud, Sutton Publishing Ltd.
Piezonka, K. (2004) Report on the burnt bone from archaeological excavations at Areas 1D, 1E and 1E ext., Caltragh, Co. Sligo. In E. Danaher (2007), *Monumental beginnings: the archaeology of the N4 Sligo Inner relief Road*. The National Roads Authority, Dublin, on accompanying CD.
Power, C. (n.d.) *Cloghers (00E0065): the cremated bone*. Unpublished specialist report, Eachtra Archaeological Projects Ltd.
Power, C. (2008) Human remains. In M. Doody, *The Ballyhoura Hills Project, Discovery Programme Monograph No. 7*, 331. Bray, Wordwell Ltd.
Schiffer, M. B. (1987) *Formation processes of the archaeological record*. Albuquerque, University of New Mexico Press.
Sofaer, J. R. (2006) *The body as material culture: a theoretical osteoarchaeology*. Cambridge, Cambridge University Press.
Taylor, K. (2007) 1179. Inchagreenoge. In E. Grogan, L. O'Donnell and P. Johnston, *The Bronze Age landscapes of the Pipeline to the West: an integrated archaeological and environmental assessment*, 281–4. Bray, Wordwell Ltd.
Tobin, R. (2007) Belan, Co. Kildare; 07E72953. excavations.ie: Database of Irish Excavation Reports. http://www.excavations.ie/Pages/Details.php?Year=&County=Kildare&id=17790 [Accessed January 2012].
van Gennep, A. (1960) *The rites of passage*. London, Routledge.
Waddell, J. (1990) *The Bronze Age burials of Ireland*. Galway, Galway University Press.
Waterson, R. (1990) *The living house: an anthropology of architecture in south-east Asia*. New York, Oxford University Press.

6

HIGH AND LOW: IDENTITY AND STATUS IN LATE BRONZE AGE IRELAND

Eoin Grogan

Introduction

Identity is primarily shaped by place, kinship and status: the location of birth and upbringing, the associated family and ancestry, and the perceived ranking of that kinship group. In prehistory it is probable that this identity, other than the progression to adulthood, for most individuals changed little throughout their lifetime. If the opportunities for social mobility were limited it is evident that travel – for trade, marriage or treaty – was also a growing feature of the Bronze Age. Two particular aspects of identity are examined here: the emblems and possessions of personal status and identity, and the formation, maintenance, projection, and display of collective identity.

Familial and communal identity

Many of the recently excavated settlement sites belonging to the Late Bronze Age consist of apparently isolated houses. However, clusters of two or three houses, often with evidence for ancillary structures and other activity, are also common. At Ballylegan, Co. Tipperary (McQuade 2009), a circular house with a porched entrance was associated with hearth and pits as well as three outbuildings. In the wider landscape the site formed part of a distinct cluster of settlement, *fulachta fiadh* (burnt mound sites characterised by their use of hot-stone technology) and funerary sites in the shelter of the Galty Mountains around Cahir (McQuade *et al.* 2009, 35–146, figs 3.2–3.4). These represent continuity of settlement from the Early Bronze Age through to the Middle and Late Bronze Age when there is an intensification of activity. The archaeological evidence suggests that such communities were local, familial and agrarian, and that many had long traditions of kinship and close attachment to their homeplace stretching – in some well documented examples, such as Lough Gur, Co. Limerick – back into early prehistory (Ó Ríordáin 1954).

Excavation, or excavation and fieldwork, have identified a number of these communities as Middle–Late Bronze Age clusters of sites such as at Grange, Co. Meath (Kelly 2008); Lisheen (Gowen *et al.* 2005), Derrybane (Lynch *et al.* 2010; Kiely and O'Mahony 2011) and Curraghatoor, Co. Tipperary (Doody 2007); Ballybrowney, Co. Cork (Cotter 2005); Rathcannon/Ballincurra, Co. Limerick (Grogan *et al.* 2007, 150–52, fig. 6.13); and Toonagh, Co. Clare (Grogan 2005b, figs 5.25, 5.27; 2005a, fig. 4.3). While open settlements, such as those at Grange and Lisheen, dominate the evidence, enclosed habitation sites are an integral part of the national picture; examples include Ballybrowney (Cotter 2006; 2005;), and Stamullin (Ní Lionáin 2007), Lagavooren (Stafford 2002), and Kilsharvan, Co. Meath (Russell and Corcoran 2001). The houses themselves show comparatively little variation (Doody 2000) although slightly more elaborate examples, for example those with porches or large internal storage pits, may indicate a level of deliberate display (see Ginn, Chapter 7). While the function of the substantial structures at Ballinderry 2, Co. Offaly, and Rathgall, Co. Wicklow (Hencken 1942; Raftery 1976; Raftery 1942), is uncertain, it is possible that they do not represent domestic buildings.

The components of these groups can include houses (both enclosed and unbounded), field systems, cremation pit cemeteries, and *fulachta fiadh*. However, they rarely include bronze artefacts or evidence for metal production, a point we will return to later. The dispersal of individual homes through the well-preserved county Clare landscapes at Gorteen and Toonagh (Grogan 2005a, fig. 4.2–4.4) suggest small enclosed familial landholdings within irregular field systems of low earth and stone boundaries. These clusters of sites suggest integrated groups based on shared lineage and history; such communities probably engaged in co-operative farming and seem to represent reasonably autonomous and prosperous units with a strong sense of shared identity.

If their identity had been forged by a shared past it is clear that it was reinforced by shared actions; apart from farm labour these probably included funerary traditions and ceremonies represented by pit and barrow cemeteries. Collective mourning and the sharing of funerary space are powerful bonding mechanisms particularly when there are visible permanent reminders. Another omnipresent aspect of these communities are the *fulachta fiadh*. At Toonagh, for example, it is evident that these are not peripheral but form an integrated component of the settled landscape (Figure 6.1). This is not the place to reprise the arguments about the function of *fulachta fiadh*; what appears certain, however, is that many of them were used for cooking meat and that most were used on multiple occasions (Grogan *et al.* 2007; Masterson 1999). Focussing on this aspect of the evidence the sites, while of necessity located in wet places, are not marginal and, in the context of extensive excavation or study, are frequently embedded in integrated, intimate, settlement landscapes. This certainly appears to be the context of their use and, since their wetland location precludes most of them being utilised in the winter or spring, clearly focussed on the summer and autumn. We might envisage a system where, perhaps at quiet times in the farming year, such as after harvest, feasting took place with, perhaps, a rota of individual families hosting the events. Such activities would help to reinforce social bonds as well as helping to maintain a strong sense of communal identity that may already have deep roots in shared history and lineage.

Another feature of a number of *fulachta fiadh* is the presence of special depositions, in most of them from the debris of the final use of the trough; these include pottery and human skull fragments and their presence is spread through the Bronze Age (see Cherry 1990). A

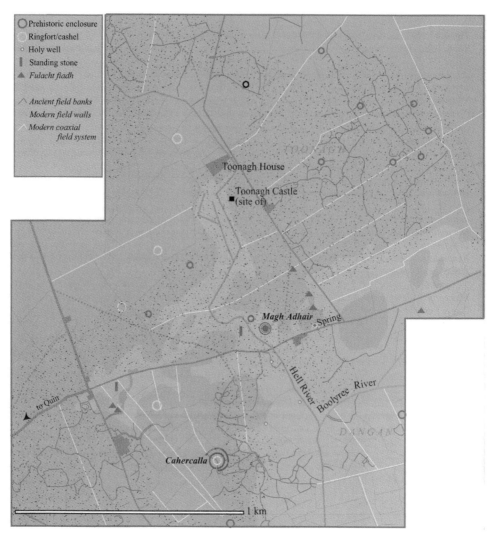

Figure 6.1: At Toonagh, southeast County Clare, the prehistoric landscape is substantially preserved and is concentrated on the thin, fertile, soils over plateaux of limestone bedrock (so-called 'rockland': stippled). An organic patchwork of small fields – defined by low earth and stone banks – with some well-defined access 'lanes' contains a reasonably evenly dispersed pattern of small domestic enclosures. Clusters of fulachta fiadh *(burnt mounds) occur on the margins of wetland areas including those at 'Magh Adhair'; here a turlough (seasonal lake) remains largely dry during the late summer and early autumn, although water can be accessed by digging close to the surface. After heavy rain the turlough fills spectacularly when water gushes from the small rock cleft ('cave') on the edge of the basin. Magh Adhair appears to have been a ceremonial enclosure in late prehistory, defined by a substantial ditch and external bank, possibly with an internal mound. The area around this, on the edge of the Hell River, appears to have been artificially levelled to create a wide flat apron. In the early medieval period, Magh Adhair became associated with the Dál gCais, and later the Uí Briain kings of Thomond. (A colour plate of this figure is at the back of the volume.)*

number of examples have been recognised. A trough at Kellymount, Co. Kilkenny, dated to 1888–1754 BC (UB-14048, 3502±21 BP), produced a substantial part of an Early Bronze Age vase urn; the vessel had been used in a domestic context for cooking and considerable external surface wear appears to be a result of its use history (Grogan and Roche 2009). Similar evidence, in the form of much worn encrusted urn sherds, came from Clogh, Co. Wexford (Grogan and Roche 2008). Such closing deposits have been identified at other burnt mound sites, such as the human skull fragments from Cragbrien, Co. Clare, and Inchagreenoge, Co. Limerick, or the cylindrical yew pipes from a composite musical instrument at Charlesland, Co. Wicklow (Grogan *et al.* 2007, 94–95; Holmes and Molloy 2006; Molloy 2006). While these deposits occasionally consist of 'high status' material one of the most remarkable discoveries is that of over 100 small brushwood bundles (170 mm long by 50 mm wide) from Muckerstown, Co. Meath (Moore and Stuijts 2006); while this dates to the Middle Bronze Age it is, perhaps, indicative of a simple personal spirituality. We might speculate about the purpose of these offerings and they may be fetishes or power bundles. Whatever their meaning these, and other 'non-precious' deposits at *fulachta fiadh*, appear to mirror the more spectacular offerings of high status material, both hoards and single items, in wet places.

Aristocratic territories

If the local communities had a measure of economic self-reliance it is clear that they were far from isolated. Extensive analysis shows that, for example, in populous areas such as east Limerick/west Tipperary, and south Clare, multiple communities existed within well-organised and ordered landscapes. The area around Toonagh also provides a snapshot of another level of social and landscape organisation (Grogan 2005a, fig. 4.3). The ceremonial site of Magh Adhair, partly embedded in a later (early medieval) 'royal' inauguration site, appears to be the ritual focus of a territory controlled by the warrior aristocracy. The identification of the nearby fortified hilltop enclosure at Cahercalla as the residence of this group is speculative. Only a small number of these enclosures have been excavated, including Haggardstown, Co. Louth (McLoughlin 2010), and Clenagh, Co. Clare (Grogan and Daly 2005), where the meagre evidence suggests a Late Bronze Age date. Nevertheless, intensive landscape analysis in the area around Toonagh/Cahercalla indicates extensive division into a number of well-defined 'territories' each with a hilltop enclosure and a ritual centre, generally a ceremonial enclosure (but with occasionally more than one), and frequently containing at least one high status hoard deposit (Grogan 2005a, 87–95, figs 4.5–4.9). These territories also, however, have evidence for more dispersed settlement in the form of apparently single homesteads, as well as more scattered *fulachta fiadh* and funerary sites including single cremation pits, suggesting more complex social networks.

A model of Late Bronze Age social organisation has been proposed for the north Munster region (designated a 'province' by Eogan in 1974; Grogan 2005a). While the level of detailed evidence for this is still inadequate it suggested a three-fold ranking system – community, territory, chiefdom – based on the analysis of the sites and artefacts. Other ranks or classes, such as specialists in craft production, trade or religious lore, may well be included in this model, but we will confine ourselves here to the basic concept.

In south Clare it was possible to propose a model of territorial organisation and to suggest actual boundaries largely based on natural features (Grogan 2005a, 73–76, 83–88, figs 3.1,

4.6). The ceremonial enclosures suggest not just collective endeavour in their construction, but also communal rituals that provided a measure of bonding between several communities within the territory. In east Limerick the enclosures are frequently embedded in barrow cemeteries, while human bone at the Grange Stone Circle at Lough Gur, Co. Limerick (Ó Ríordáin 1951; Roche 2004), and cremation burials at Lugg, Co. Dublin (Kilbride-Jones 1950; Roche and Eogan 2007), indicate that the dead played some part in the formation of another layer of identity. The association of a warrior aristocracy with this level of landscape organisation is, of course, speculative, but such a class is suggested by the considerable array of Late Bronze Age weaponry. In addition, a number of high status domestic sites have been identified, perhaps related to this high status; certainly, some of these sites have produced the paraphernalia – weapons, tools and ornaments – that may also represent the wealth, status and identity of this group. Among this limited list are the lakeshore sites of Ballinderry 2, Co. Offaly (Hencken 1942); Moynagh Lough, Co. Meath (Bradley 2004); Rathtinaun, Co. Sligo (Raftery 1994, 32–35); Knocknalappa, Co. Clare (Raftery 1942; Grogan *et al.* 1996); and Killymoon, Co. Tyrone (Hurl 1999; 1995; Hurl *et al.* 1995), while other sites include Site C, Knockadoon, Lough Gur, Co. Limerick, and Rathgall, Co. Wicklow (Becker 2010; Ó Ríordáin 1954).

In any case, the collaboration of multiple communities involved larger population groups that now moved beyond the ties of family and lineage; the dynamic behind the forging of these links is unknown, but the creation of substantial extra-familial groups was already occasionally manifest in the Middle Bronze Age at, for example, Corrstown, Co. Londonderry, and on the Knockadoon peninsula at Lough Gur (Ginn and Rathbone 2012; Grogan 2005b, 50–6). It is tempting to see a role for the aristocracy in the Late Bronze Age developments and certainly, in some areas, significant increases in population density may have created tensions and the potential for conflict that required forceful mediation. The rise of a special warrior class, and the need for discipline and training, perhaps in groups or cadres, from boyhood as well as the production of war gear, is a widespread phenomenon in the latter part of the European Bronze Age, and the development of this group is too complex to be elucidated at a local or regional level.

What is relevant at this scale is the source of the economic wealth required to produce the rich artefactual assemblage of the period. In north Munster, as in many other regions, there was no direct access to metals. Other areas of potential may have included trade, and well-developed craft and production skills – importing raw materials and converting them into high value goods – although the only possible evidence for such a 'manufactory' process comes from the hillfort site at Rathgall, Co. Wicklow (Raftery 1976). Another source may have been the sustained production of agricultural surplus. Too little is known about the Bronze Age farming economy and the record has recently been swamped by largely undigested new data (but see O'Donnell and Johnston 2007). There are, however, indications, including improved land management, farming tools and the expansion of settlement onto soils that had previously been too heavy to work, possibly facilitated by deeper ploughing, that agriculture was more than capable of meeting the demands of population growth. The suggestion that Late Bronze Age society was capable of generating and channelling surplus towards conversion into portable wealth that was controlled, if not owned by, elites is, of course, speculative. However, it does fit with the widespread paucity of artefactual wealth on the majority of domestic sites that otherwise appear to reflect a comfortable, self-sufficient, lifestyle, and the concentration of high status objects, other than those from ritual contexts including hoards, on a comparatively small number of settlements.

If we might follow this speculative strand a little further, one of the motivations behind greater cross-community co-operation and bonding may have been this new shared obligation to generate surplus. In this context the territories emerge as both social and economic units within, at least in the Mooghaun area, fixed landscape boundaries.

Collective and regional identity

At a regional level the clear preference for particular objects, most of them of high status, indicates, at the very least, differing stylistic tastes. Moreover, these have been used, primarily by Eogan (1993; 1979) with subsequent expansion (Grogan 2005b), to characterise separate regional entities. This material includes personal ornaments (gorgets, lock rings, fine gold bracelets: north Munster), items associated with public ceremonial (horns, cauldrons and buckets: south Munster) and possibly horse harnesses (bronze rings: the midlands). This variation also reflects differences in the context of use and display (see below). In addition, some of these regional groups are further highlighted by contrasting preferences in the mix of sites types (including, for example: *fulachta fiadh*, stone circles, rows and alignments, barrows and ringditches, ceremonial enclosures: Grogan 2005b, 173–86).

There are, of course, elements of the Late Bronze Age material assemblage that have a national distribution. There are few parts of the country, for instance, that do not have at least occasional examples of a wide variety of site types, such as *fulachta fiadh*, barrows, ceremonial circles, or enclosures. While site preservation is varied and, even in the construction boom of the first decade of this century, excavation was not evenly dispersed, one major feature of settlement distribution is apparent: the principal population focus was in the east and south of the country with very limited occupation in the midlands and parts of the west and northwest. Tools and weapons have very wide distributions, although these artefacts also display significant concentrations, such as the high number of swords along the Shannon and Bann Rivers. There is some regional variation among the socket axe types, although the most numerous type, Eogan's (2000) Group 13, is found throughout the overall distribution range. In short, the evidence suggests a strong element of homogeneity in some areas of cultural expression, as well as a high level of on-going awareness of technological and stylistic trends and, perhaps, an undercurrent of basic shared beliefs and customs. Current research indicates, for example, that the most common and basic material – the pottery – represents a single, apparently undifferentiated, island-wide tradition (Grogan and Roche 2010, 41–4, illus. 10). The universal use of cremation in pits or enclosing ditches and the virtual absence of grave goods, other than pottery, also demonstrate an element of cultural unity.

North and south Munster

To extend this line of enquiry, it is worth considering two adjacent, but contrasting, regions: north and south Munster. North Munster, the lower part of the Shannon valley, is a largely low-lying area dominated, especially in east Limerick and west Tipperary, by very fertile land in modern times principally devoted to dairying. South Munster consists of mainly upland terrain, including the Glanaruddery and Slieve Mish, Derrynasaggart and Boggeragh Mountains, and Macgillycuddy's Reeks. While extensive settlement, indicated principally by very large numbers of *fulachta fiadh*, occurs along the lower river valleys and on the flanks of the uplands, there are also clusters of settlement evidence on pockets of more fertile soils along the high passes that cross the mountainous zones (see Grogan 2005b, figs 9.6–9.8). These routeways also preserve large numbers of small stone monuments (circles, enclosures, radial cairns, boulder burials, and stone alignments) that give further character to the region. North Munster is characterised by barrows (and ringditches) and large ceremonial enclosures, but the site repertoire also includes flat cremation pit cemeteries as well as some stone circles and *fulachta fiadh*. The distribution includes large, very tight clusters of sites in, for example, southeast Clare and east Limerick (Grogan 2005a, fig. 3.1; 2005b, figs 5.13, 5.25; Grogan *et al.* 2007, 149–52, fig. 6.13).

As already noted, the mix of artefacts from south Munster includes a significant number of ceremonial items – Class 2 horns (Coles 1963), Class B cauldrons (Gerloff 1986), and some bronze buckets – that generally occur as votive deposits including horn hoards (Eogan 1983). These suggest a very public display of prestige possibly associated with feasting accompanied and enhanced by music; the presence of up to six instruments in the horn hoards suggest dramatic sound effects. In this context we can suggest that communal feasting hosted by an elite provided the opportunity to display and reinforce status, as well as reiterate the subservient rank of the 'guests'.

In north Munster high status objects are characteristically high value personal ornaments of gold perhaps matched, in terms costliness and desirability, by amber imported from the Baltic (Cahill 2004, 102–04). While these also occur as single items in votive deposits, discoveries, such as the hoard of gold ornaments from Gorteenreagh, Co. Clare (Raftery 1967), indicate that these were on occasion worn as prestige sets. The context for the display of this finery may well include communal gathering in the large ceremonial enclosures as well as at the public deposition of votive gifts. In this context it is possible to envisage the overlap between the display of separate identities (represented by the distinct ranking of elites and others) and the proclamation of shared identity between the respective ranks within a particular community. It is also probable that communal identity was reinforced by shared endeavour, such as in the construction of the ceremonial enclosures. Another example of pooled labour may be provided by the morphology of Mooghaun hillfort: here the ramparts were constructed in linked straight sections rather than a seamless curve (Grogan 2005a, 226–29). It has been suggested that each of these sections (which vary in the detail of their construction techniques) was the responsibility of the individual communities that formed the overarching social group. In this way the erection of specific portions of the hillfort were the responsibility of workgroups made up of neighbours and kin; these appear to have been drawn from a wide landscape working in conjunction, and perhaps in friendly competition, with other communities with whom they were neither acquainted or related.

These bonding exercises helped to create a wider, and more close-knit, circle of 'stakeholders' in both the enterprise and in the on-going use of important centres such as the hillforts and ceremonial sites. These endeavours must have been important social mechanisms in the context of expanding populations and enlarged social territories where traditional communities had been confined to smaller and more kin-bound social and economic units.

Obligation and reciprocation undoubtedly still formed part of the maintenance of social fabric, at both a local and regional level, but the forging of larger, including regional, identities required systems that moved beyond established, familiar and often personal, relationships.

A material world

The evidence of metalwork can be used to explore both the projection of personal status, and the formation and display of collective identity. While some current debate has queried the characterisation of very high status material, for example gold gorgets or heavy dress-fasteners, as strictly personal possessions, it is clear that other costly objects, such as swords and some personal ornaments, represent the belongings of specific individuals. The complete absence of direct association between individuals and these items certainly hampers interpretation and in this the lack of grave goods, other than pottery, is certainly a further hindrance. Indirect evidence, such as the occasional appearance of high status material on domestic sites, suggests that ownership rested at a familial level. However, it is probable that weapons, spearheads, a small number of knives and shields and particularly swords, were emblems of personal wealth and rank, and were also symbols of group identity, membership of an elite warrior class. Although body armour has not been identified in Ireland, Cahill's (2005) inspired analysis of the decoration on the gorgets suggests a derivation from the continental and especially French bronze cuirasses. If the gorgets are symbols of warrior status and prowess then it may be that they are reflective of very high standing and are the insignia of social and military leaders. Cahill (*ibid.*, 27–8) noted similar decorative features on ear-spools, shields and sunflower pins (see also Cahill 2001). While the shields clearly have a direct martial connection it may be that largely decorative items were worn to evoke or symbolise a warrior spirit.

There can be little doubt that, by their nature, weapons (here including shields and armour) are personal possessions. Furthermore, their high value, in terms of resources, craftsmanship and labour input, indicate that they were well beyond the aspirations of the inhabitants of the vast majority of settlements. As highly specialised implements swords, in particular, very strongly suggest the existence of a warrior class or caste; the occasional occurrence of weaponry on, or in close association with, the small number of settlements that have produced other valuable or prestige material (see above) further emphasises the high status of this group. The frequency of weapons in votive deposits, particularly as single items in rivers (Cooney and Grogan 1999, figs 8:13–8:15), suggests not only sufficient wealth to make these sacrifices, but also that these were not just the insignia of social status and that they also reflected a spiritual dimension to the identity of the warrior. We can envisage, although regrettably not prove, that the occasions of these deposits were public events with guests or participants drawn primarily from social peers. These shared experiences no doubt helped to cement the status of the warrior as well as advertising his martial prowess and strengthen his actual or potential success in combat.

In his work on Late Bronze Age hoards, Eogan (1983) identified three basic types of material – tools, weapons and ornaments. While more complex subdivisions can be made, these are useful categories given the overall composition of the hoards. If weaponry can be accepted as personal possession, what is to be made of the tools of which the vast majority are axes (Eogan 2000)? Some associations suggest that axes were occasionally used as weapons and there is ample evidence, in the form of axe marks on timber, that they were also used as woodworking implements. A wide range of owners (elites, farmers or artisans) is possible, but the contexts from which this material is derived may shed further light on this issue. Apart from hoards, including those with weapons, and other apparently votive deposits of single items, bronze tools have only occasionally come from domestic sites (principally the high status examples mentioned earlier), although crude flint and chert implements are reasonably common. While we must be aware of the care taken with valuable metal artefacts, and the re-cycling of this material, it is instructive that the discovery of these is effectively restricted to sites that display other indications of wealth. In terms of closed associations, tools and especially axes, occasionally occur in hoards with swords (Eogan 1983); in these contexts they may be interpreted as weapons rather than more mundane implements. Moreover, given their association with high status material, and the absence of simple tools from most habitation sites, the evidence may suggest that costly metal, including bronze, may largely have been the preserve of social elites. It is not clear whether this was simply because of the generally unobtainable value of metals, as well as other materials such as amber and jet, or if there were social restrictions on its ownership.

However, even if possession was ultimately confined to a few, the movement and distribution of both the raw materials and the finished articles was most probably in the hands of an entrepreneurial class. While there is no direct evidence for this in an Irish context, tin and amber were certainly being imported and, with the proximity of the major copper mining complex at the Great Orme in north Wales, it is probable that some of that material was making its way to Ireland. Certainly, the shipwrecks off the British coast, such as Salcombe, south Devon, and Ferriby, Yorkshire, suggest that copper was an important bulk cargo during the period (Roberts 2005; Roberts and Vesley 2011). The dramatic upsurge in demand for commodities such as tin, copper, gold, amber, and jet contributed to developments in sourcing and extraction, as well as an increasing expertise in mining and smelting. These changes also appear to be reflected in the greater formalisation of established routeways. There are two elements to the evidence. Firstly, there is an increased concentration of ribbon settlement along, or in close proximity to, routeways although, conversely, it is probable that some routes, especially those associated with local travel, will develop between existing population nodes. Secondly, the strategic placement of hillforts and hilltop enclosures overlooking important travel ways may well reflect an increased concern with the control of movement and, potentially, the profit to be made from monitoring trade. Some routes, at both a regional and local level, can be identified with reasonable accuracy (Grogan 2006; 2005b, figs 6.5, 6.7); the evidence indicates a well-trod network that facilitated local traffic as well as the less frequent travel of 'strangers'. A feature of the regional routes is their convergence on fording points across major rivers such as the Shannon, Barrow, Erne and Bann (Bourke 2001; Cooney and Grogan 1999, 167; Ramsey *et al.* 1991–92). These crossroads – where land and water thoroughfares intersect – many of which had been in use since early prehistory, are frequently marked by artefact deposition. Other evidence for an increased desire to access and traverse the landscape is provided by the timber trackways (*e.g.* Raftery 1996; 1990).

Conclusions

Recent infrastructural associated excavations have demonstrated that, while well-defined settlement clusters are a feature of the Late Bronze Age landscape in many parts of the east of the country, the hierarchical model proposed for north, and to a lesser extent for south, Munster is clearly not universally applicable. There are, of course, other regions – southeast Ulster, north Leinster and perhaps Roscommon-Sligo – that suggest similar developments were occurring around the beginning of the first millennium. Indeed, at a local level almost throughout the country it is evident that there are reflections of this social system even if, in most instances, these may have been limited, relatively short-lived, thrusts for power as well as the projection of separate and superior status. Nevertheless, the considerable evidence – domestic sites, *fulachta fiadh* and the apparently undifferentiated funerary traditions – demonstrates that the majority of the Late Bronze Age population, which may have been present in significant densities in some parts of the country, lived in reasonable comfort and security within well-established communities that did not have access to material wealth. For these people identity was a received part of their familial and communal history and was maintained through shared experience. In the growing social and economic complexity of the Late Bronze Age, new bonds and alliances may have been formed between groups of communities which, in turn, could have provided the source of the wealth that underpinned a new warrior elite.

References

Becker, K. (2010) Rathgall, Co. Wicklow, Heritage Guide No. 51. *Archaeology Ireland.*

Bourke, L. (2001) *Crossing the Rubicon: Bronze Age metalwork from Irish rivers.* Bronze Age Studies 5, Department of Archaeology. Galway, National University of Ireland.

Bradley, J. (2004) Moynagh Lough, Co. Meath, in the Late Bronze Age. In H. Roche, E. Grogan, J. Bradley, J. Coles, and B. Raftery (eds) *From megaliths to metals. Essays in honour of George Eogan,* 91–8. Oxford, Oxbow.

Cahill, M. (2001) Unspooling the mystery. *Archaeology Ireland* 57, 8–15.

Cahill, M. (2004) The gold beads from Tumna, Co. Roscommon. In H. Roche, E. Grogan, J. Bradley, J. Coles, and B. Raftery (eds) *From megaliths to metals. Essays in honour of George Eogan,* 99–108. Oxford, Oxbow.

Cahill, M. (2005) Ornaments: cuirass to gorget? An interpretation of the structure and decorative elements of some gold ornaments from the Irish Late Bronze Age. *Archaeology Ireland* 74, 26–30.

Cherry, S. (1990) The finds from *fulachta fiadh.* In V. Buckley (ed.) *Burnt offerings. International contributions to burnt mound archaeology,* 49–54. Bray, Wordwell.

Coles, J. (1963) Irish Bronze Age horns and their relations with northern Europe. *Proceedings of the Prehistoric Society* 11, 326–56.

Cooney, G. and Grogan, E. 1999 *Irish prehistory: a social perspective.* Bray, Wordwell (2nd edition).

Cotter, E. (2005) Bronze Age Ballybrowney, Co. Cork. In J. O'Sullivan and M. Stanley (eds) *Recent archaeological discoveries on National Road Schemes 2004,* 25–35. Archaeology and the National Roads Authority Monograph Series 2. Dublin, The National Roads Authority.

Cotter, E. (2006) *Final report on Ballybrowney Lower 1.* Unpublished report prepared by Archaeological Consultancy Services Ltd.

Doody, M. (2000) Bronze Age houses in Ireland. In A. Desmond, G. Johnson, M. McCarthy, J. Sheehan, and E. Shee Twohig (eds) *New agendas in Irish prehistory. Papers in commemoration of Liz Anderson,* 135–59, Bray, Wordwell.

Doody, M. (2007) *Excavations at Curraghatoor, Co. Tipperary*. Cork, University College Cork Department of Archaeology, Archaeology Monograph.

Eogan, G. (1974) Regionale gruppierungen in der Spätbronzeit Irland. *Archaeologisches Korrespondenzblatt* 4, 319–27.

Eogan, G. (1983) *Hoards of the Irish later Bronze Age*. Dublin, University College Dublin.

Eogan, G. (1993) The Late Bronze Age. Customs, crafts and cults. In E. Shee Twohig and M. Ronayne (eds) *Past perceptions: the prehistoric archaeology of south-west Ireland*, 121–33. Cork, University College Cork.

Eogan, G. (2000) *The socketed bronze axes in Ireland. Prähistorische Bronzefunde, Abteilung* 9, 22.

Gerloff, S. (1986) Bronze Age class A cauldrons: typology, origins and chronology. *Journal of the Royal Society of Antiquaries of Ireland* 116, 84–115.

Ginn, V. and Rathbone, S. (eds) (2012) *Corrstown: a coastal community. Excavations of a Bronze Age village in Northern Ireland*. Oxford, Oxbow.

Gowen, M., Ó Néill, J. and Phillips, M. (eds) (2005) *The Lisheen Mine Archaeological Project 1996–8*. Margaret Gowen and Co. Ltd. Bray, Wordwell.

Grogan, E. (2005a) *The later prehistoric landscape of south-east Clare*. Discovery Programme Monograph 6, Volume 1. Bray, The Discovery Programme/Wordwell.

Grogan, E. (2005b) *The prehistoric landscape of north Munster*. Discovery Programme Monograph 6, Volume 2. Bray, The Discovery Programme/Wordwell.

Grogan E. (2006) The place of routeways in later prehistory. In F. Coyne *Islands in the clouds: an upland archaeological study on Mount Brandon and the Paps, County Kerry* 74–82. Kerry, Kerry County Council and Aegis Archaeology Limited.

Grogan, E. and Daly, A. (2005) Excavations at Clenagh, Co. Clare. In E. Grogan *The later prehistoric landscape of south-east Clare*, 247–53. Discovery Programme Monograph 6, Volume 1. Bray, The Discovery Programme/Wordwell.

Grogan, E., O'Donnell, L. and Johnson, P. (2007) *The Bronze Age landscapes of The Pipeline to the West*. Bray, Wordwell.

Grogan, E., O'Sullivan, A., O'Carroll F., and Hagen, I. (1999) Knocknalappa, Co. Clare: a reappraisal. *Discovery Programme Reports* 6, 111–23, Dublin, The Discovery Programme/Royal Irish Academy.

Grogan, E. and Roche, H. (2008) *The prehistoric pottery assemblage from Clogh, Co. Wexford (A003/059, E3468). N11 Gorey – Arklow Link Road, Co. Wexford*. Unpublished report prepared for V. J. Keeley Ltd.

Grogan, E. and Roche, H. (2009) *The prehistoric pottery assemblage from Kellymount 5, Co. Kilkenny (AR127, E3858). N9/N10 Rathclogh to Powerstown*. Unpublished report prepared for Irish Archaeological Consultancy Ltd.

Grogan, E. and Roche, H. (2010) Clay and fire: the development and distribution of pottery traditions in prehistoric Ireland. In M. Stanley, E. Danaher and J. Eogan (eds) *Creative minds*, 27–45. Archaeology and the National Roads Authority Monograph Series 7. Dublin, The National Roads Authority.

Hencken, H. (1942) Ballinderry crannóg no. 2, *Proceedings of the Royal Irish Academy* 47C, 1–76.

Holmes, P. and Molloy, B. (2006) The Charlesland (Wicklow) pipes. In E. Hickmann, A. A. Both, and R. Eichmann (eds) *Music archaeology in contexts. Studien zur Musikarchäologie V*, Orient-Archäologie 20, 15–40. Rahden/Westf.

Hurl, D. (1995) Killymoon: new light on the Late Bronze Age. *Archaeology Ireland* 36, 24–7.

Hurl, D. (1999) More light on Killymoon. *Archaeology Ireland* 52, 5.

Hurl, D., Nelis, E., and Murray, B. (1995) *Data structure report, Killymoon, County Tyrone 1995*. Unpublished report. Belfast, School of Geography, Archaeology and Palaeoecology, Queen's University Belfast.

Kelly, A. (2008) *Interim report on archaeological excavation of A029/005, E3123, Grange 3. M3 Clonee–North of Kells. Contract 4 – Navan-Kells and Kells Bypass*. Unpublished report prepared for Irish Archaeological Consultancy Ltd.

Kiely, J. and O'Mahony, E. (2011) Bronze Age domestic and funerary activity at Derrybane, Co. Tipperary, *Eachtra Journal* 11. Eachtra Archaeological Projects.

Kilbride-Jones, H. E. (1950) The excavation of a composite early Iron Age monument with 'henge' features at Lugg, Co. Dublin. *Proceedings of the Royal Irish Academy* 53C, 311–32.

Lynch, L., Johnston, P., and Kiely, J. (2010) Cremains and questions: Bronze Age burial at Derrybane 2. *Seanda* 5, 18–21.

McLoughlin, G. (2010) *Archaeological excavations at Haynestown–Haggardstown, Dundalk Co. Louth: Site 13 Haggardstown (06E0485).* Unpublished final report prepared for Irish Archaeological Consultancy Ltd.

McQuade, M. (2009) Ballylegan, Co. Tipperary. Four structures. Site 207.2 (E2265). In M. McQuade, B. Molloy, and C. Moriarty, *In the shadow of the Galtees: archaeological excavations along the N8 Cashel to Mitchelstown Road Scheme*, 69–73. National Roads Authority Scheme Monograph 4. Dublin, The National Roads Authority.

McQuade, M., Molloy, B. and Moriarty, C. (2009) *In the shadow of the Galtees: archaeological excavations along the N8 Cashel to Mitchelstown Road Scheme.* National Roads Authority Scheme Monographs 4. Dublin, The National Roads Authority.

Masterson, B. (1999) Archaeological applications of modern survey techniques. *Discovery Programme Reports* 5, 131–46. Dublin, The Discovery Programme/Royal Irish Academy.

Molloy, B. (2006) Site CA1, Charlesland, Co. Wicklow. In I. Bennett (ed.) *Excavations 2003*, 545–46. Bray, Wordwell.

Moore, C. and Stuijts, I. (2006) A Bronze Age enigma: some unusual artefacts from County Meath. *Seanda* 1, 44–45.

Ní Lionáin, C. (2007) Life, death and food production in Bronze Age Ireland: recent excavations at Stamullin, Co. Meath. *Archaeology Ireland* 82, 18–21.

O'Donnell, L. and Johnston, P. (2007) Environmental archaeology: identifying patterns of exploitation in the Bronze Age. In E. Grogan, L. O'Donnell and P. Johnston (eds) *The Bronze Age landscapes of the Pipeline to the West: an integrated archaeological and environmental assessment*, 27–79. Bray, Wordwell Ltd.

Ó Ríordáin, S. P. (1951) Lough Gur excavations: the great stone circle (B) in Grange townland. *Proceedings of the Royal Irish Academy* 54C, 37–74.

Ó Ríordáin, S. P. (1954) Lough Gur excavations: Neolithic and Bronze Age houses on Knockadoon. *Proceedings of the Royal Irish Academy* 56C, 297–459.

Raftery, B. (1976) Rathgall and Irish hillfort problems. In D. Harding (ed.) *Hillforts: later prehistoric earthworks in Britain and Ireland*, 339–57. London, Academic Press.

Raftery, B. (1990) *Trackways through time.* Rush, Headline Publishing.

Raftery, B. (1994) *Pagan Celtic Ireland. The enigma of the Irish Iron Age.* London, Thames and Hudson.

Raftery, B. (1996) *Trackway excavations in the Mountdillon Bogs, Co. Longford, 1985–1991.* Dublin, Irish Archaeological Wetland Unit Transactions 3, Crannog Publications.

Raftery, J. (1942) Knocknalappa crannóg, Co. Clare. *North Munster Antiquarian Journal* 3, 53–72.

Raftery, J. (1967) The Gorteenreagh hoard. In E. Rynne (ed.) *North Munster studies: essays in commemoration of Monsignor Micheal Moloney*, 61–71. Limerick, Thomond Archaeological Society.

Ramsey, G., Bourke, C., and Crone, D. (1991–92) Antiquities from the River Blackwater I, Bronze Age metalwork. *Ulster Journal of Archaeology* 54–5, 138–49.

Roberts, B. and Veysey, C. (2011) Trading places. *British Museum Magazine* (Autumn 2011), 44–5.

Roberts, O. T. P. (2005) Interpretations of prehistoric boat remains. *International Journal of Nautical Archaeology* 35, 72–78.

Roche, H. (2004) The dating of the embanked stone circle at Grange, Co. Limerick. In H. Roche, E. Grogan, J. Bradley, J. Coles, and B. Raftery (eds), *From megaliths to metals. Essays in honour of George Eogan*, 109–16. Oxford, Oxbow.

Roche, H. and Eogan, G. (2007) A re-assessment of the enclosure at Lugg, County Dublin, Ireland. In C. Gosden, H. Hamerow, P. de Jersey, and G. Lock (eds), *Communities and connections: essays in honour of Barry Cunliffe*, 154–68. Oxford, Oxford University Press.

Russell, I. and Corcoran, E. (2001) *Kilsharvan 16, final excavation report.* Unpublished report prepared by Archaeological Consultancy Services Ltd.

Stafford, E. (2002) *Site 17, Lagavooreen, excavation report.* Unpublished excavation report prepared by Irish Archaeological Consultancy Ltd.

WHO LIVES IN A ROUNDHOUSE LIKE THIS? GOING THROUGH THE KEYHOLE ON BRONZE AGE DOMESTIC IDENTITY

Victoria Ginn

It is through the symbolic orderings of space and time that roles in society are experienced (Bourdieu 1972). People establish individual and collective identity by manipulating spaces and places; in this way spatial order is created through dwelling, social activity or existence. Houses, as central places, are well-suited to topoanalysis (the exploration of identity through place, see *e.g.* Buttimer 1980, 167). The interaction between spatial configuration, cognition and behaviour and the physical environment means that houses and settlements are also inherently associated with social constructs and identities. They 'form a nexus for expression as well as perpetuation and reiteration' (Roberts 1996, 5). House characteristics are constructed from physical and socio-cultural processes and 'perhaps more than any other physical construction, the house embodies and emphasises links between materiality, people and ideas' (Downes and Richards 2005, 57). The Neo-classicist approach decrees that the essence of building, as distinguished from architecture, also requires a symbolic function (St John Wilson 1992, x, 50). This goes some way to explaining why certain patterns have been observed in Bronze Age settlements. For example, although the marked favouritism of eastern-orientated entrances (*e.g.* Carlin 2006; Doody 2000; Ó Néill 2009) can be considered as a pragmatic response to diminish the effects of the prevailing winds, eastern orientation of entrances occurs regardless of the topography, leading some archaeologists to seek a more ritual rationale for this behaviour (*e.g.* Oswald 1997; Parker Pearson 1999). This chapter will concentrate on how identity was established through the manipulation of Bronze Age houses in Ireland, with an emphasis on entrances as they represent a threshold to both internal and also external space: an entrance and an exit. Sites mentioned in the chapter are shown in Figure 7.1.

In Ireland and Britain the vanguard of the Bronze Age domestic architecture was the roundhouse. Circular architecture has certain requirements when it comes to construction and roundhouses from different regions had to be very similarly built. Strong, sturdy posts are required to support the roof and need to be set in such a way as to keep the pitch of the roof at 45° or greater; the roof also needs to be supported over the entrance. A roundhouse has a maximum diameter determined by the roof pitch and also by the length of timbers. Expansion

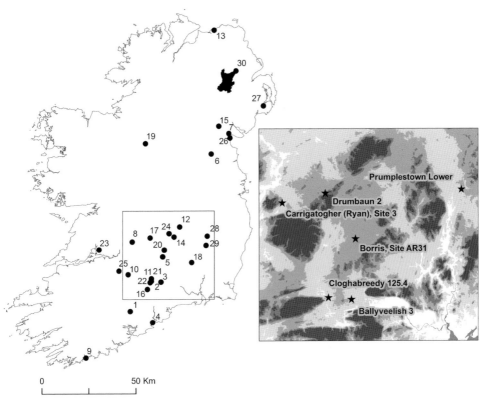

Figure 7.1: Distribution map of sites mentioned in text: (1) Ballybrowney; (2) Ballydrehid; (3) Ballyveelish 3; (4) Ballyvergen West; (5) Borris and Blackcastle AR31; (6) Brittas, Moynagh Lough; (7) Carn More 1; (8) Carrigatogher (Ryan) 3; (9) Carrigillihy; (10) Chancellorsland 1A; (11) Cloghabreedy 125.4; (12) Clondacasey 2: (13) Corrstown; (14) Cuffsborough 4; (15) Cullyhanna; (16) Curraghatoor; (17) Drumbaun 2; (18) Dunbell Big 2; (19) Kildorragh; (20) Killoran 8; (21) Knockgaffron 137.1; (22) Knockgaffron 137.3; (23) Knocksaggart; (24) Lismore 2; (25) Lough Gur; (26) Marshes Upper 9; (27) Meadowlands; (28) Prumplestown Lower; (29) Tinryland; (30) Townparks.

of a roundhouse is therefore only possible by the addition of an annex or an entirely new, separate structure, unlike longhouses which can be more readily elongated. Ó Néill (2009) and Doody (2000, 144) identified regional construction traits of Irish roundhouses which they attributed to wood availability, the size and type of structure, and climatic factors. Yet these regional traits were limited by a restricted repertoire of possibilities, such as the choice of hazel instead of oak, stone wall foundations instead of turf, and so forth. However, there are certain aspects of roundhouse architecture discernible in the archaeological record, particularly the entrance, that can be more significantly altered, and that differ temporally and or spatially.

The standard entrance

On many ground plans it is difficult to discern the precise nature of the roundhouse entrance due to inter-cutting features or the effects of truncation. Where identifiable, it is apparent that several different forms of entrances were used. Some roundhouses have little elaboration and the entrance is only notable by way of a slightly larger gap between the spacing of postholes which formed the structural elements. Examples of this type include Cuffsborough Site 4, County Laois (oak charcoal samples radiocarbon dated to the early Middle Bronze Age) (Murphy 2009) (Figure 7.2), Townparks, County Antrim (House C dating to the Early Bronze Age (hazel charcoal) and House B to the Middle Bronze Age (separate willow, hazel and birch charcoal)) (Ballin Smith 2003) and at Tinryland, County Carlow (charred hazelnuts dated to the Middle Bronze Age) (O'Connell 2009), suggesting that this trend was neither geographic nor temporally specific.

A more prominent entrance type is the standard porch. Observed in the archaeological record through the placement of at least two postholes which jut out from the structural postring, there are well-preserved examples of this entrance type at four roundhouses from Clonadacasey Site 2, County Laois (oak and short-lived samples dated to the Late Bronze Age) (Ó Néill 2008) (Figure 7.2), Lismore 2, County Laois (short-lived samples dated to the Late Bronze Age) (Wiggins 2008), and Knockgaffron 137.1 and 137.3, County Tipperary (mixed sample dated to the Middle/Late Bronze Age and fruitwood to the Late Bronze Age) (Gowen 2006; Moriarty 2007a). These examples suggest that this type of porch was common to the Late Bronze Age period. A possibly earlier example was identified at Ballybrowney, County Cork, which had small slot-trenches running from the wall line to the porch. It was undated but associated with Middle Bronze Age pottery which was also recovered from an adjacent roundhouse which was dated (sample: alder and oak) to the Middle Bronze Age (Cotter 2006).

The elaborate entrance

More elaborate entrances have also been observed. Cleary (2007) noted a trend of inward turning wall slots which formed entrances at Structures 2, 4 and 6 from Late Bronze Age Curraghatoor, County Tipperary (Doody 1987a, 2007), and also at the undated site of Kildorragh, County Leitrim (Opie 1995). At the Middle Bronze Age site of Corrstown, County Londonderry, the majority of the 74 nucleated roundhouses had long sunken entrances, ranging from (where discernible) 2m by 1.8m (Structure 1) to 10m by 1.6m (Structure 41) and 4.5m by 4.3m (Structure 7) (Ginn and Rathbone 2012) (Figure 7.2). Flanked by postholes, Ginn and Rathbone considered that part of the sunken entrances may have had porches, or at least had some form of windbreak along one side. The roundhouses at Corrstown were not architecturally dissimilar to those from other contemporary settlements, apart from this elongation and elaboration of the entrances which has not been observed at any other settlement sites.

Figure 7.2 (opposite): Porches: (a) Cuffsborough 4 (after Murphy 2009, fig. 6); (b) Clonadacasey 2 (after O'Neill 2008, fig. 8); (c) Corrstown Structure 4 (after Ginn and Rathbone 2011, fig. 2.4); (d) Ballyveelish 3 (after Doody 1987b, fig. 1.4); (e) Carrigatogher Ryan Site 3 (after Mulcahy and Taylor 2009, fig. 5); (f) Structure A from Cloghabreedy 125.4 (after Moriarty 2007, plate 5); (g) Borris and Blackcastle AR31 (after Stevens 2010, plate 3).

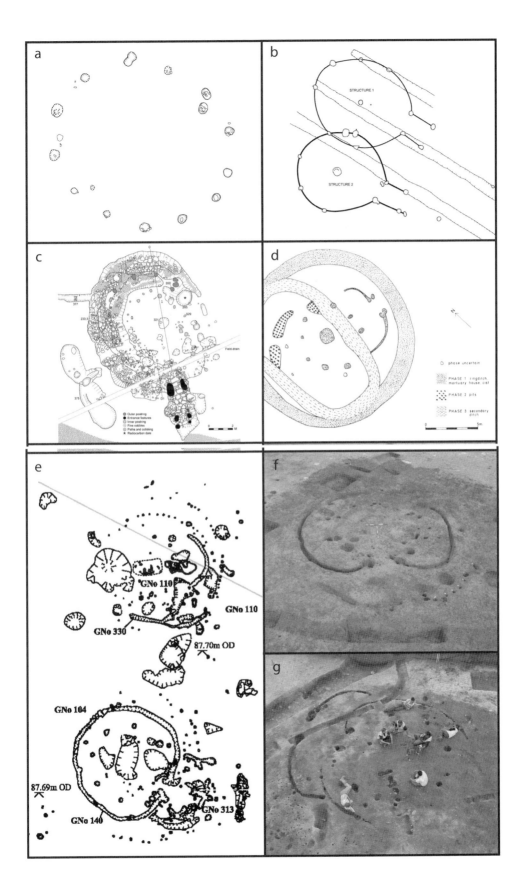

a

b

STRUCTURE 1

STRUCTURE 2

c

350

377

233.3

321

329

Field drain

375

○ Outer posting
● Entrance features
● Inner posting
◎ Fine cobbles
◉ Paths and cobbling
★ Radiocarbon date

0   2 M

d

N

○ phase uncertain

▦ PHASE 1 ringditch,
   mortuary house, cist

⦙ PHASE 2 pits

▧ PHASE 3 secondary
   ditch

0   5m

e

GNo 110

GNo 110

GNo 330

87.70m OD

GNo 104

87.69m OD

GNo 313

GNo 140

f

g

There is another trend concerning entrance elaboration which appears to be regionally specific. Several sites in County Tipperary have noticeably large porches formed with curving slot-trenches. Some of the houses are also 'missing' their western sides. At Carrigatogher (Ryan) Site 3, the outer gullies which formed the porch of Structure RH104 enclosed an area 4.2m by 2.5m (Mulcahy and Taylor 2009) (Figure 7.2). The porch of Structure RH110 was just as wide, although not quite as long but still significant at 1.25m. Structure RH110 appeared to be missing much of its western side, although a large pit which post-dated the Bronze Age occupation may have obscured the evidence. Both of these roundhouses dated to the Middle Bronze Age (Figure 7.3). A copper-alloy razor, which appeared to have been burnt, was interpreted by the excavators as a foundation deposit associated with a structural posthole from RH104. Additionally, decorated pottery sherds and some metalworking waste were recovered (Mulcahy and Taylor 2009). The entrance to Ballyveelish 3 was also 4m wide and 2.5m long and formed with two curving linear features (Doody 1987b) (Figure 7.2). Terminals at the end of these curvilinear features suggested the former presence of large posts. This roundhouse is among the earliest securely dated houses of this entrance type with hazel/willow charcoal from the porch dating to the early Middle Bronze Age

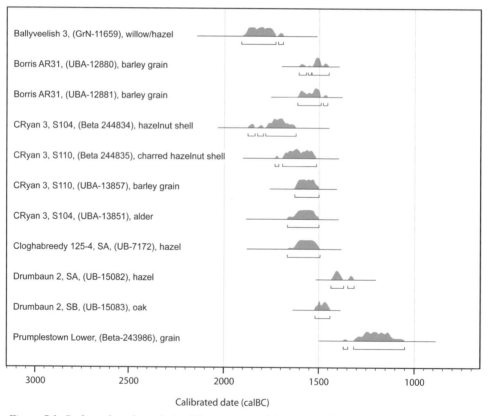

Figure 7.3: Radiocarbon dates derived from structural features on houses with elaborate porches.

(Figure 7.3). A heart-shaped house, Structure A, at Cloghabreedy 125.4 had a significant porch added to it, again 4–5m wide and *c.* 2.5m long (Gowen 2006; Moriarty 2007b) (Figure 7.2). Structure A also had large postholes at the terminals of the slot-trench which suggested that these porches were designed to create a two-phased entrance into the house, with an additional door between the porch and the house proper. A radiocarbon date from the slot-trench indicated that this house firmly dated to the Middle Bronze Age (Figure 7.3).

At Borris and Blackcastle Site AR31 a porch with similar dimensions expanded a house which was originally 6.7m in diameter (Stevens 2010) (Figure 7.2). At this Middle Bronze Age house (Figure 7.3), large postholes were also observed at the terminals of the curvilinear features, reinforcing the creation of the porch as a separate space. The slot-trench which formed the perimeter of the structure appeared not to extend along the western side of the house. Charred cereal grains associated with the house prompted the suggestion that grain had been stored in the structure (Lyons 2010). Two houses from Drumbaun 2 had partial evidence for the same type of porch elaboration (Kiely *et al.* 2011). This was most apparent at Structure B, where one curvilinear feature was discernible, running from the entrance towards the north of the house. Structure A had two surviving lengths of such a curvilinear feature, as well as an apparent threshold, and also a further section of curvilinear ditch which appeared to act as a windbreak. Structure B was earlier in the sequence, and post-dated by Structure A; both were Middle Bronze Age in date (Figure 7.3). The outer concentric postring of Structure A was not apparent along the western side of the structure. An additional example, although slightly smaller, exists nearby, in County Kildare. Re-modifications to a roundhouse at Prumplestown (Clarke and Long 2010) indicate that instead of the curvilinear features forming a porch, they formed two annexes on either side of the entrance; truncation obscured the eastern annex but the western measured approximately 4m by 1.5m (Figure 7.3).

An expression of identity?

The fact that the houses with this particular type of entrance façade are relatively clustered within County Tipperary suggests that this type of elaborate entrance represents a specific trend, restricted in use geographically. That the roundhouses all date to the Middle Bronze Age indicate that the duration of this entrance style did not have considerable longevity. So does the manipulation of entrance features, of which these roundhouses provide such pertinent examples, have anything to do with conscious expressions of identity? Aspects of spatial patterning have been attributed to a close link between the structure and its inhabitants, both on a practical and also a metaphorical level (Brück 2001). As Brück also outlines, there is 'a deep symbolic relationship between a particular settlement and the kin group that inhabits it' (Brück 1999, 153). In this way spatial ordering within structures and settlement can reflect symbolic representations of life and death (Brück 2001; Cleary 2006).

Brück argues that the possibility of anthromorphic symbolism in house architecture may facilitate explanations of structured artefact and ecofact depositions (Brück 1999), as well as understanding settlement patterns and spatial organisation. The entrance is one architectural aspect of the domestic roundhouse which can be more readily manipulated and embellished than other constructional components (see above). Acting as a threshold to the interior, and also the exterior, entrances are important liminal spaces. Structured deposition, when it does occur in Irish Bronze Age houses, often focuses upon such spaces. Burnt bone remains from at least one of the entrance postholes at Ballyveelish 3, and three incomplete, token cremation deposits (species unknown) from the porch entrance at Structure B, Knocksaggart, County Clare (Hanley 2001), as well as large quantities of cereal grains at the entrance postholes of Structure B, Cloghabreedy Site 125.4 (Moriarty 2007b), all demonstrate that the entrances to houses transcended functional necessity, that the symbolic boundary which the entrance represents was subject to highly ordered regulations.

Certainly, it is becoming apparent that the material culture of the Middle and Late Bronze Age which is associated with domestic sites was not as readily used to construct and maintain identity as architecture. Indeed, on-going research by the author is re-affirming that notable artefact deposition occurred away from the domestic sphere, and that hoards and singly deposited artefacts do in fact represent the main-stay of the Irish Bronze Age artefact assemblages. These notable single finds and hoards consist of gold and bronze artefacts, including weapons, personal ornaments, ceremonial items and tools. There is a strong correlation between where they are located in the landscape (bogs, rivers, marshes) and the artefact type (Becker 2006). Artefacts from domestic sites encompass, for the most part, pottery, lithics and occasional moulds for metalworking (although further evidence of metalworking on domestic house sites is generally absent). With an expedient lithic technology (O'Hare 2005) and a ceramic tradition with considerable longevity (especially with the extension of the domestic variety of the cordoned urn from as early as *c*. 1730 through to 1200 BC (Brindley 2007, 328)), it is evident that expressions of identity within the domestic sphere were not primarily conducted through artefacts and artefact deposition. The possible structured deposition of the (?burnt) copper-alloy razor from Carrigatogher (Ryan) Site 3 is the only artefact of particular interest from these sites, with most artefact assemblages formed of only a few pottery sherds and lithic flakes. The lack of regional pottery or lithic variations (contra that in Late Neolithic Orkney where settlement-specific identities were expressed through Grooved Ware assemblages, see Jones 2007, 128–31), and the importance of the highly structured practice of hoarding and ritual deposition of single artefacts at a remove from domestic settlement sites, implies instead that the manipulation of architecture may have been more important. It is therefore highly likely that entrances, the experience of crossing the threshold (either into or out of the roundhouse), and the use of this space, formed a component of identity construction and or maintenance.

Further differential evidence

It was stated above that, with the exception of the copper-alloy razor, no significant artefacts were recovered from these sites. However, there is another facet of the archaeological record that indicates that these roundhouses may have been different. In addition to the deposited large quantities of cereal grains in the two entrance postholes of Structure B, Cloghabreedy Site 125.4, barley, wheat and emmer wheat grains were recovered in significant concentrations (without any chaff or weeds) from the slot-trench of the roundhouse at Borris and Blackcastle Site AR31 (Lyons 2010; Stevens 2010). In her analysis of the cereal assemblage from Borris and Blackcastle Site AR31, Lyons notes that the structure was not cleaned out, but left abandoned with the charred grain deposits (Lyons 2010). It is equally plausible that the remains represent a closing deposit, left as part of an abandonment ritual.

At Corrstown significant grain deposits were recovered from several structures across the site and the most notable of these included 450 grains from an internal small posthole of Structure 25, 450 grains from the outer ditch and 300 cereal grains from the entrance pathway of Structure 69A further three deposits of grain were associated with Structure 58: a cache of 80 grains in a posthole, 100 grains from an outer ditch fill, and 150 from an internal small posthole/stakehole (Ginn and Rathbone 2012). It is clear that the occurrence of cereal remains in these quantities and in these structural contexts are not merely the results of post-depositional processes.

So who lived in a roundhouse like this?

Having argued that manipulation of architecture was used during the Bronze Age in order to express identity, what can the nature of entrance elaboration convey about the identity of the inhabitants? With regards to the reproduction of community identity, Downes and Richards (2005, 126) suggest that the 'inhabitants may have needed to express continuity in increasingly visible and public actions'. The Tipperary porches are of monumental proportions, increasing the usable floor space by approximately 6m^2 and would have represented a strikingly visible addition to the roundhouse: there is an aggrandisement of the domestic roundhouse which can only be described as dramatic. The large postholes at the terminals of the porch curvilinear features indicate that substantial posts would have further enhanced the porch appearance. These changes altered the public aspect of the houses; they are very much designed to be visible to neighbours and strangers.

The addition of these porches, which may have happened after construction but during occupation of the roundhouse, could mean one of several things. The occupants may be displaying improved or new-found wealth, reaffirming ownership of their settlement site, or demonstrating an increased family/kin-group demographic. The inhabitants may have acquired more animals, and stalled these in their porches which acted as byres; there was certainly sufficient space. Additionally, that this type of elaborate porch has only been identified in one particular area, and the elongated entrances at Corrstown are known only to that village, suggests that domestic architecture was used to reinforce communities, signifying who belonged, and who did not belong, to a particular identity. Architecturally, these exaggerated porches serve as a physically imposing boundary and facilitate an actual bodily transition of the enclosed space. Even if these spaces were occasionally employed for domestic storage, they still formed an additional space which must be negotiated in order to enter the roundhouse proper.

The combination of the significant grain surpluses and the elaboration of the porches suggest that these particular roundhouses may have been associated with inhabitants of a certain social status. This was suggested by Cotter (2006) for Structure D at Ballybrowney who thought that this house could have had a higher status than the other contemporary houses on site due to its architectural sophistication indicated by the presence of its porch.

The framework of settlement hierarchies is not fully understood in Bronze Age Ireland. Until the recent rise of development-led archaeological excavation it was considered that enclosed settlement sites reflected a social ordering (*e.g.* Grogan 2005a; 2005b; Grogan *et al.* 1996); the relationship between enclosed sites and status and prestige was also explored for Bronze Age Britain (Hingley 1990; 1984). The rich artefact assemblages and metalworking evidence from archetypal sites such as Lough Gur, County Limerick (Ó Ríordáin 1954; Ó Ríordáin and MacDermott 1949), and the enclosed lakeside sites (*e.g.* Moynagh Lough, County Meath (Bradley 1997), and Cullyhanna, County Armagh (Hillam 1976; Hodges 1958)) facilitated the interpretation of enclosed sites as being the homes of the relatively wealthy (Cullyhanna was originally interpreted as a seasonal hunting lodge but in light of subsequent excavations this can be re-addressed). In Grogan's model based on the Mooghaun evidence, he suggested that enclosed sites, which would be less numerous than their unenclosed counterparts, were occupied by farmers of a relative status (Grogan 2005a, 92). Certainly, the numbers of enclosed sites are significantly smaller than settlements without enclosures; however, the associated artefact assemblages from the more recently excavated enclosed sites send an ambiguous message about the social status of their inhabitants. Many of the sites have little in their assemblages to differentiate them from unenclosed sites, for example at Dunbell Big 2 the artefacts consisted solely of 21 sherds of Middle Bronze Age pottery (Whitty 2009). At Ballybrowney, which had enclosed and unenclosed houses, the assemblage was only slightly more noteworthy, containing prehistoric pottery sherds, saddle querns, hammerstones, and a possible sandstone anvil (Cotter 2006). Certainly, the evidence from Chancellorsland Site 1A, with its pottery sherds, worked jasper, chert, and amber beads suggests that it was occupied by relatively wealthy residents (Doody 2008; 1999). The excavation of the undated but enclosed site of Carrigillihy, County Cork, revealed a socketed bronze axe (from the topsoil), a D-shaped lignite fragment, a bronze awl and a stone disc, alongside a broken hone stone and several coarseware sherds, again suggested prosperous inhabitants (O'Kelly 1951).

The unenclosed domestic settlement sites of this period generally have a limited range of associated artefacts and these are predominantly confined to pottery sherds, whetstone and quern stone fragments, worked flint and chert (*e.g.* at Ballyvergan West, County Cork (O'Hara and Kehoe 2002), Killoran 8, County Tipperary (Ó Néill 2005), and Marshes Upper 9, County Louth (O'Hara 2002)). A restricted number of sites have other artefacts, as at Carn More 1, County Louth, where a polished stone adze head and a fragment from a circular lignite hoop were excavated (Delaney 2009) and at Ballydrehid, County Tipperary, where a possible gaming piece and a copper-alloy tube were recovered along with pottery sherds, lithic tools, a spindle whorl (found in association with probably domestic cordoned urn sherds and is therefore unlikely to be later than 1300 BC) and quern fragments (McQuade 2007). It could therefore be tentatively concluded that enclosed sites were, for the most part, artefactually rich, at least in comparison to their unenclosed counterparts and for the period pre-1500 BC. Yet the presence of artefact rich unenclosed settlements indicates that the association between enclosure and wealth is not clear cut.

There is a recognised anthropological link between settlement enclosure and agricultural intensification which leads to land becoming more valued as a form of property (Thomas 1997). The focus on the possible origins of enclosure through changes in land ownership highlights the importance of divisions between insiders and outsiders. Structured deposition in boundary areas, such as entrances and enclosure ditches, therefore becomes important as a way of reinforcing such divisions. Structured deposits of grain, like those identified at Cloghabreedy 125.4 and Borris and Blackcastle Site AR31, have an increased significance if social wealth and prestige is based upon farming. A normal surplus of the domestic economy, in terms of cereals or animals, could easily transform into a bankable commodity;

appropriation and control of this commodity could facilitate or further the emergence of elites. It is therefore certainly plausible that the sites which have surplus grains that went beyond the needs of domestic subsistence were the homesteads of an economically and therefore socially elevated group. It is subsequently apparent that the strongest vehicle for the emergence of the architectural change that enclosure represents must have been agricultural intensification which brought about an altered, stronger sense of property rights, of owning the land. In this way the enclosure does not need to be physically impressive or substantial to function as a social mechanism which defined, re-enforced and re-affirmed rights to land. Such rights do not even have to be conceptualised through enclosures. Rather, the aggrandisement and elaboration of porches discussed in this chapter may in fact represent the physical remains of this conceptualisation.

Conclusions

The house is a 'material manifestation of people's identity' (Downes and Richards 2005, 125) and it is therefore apparent that the manipulation of the very access to the house that establishes a new spatial order is of potentially great significance. The dramatic aggrandisement of the domestic residence which the monumental Tipperary porches create happens within the public arena. It is very much a conscious expression of a new self. Whether that new self represents wealth or status is unclear. Ginn (2013; 2012) has also addressed the lack of understanding about the framework of domestic settlement hierarchies. It is now understood that enclosure is not necessarily associated with status; however, in the Middle Bronze Age especially the combination of agricultural surplus, a preoccupation with land divisions (including enclosure), and occasional conspicuous consumption that the elaboration of these entrances suggests, some form of identity is being expressed through the domestic architecture. Identity expression that occurs through material culture happens at a remove from the domestic settlement (excluding here the structured deposition of particular artefacts) and therefore the manipulation of space and place is all the more significant. Whether or not the inhabitants of these houses were part of an elite population is unknown but it *is* apparent that they were concerned with appearances and desired to differentiate themselves from their neighbours, to show outwardly their identity.

Acknowledgements

Many thanks go to Dr Gill Plunkett, Rebecca Enlander, and Rebecca Crozier for reading and commenting on earlier drafts of this chapter. Thanks also extend to the archaeological companies who willingly shared their data with me: notably, Archaeological Consultancy Services Ltd, Archaeological Development Services Ltd, Margaret Gowen and Co., Headland Archaeology Ltd, and Irish Archaeological Consultancy Ltd. Libby Mulqueeny, Queen's University Belfast, kindly tidied up Figures 7.2 and 7.3. This research forms part of a PhD, funded by the DEL.

References

Ballin Smith, B. (2003) The excavation of two Bronze Age roundhouses at Townparks, County Antrim. *Ulster Journal of Archaeology* 62, 16–44.

Bourdieu, P. (1972) *Esquisse d'une théorie de la pratique*. Paris, PUF.

Bradley, J. (1997) Archaeological excavations at Moynagh Lough, County Meath, 1995–1996. *Riocht na Midhe* 9(3), 50–61.

Becker, K. (2006) *Hoards and deposition in Bronze Age Ireland*. Unpublished PhD thesis. Dublin, University College Dublin.

Brindley, A. (2007) *The dating of food vessels and urns in Ireland*. Galway, Galway University Press.

Brück J. (1999) Houses, lifestyles and deposition on Middle Bronze Age settlements in southern England. *Proceedings of the Prehistoric Society* 65, 145–66.

Brück J. (2001) Body metaphors and technologies in the English Middle and Late Bronze Age. In J. Brück (ed.) *Bronze Age landscapes, tradition and transformation,* 149–60. Oxford, Oxbow.

Buttimer, A. (1980) Home, reach, and the sense of place. In A. Buttimer and D. Seamon (eds) *The human experience of space and place*. London, Croom Helm Ltd.

Carlin, N. (2006) *Bronze Age houses*. Unpublished research report prepared for Archaeological Consultancy Services Ltd.

Clarke, L. and Long, P. (2010) *Final report on archaeological investigations at Site E2967, in the townland of Prumplestown Lower, County Kildare*. Unpublished report prepared by Headland Archaeology Ltd.

Cleary, K. (2006) Irish Bronze Age settlements: more than meets the eye? *Archaeology Ireland* 20 (2), 18–21.

Cleary, K. (2007) *Irish Bronze Age settlements: spatial organisation and the deposition of material culture*. Unpublished PhD thesis for University College Cork.

Cotter, E. (2006) *Final report on Ballybrowney Lower 1*. Unpublished report prepared by Archaeological Consultancy Services Ltd.

Delaney, S. (2009) *Carn More 1, draft final excavation report*. Unpublished report prepared by Irish Archaeological Consultancy Ltd.

Doody, M. G. (1987a) Late Bronze Age huts at Curraghatoor, County Tipperary. In R. M. Cleary, M. F. Hurley, E. A. and Shee Twohig (eds) *Archaeological excavations on the Cork–Dublin Gas Pipeline (1981–32),* 22–35. Cork, Cork Archaeological Studies No. 1.

Doody, M. G. (1987b) Early Bronze Age burials, Ballyveelish 3, County Tipperary. In R. M. Cleary, M. F. Hurley, E. A. and Shee Twohig (eds) *Archaeological excavations on the Cork–Dublin Gas Pipeline (1981–32),* 9–21. Cork, Cork Archaeological Studies No. 1.

Doody, M. G. (2007) *Excavations at Curraghatoor, County Tipperary*. Edited by R. M. Cleary. University College Cork, UCC Department of Archaeology, Archaeological Monograph.

Doody, M. G. (1999) *The Ballyhoura Hills Project. Discovery Programme Reports 5,* 97–110.

Doody, M. G. (2000) Bronze Age houses in Ireland. In A. Desmond, G. Johnson, M. McCarthy, J. Sheehan, and E. Shee Twohig (eds) *New agendas in Irish prehistory*, 135–60. Bray, Wordwell.

Doody, M. G. (2008) *The Ballyhoura Hills Project*. Discovery Programme Monograph No. 7. Bray, Wordwell.

Downes, J. and Richards, C. (2005) Spatial organisation of houses. In C. Richards (ed.) *Dwelling among the monuments: the Neolithic village of Barnhouse, Maeshowe passage grave and surrounding monuments at Stenness, Orkney, 57–127. Cambridge, Cambridge University Press.*

Ginn, V. (2013) Power to the people: re-interpreting Bronze Age society. *Emania* 21, 47–58.

Ginn, V. (2012) *Settlement structure in Middle–Late Bronze Age Ireland*. Unpublished PhD thesis. Belfast, Queen's University Belfast.

Ginn, V. and Rathbone, S. (eds) (2012) *Corrstown: a coastal community. Excavations of a Bronze Age Village in Northern Ireland*. Oxford, Oxbow.

Gowen, M. (2006) Prehistoric settlement on the M8. *Seanda* 1, 54–57.

Grogan, E. (2005a) *The North Munster Project Vol. 1: the later prehistoric landscape of southeast Clare*. Discovery Programme Monograph 6. Dublin, Wordwell.

Grogan, E. (2005b) *The North Munster Project Vol. 2: the prehistoric landscape of north Munster*. Discovery Programme Monograph 6. Dublin, Wordwell.

Grogan, E., Condit, T., O'Carroll, F., O'Sullivan, A. and Daly, A. (1996) *Tracing the later prehistoric landscape in north Munster*. Discovery Programme Reports 4, 26–46. Dublin, Wordwell.

Hanley, K. (2001) *Excavation Report on Knocksaggart, 00E0416*. Unpublished report prepared by Valerie J. Keeley Ltd.

Hillam, J. (1976) The dating of Cullyhanna hunting lodge. *Irish Archaeology Resource Forum* 3(1), 17–20.

Hingley, R. (1984) Towards social analysis in archaeology: Celtic society in the Iron Age of the Upper Thames Valley. In B. Cunliffe and D. Miles (eds) *Aspects of the Iron Age in central southern Britain*, 72–88. Oxford, Oxford University Committee for Archaeology Monograph No. 2.

Hingley, R. (1990) Boundaries surrounding Iron Age and Romano-British settlements. *Scottish Archaeological Review* 7, 96–103.

Hodges, H. W. M. (1958) A hunting camp at Cullyhanna Lough, near Newtown Hamilton, County Armagh. *Ulster Journal of Archaeology* 21, 7–13.

Jones, A. (2007) *Memory and material culture*. Cambridge, Cambridge University Press.

Kiely, J., Tierney, J. and Chrobak, E. (2011) Archaeological excavation report, Drumbaun, County Tipperary, Bronze Age houses and medieval iron-working site. *Eachtra Journal*, Issue 11. http://www.slideshare.net/eachtra/archaeological-report-moatquarter-co-tipperary-ireland [Accessed July 2012].

Lyons, S. (2010) Appendix 9.2: Plant remains. In P. Stevens *M8/N8 Cullahill to Cashel Road Improvement Scheme: archaeological resolution. Final report, Ministerial Direction: A027/000, Registration No. E2374, Site AR31, Borris and Blackcastle townlands, County Tipperary*. Unpublished report prepared by Valerie J. Keeley Ltd.

McQuade, M. (2007) *Final report at Ballydrehid, County Tipperary, N8 Cashel to Mitchelstown Road Improvement Scheme*. Unpublished report prepared by Margaret Gowen & Co. Ltd.

Moriarty, C. (2007a) *Final report, Knockgaffron, County Tipperary, N8 Cashel to Mitchelstown Road Improvement Scheme*. Unpublished report prepared by Margaret Gowen & Co. Ltd.

Moriarty, C. (2007b) *Final report for Cloghabreedy, County Tipperary, N8 Cashel to Mitchelstown Road Improvement Scheme*. Unpublished report prepared by Margaret Gowen & Co. Ltd.

Mulcahy, A. and Taylor, K. (2009) *N7 Nenagh to Limerick High Quality Dual Carriageway Archaeological Resolution Project, E2285, Carrigatogher (Ryan) Site 3, County Tipperary*. Unpublished report prepared by TVAS Ireland Ltd.

Murphy, D. (2009) *Cuffsborough 4, final excavation report*. Unpublished report prepared for Archaeological Consultancy Services Ltd.

Ó Néill, J. (2009) *Inventory of Bronze Age structures*. Unpublished report prepared for the Heritage Council.

Ó Néill, J. (2005) Killoran 8. In M. Gowen, J. Ó Néill and M. Phillips (eds) *The Lisheen Mine Archaeological Project 1996–8*, 288–90. Dublin, Wordwell.

Ó Ríordáin, S. P. and MacDermott, M. (1949) Lough Gur excavations. *The Journal of the Royal Society of Antiquaries of Ireland*, 79, No.1/2, 126–45.

Ó Ríordáin, S. P. (1954) Lough Gur excavations: Neolithic and Bronze Age houses on Knockadoon. *Proceedings of the Royal Irish Academy* 56C, 297–459.

O'Connell, T. J. (2009) *N9/N10 Kilcullen to Waterford Scheme: Kilcullen to Powerstown. Archaeological Services Contract No. 4: Resolution, Prumplestown to Powerstown. Final report on Archaeological Investigations at Site E2589, in the townland of Tinryland, County Carlow*. Unpublished report prepared by Headland Archaeology Ltd.

O'Hare, M. (2005) *The Bronze Age lithics of Ireland*. Unpublished PhD thesis for Queen's University Belfast.

O'Hara, R. (2002) *Marshes Upper Site 9, final excavation report*. Unpublished report prepared by Archaeological Consultancy Services Ltd.

O'Hara, R. and Kehoe, H. (2002) *Ballyvergan West, final report*. Unpublished report prepared by Archaeological Consultancy Services Ltd.

O'Kelly, M. (1951) An Early Bronze Age ringfort at Carrigillihy, County Cork. *Journal of the Cork Historical and Archaeological Society* 56, 69–86.

Ó Néill, T. (2008) *Clonadacasey 2, final excavation report*. Unpublished report prepared by Archaeological Consultancy Services Ltd.

Opie, H. (1995) *Kildorragh, 1994:149, County Leitrim*. www.excavations.ie

Oswald, A. (1997) A doorway on the past: practical and mystic concerns in the orientation of roundhouse doorways. In A. Gwilt and C. Haselgrove (eds) *Reconstructing Iron Age societies*, 87–95. Oxford, Oxbow.

Parker Pearson, M. (1999) Food, sex and death: cosmologies in the British Iron Age with particular reference to east Yorkshire. *Cambridge Archaeological Journal* 9(1), 43–69.

Roberts, B. K. (1996) *Landscapes of settlement: prehistory to the present.* London, Routledge.

St John Wilson, C. (1992) *Architectural reflections.* Oxford, Butterworth.

Stevens, P. (2010) *M8/N8 Cullahill to Cashel Road Improvement Scheme: Archaeological Resolution. Final report, Ministerial Direction: A027/000, Registration No.: E2374, Site AR31, Borris and Blackcastle Townlands, County Tipperary.* Unpublished report prepared by Valerie J. Keeley.

Thomas, R. (1997) Land, kinship relations and the rise of enclosed settlement in first millennium BC Britain. *Oxford Journal of Archaeology* 16(2), 211–18.

Whitty, Y. (2009) *Dunbell Big 2, interim excavation report.* Unpublished report prepared by Irish Archaeological Consultancy Ltd.

Wiggins, K. (2008) *Lismore 2, Final Excavation Report.* Unpublished report prepared by Archaeological Consultancy Services Ltd.

8

POTTY ABOUT POTS: EXPLORING IDENTITY THROUGH THE PREHISTORIC POTTERY ASSEMBLAGE OF PREHISTORIC MALTA

Sara Boyle

Introduction

Since Palaeolithic times, humans have used material objects as physical manifestations of their beliefs and ideologies, giving such objects meaning beyond their corporeal form. What do these objects say about the people behind their creation and use? The communicative role of material culture in the expression of identities has, in recent times, been given prominence in the archaeological arena and is a subject that has been enthusiastically discussed by a variety of scholars (*e.g.* Blake 1999; Casella and Fowler 2005; Conkey and Hastorf 1990; Hegmon 1992; Hodos 2010; Lucy 2005; Sackett 1977).While these discussions have highlighted the inherent difficulties of inferring identity from material culture, there is still much to be gained from such considerations, provided that they are placed within the wider context of cultural developments. These notions can be carefully applied to the study of pottery, and in particular, the consideration of pottery style, in the investigation of cultural identities. There have been few studies which have moved beyond the traditional typological and chronological approaches to pottery analysis (an exception is Fletcher 2004). Yet, a consideration of the stylistic variations of pottery, and particularly, the decorative features, has the potential to offer great insight into the social aspects of past societies.

The Maltese Islands are home to one of the finest prehistoric pottery assemblages found within the central Mediterranean region today. Yet, the major pottery studies have remained within a traditional framework that is very much concerned with typological and chronological classification (Evans 1971; 1959; 1953; Trump 2008; 1966; 1961a). While these studies were revolutionary at the time, there is a growing awareness that the prehistoric pottery sequence on Malta requires further refinement. Such classification should, for example, differentiate more clearly between the ritual and domestic aspects of pottery within the phases of Maltese prehistory. There is a need for archaeologists to move away from the constraints of antiquated approaches in order to gain further insight into the social dialogues of the past. This revolution in archaeological thought has begun to be addressed on the Maltese Islands with the publication of a number of key studies which attempt to explore the cultural constructions of difference and the changing identities of the islands' prehistoric inhabitants (Malone *et al.* 2009; Rainbird 2007; Robb 2001; Skeates 2010; Tilley 2004). The majority of these studies have tended to focus upon the dominant megalithic monuments of Temple Period Malta (3600–2400 BC) and have unintentionally relegated less obvious aspects of the material record. The time is now ripe to address the subtleties of the material record through the exploration of cultural identities. With this in mind, the aim of this chapter is to explore the identities of prehistoric Malta's inhabitants through a contextual analysis of the changing styles of their prehistoric pottery sequence. Stylistic, and, in particular, decorative features of Malta's prehistoric pottery assemblage will be discussed, although other key features have been summarised in Table 8.1. Within this approach, it is necessary to provide an overview of the prehistoric period on the islands in order to provide a context for the interpretation of the changing styles of prehistoric pottery, and thus, to explore the changing identities of the Maltese Islands' prehistoric inhabitants.

Malta, pots and potters

The Maltese Islands are a group of small, low-lying islands located in the central Mediterranean some 96km south of Sicily and 290km north of Libya (Figure 8.1). Consisting of three inhabited isles, Malta, Gozo and Comino, they are among the most remote islands of the Mediterranean and this isolation, alongside their relatively small size and arid nature, has influenced both the physical and cultural development of the archipelago over the millennia. Throughout history, the Maltese Islands have an arena within which identities have been forged, forgotten, contested and reinvented and their bounded, relatively isolated and insular nature makes them an ideal setting to explore identity (see Table 8.2 for general themes).

The Neolithic (*c.* 5000–4100 BC): remembering

The archaeological context
The Maltese Islands were first colonised in the Għar Dalam phase (*c.* 5000–4300 BC) by a group of agriculturalists from Sicily, and limited evidence suggests that these early settlers exploited natural caves and established open villages in strategic locations (*e.g.* Skorba on Malta and Taċ-Ċawla on Gozo). An abundance of imported raw materials, such as red ochre and obsidian (which do not occur naturally on the islands), from an extensive geographic region implies that contacts across the Sicily–Malta channel were maintained during this time (Bonanno 1990; Pace 2004; Trump 2010, 2008). The following Grey Skorba (*c.* 4500–4400 BC) and Red Skorba (*c.* 4400–4100 BC) phases provide a much clearer picture of Neolithic life due to the important excavation of Skorba on Malta (Trump 1966) which uncovered the remains of a Neolithic village underlying a later megalithic temple. It is not known how the Neolithic inhabitants disposed of their dead, although whispers of ritual activity begin to emerge in the Red Skorba phase as evidenced by the discovery of a 'shrine' within the Neolithic village at Skorba (*ibid.*). This suggests that distinct spaces were set aside for ritual purposes and it was this distinction between the sacred and the secular that was to flourish during the Temple Period (Bonanno 1990; Pace 2004; Stoddart 1999).

Table 8.1: Principal features of Malta's prehistoric pottery assemblage (after Evans 1971, 1953; Malone et al. 2009; Trump 1966).

PHASE	FABRIC	SURFACE	DECORATION		PRINCIPAL SHAPES
			Technique	Motifs	
Ghar Dalam	Grey to Black	Grey or Black, Unslipped, Highly polished	Repeat impressions, Incision, Finger-tip pinching	C-motifs and dots, Close-set hatching, Haphazard lines	Globular jars, Small deep bowls, Open dishes, Pedestal vases, Heavy ovoid jars
Grey Skorba	Dark Grey	Variable Grey, Unslipped, Highly polished	Usually no decoration, Occasionally plastic cordons	No decoration, Occasionally wavy lines, Zoomorphic figures (rare)	Open tronco-conic bowls, Deep S-shaped bowls, Simple ovoid jars with thick rims
Red Skorba	Dark Grey	Bright Red, Slipped, Highly polished	Incision before firing	C-motifs (Ss, loops, crescents, simple spirals), V-motifs, 'Ear of Corn'	Carinated bowls, Inverted pedestal bowls, Ladles, Globular jars
Żebbuġ	Brownish-Black	Brownish-Black, May be slipped and polished	Grooved incision, White inlay, Occasionally painted	Standing arcs, Chevrons, Fringed lines, Incised triangles, Cross-hatching, 'Stick-men'	Jars with bell-shaped neck, Deep tronco-conic bowls, Single-handled cups, Hole-mouth jars, Domed lids
Mġarr	Dark Grey to Black	Dark Grey or Black, Unslipped, Highly polished	Broader-grooved incision, White inlay, Occasionally painted	Scratch-nicked rims, Fringes of diagonal lines, Curvilinear ribbon patterns, Ladders	Thickened-lip jars, Cylindrical platters or lids, Squat neckless jars, Bag-shaped bowls, Cups
Ġgantija	Dark Grey to Black, Brown	Brown, Very highly polished	Scratched after firing, Red ochre encrusted	Converging curves, Curvilinear 'comet' motifs with terminal 'cherry', Cross-hatching, 'Chequerboard' motifs	Shouldered cups and bowls, 'Hanging vases', Carinated hole-mouth bowls, Flanged globular bowls, Circular covers
Tarxien	Black	Grey or Black, Very highly polished	Scratched after firing, Red ochre encrusted, Plastic, Cut-out, Rustication, Studded	Volutes, Lattices, Interlocking arcs, True spirals, Vertical striations, Applied scales, Human, animal and plant imagery	Carinated bowls (sometimes on hollow pedestal), Hole-mouth 'Saflieni' bowls, 'Amphorae', Tripartite bowls, Covers
Saflieni-style	Black	Variable, Very highly polished	Scratched after firing, Red ochre encrusted	Straight or curving diagonals, Fringed lines, Fleck-filled areas between curves, Rectangular chequers	Deep open or splayed bowls, Splayed flat-bottomed dishes, Hole-mouth 'Saflieni' bowls, Carinated bowls
Tarxien Cemetery	Black	Yellow to Brown, Thick-slipped	Deep incision, Impressions, Rarely applied cordons	Bands of parallel lines in horizontal and zigzag forms, Hatched triangles, Chequers,	'Helmet' vases, Askos, Siamese-twin bowls and jars, Multiple spouts, 'Thermi' bowls
Borġ in-Nadur	Orange-Buff with Black core	Bright Red, Slipped	Cut-out, White inlay, Deep incision, Applied pellets, Painted	Multiple zigzags between dash-filled bands, Hatched triangles, Inverted chevrons, Pellets	Chalices, High-footed 'lamps', Large storage jars, Oblong basins, S-profile bowls
Bahrija	Dark Grey to Black	Black, Red, Slipped, Polished	Cut-out and Painted	Dovetails, Spiral meanders, Excised triangles, Zigzags, Geometric motifs	Inverted-lip bowls, Angular bowls, Trilychnis lamps, Globular jugs, Strainer-spouted vessels

Sara Boyle

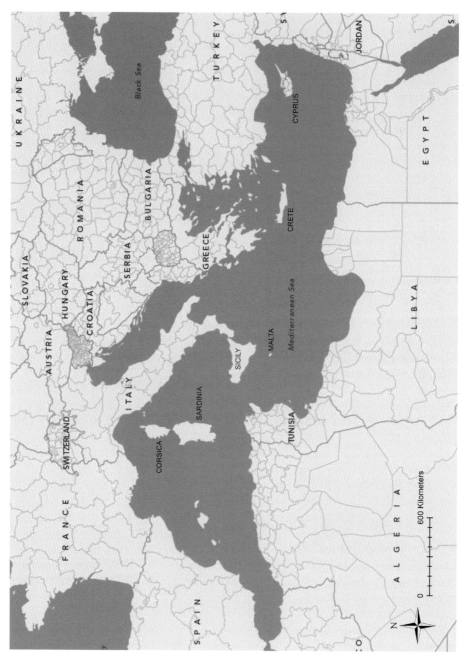

Figure 8.1: Map of the Mediterranean region.

Table 8.2: Themes of identity during Maltese prehistory.

CULTURE NAME	APPROX. DATE	IDENTITY THEME
Neolithic		
Għar Dalam	5000–4300 BC	
Grey Skorba	4500–4400 BC	Remembering
Red Skorba	4400–4100 BC	
Early Temple Period		
Żebbuġ	4100–3700 BC	
Mġarr	3800–3600 BC	Forgetting and Reinventing
Full Temple Period		
Ġgantija	3600–3100 BC	
Tarxien (and Saflieni)	3100–2400 BC	Elaborating
Bronze Age		
Tarxien Cemetery	2000–1500 BC	
Borġ in-Nadur	1500–700 BC	Redefining and Assimilating
Baħrija	900–700 BC	

The pottery styles

Pottery of the Għar Dalam phase is a member of the Impressed ware family, widely distributed throughout the central and western Mediterranean region. Decoration on Għar Dalam pottery is fairly common, although simple impressions, such as C-shaped impressions, dots and scalloped edging, were a secondary element. More common was line decoration which was often grooved and comprised bands of close-set hatching, broader diagonally hatched or cross-hatched bands, chevrons, and cross-hatched triangles. Such decorative techniques are paralleled with the Sicilian Stentinello wares, although some very characteristic Stentinello-type decoration is completely absent from the Maltese assemblage. This includes the use of rocker decoration, true cardinal impressions and lozenge stamps (Evans 1971; Leighton 1999; Trump 1966).

The Grey Skorba and Red Skorba phases were not known until Trump's excavations at Skorba (1966). Up until such revelations, a small number of distinguishable sherds were incorrectly assigned as imports of Diana ware from the Sicily–Lipari region (Evans 1953, 47). It is thanks to the excavations at Skorba that these are now considered to be an indigenous development on the islands, although very much influenced by the wider Diana style and technology (Malone 2008). Decoration on Grey Skorba ware is extremely rare, and its absence is considered to be one of the main characteristics of the phase, since decoration occurs liberally in all other phases of Maltese prehistory (Evans 1971). There is close continuity between the Grey Skorba and the Red Skorba ware, although two major changes are evident. Firstly, as the name implies, Red Skorba fabric is covered with a red slip, and secondly, there is a considerable increase in decoration, which includes incised C-motifs, variously combined into crescents, S-shapes and loops, and V-motifs similarly employed. While influence from the contemporary red slip of Diana ware is highly probable, Trump (2008, 48) postulates that the Red Skorba slip is simply a superficial addition to a fundamentally local ware; it is considered that Red Skorba evolved directly out of Grey Skorba (Evans 1971; Trump 1966).

It may be suggested that during the Neolithic period the islanders were remembering their ancestral roots and expressing an identity that was linked to their origins. This sense of remembrance can be seen in the decorative similarities that are evident between the pottery of the Għar Dalam phase and the Stentinello culture of Sicily and that of the Red Skorba phase and the contemporary Diana culture of Sicily and Italy. However, at the same time, the islanders were also beginning to forge their own identity as evidenced by the selective use of decorative elements from the Stentinello ware in the Għar Dalam phase, and the development of a fundamentally local ware in the following Skorba phases. During the Neolithic, as they became more established on their island home, the islanders' identity was transformed from one which was reminiscent of their Sicilian origins to one which reflected their cohesiveness and solidarity as they looked towards the future.

The Early Temple Period (*c.* 4100–3600 BC): forgetting and reinventing

The archaeological context

Divergence of the Maltese Islands' inhabitants from their Mediterranean neighbours first becomes clear in the Żebbuġ phase (4100–3700 BC). During this time the islanders begin to carry out collective formal burial in artificial rock-cut tombs 'ahead of patterns in Sicily and peninsular Italy [which] suggest a precocious social and political process in Malta' (Stoddart 1999, 139). The Żebbuġ rock-cut tombs were used for repeated collective burial as a means of asserting the past and actively maintaining kinship ties. The deceased were often buried with votive offerings, such as highly decorated pottery vessels and imported materials, which may have related to their social status in life. The Żebbuġ phase represents the first clear separation of the domestic and ritual spheres of activity, an action which would climax with the construction of the megalithic monuments of the Full Temple Period. The following phase, Mġarr (3800–3600 BC), is a short transitional one, during which time the first ritual lobed structures were constructed which would later develop into temples (Bonanno 1990; Malone *et al.* 2009, 1995; Pace 2004; Stoddart 1999; Trump 2010).

The pottery styles

The prehistoric pottery repertoire of the Maltese Islands reaches its peak in development during the Temple Period. There is a clear line of development in the typology of the Żebbuġ, Mġarr, Ġgantija, Tarxien, and Saflieni-style wares in terms of fabric, form and decorative styles. Yet, from this point a number of new characteristics appear, especially in the decoration, that have neither been seen before, nor can be traced to influences from overseas. Trump (2008, 217) explains such changes as 'deliberate innovation by the pot-makers and, even more remarkably, a willingness by society to accept that innovation'. This makes the study of this period all the more intriguing.

The pottery of the Żebbuġ phase contrasts strongly with that found before it which led both Trump (1966) and Evans (1971) to consider that it derives from a very different and foreign tradition. More recent investigations at the Brochtorff Circle on Gozo have allowed a distinction to be made between pottery used for funerary and domestic purposes and uncovered what may be 'a late 'devolved' Żebbuġ style' (Malone *et al.* 2009, 221). Decoration consists of grooved incision before firing, with motifs casually drawn and patterns correspondingly irregular, displaying partly rectilinear and partly curvilinear styles. Incised triangles are common. Such design is broadly similar to the San Cono–Piano Notaro ware of Early Copper Age Sicily. Of particular note are a number of sherds decorated with schematised human figures with triangular heads and 'stick-man' bodies. Such decorative features, alongside the extensive use of rock-cut tombs during this time, may be indicative of the importance of the individual as part of the broader collective. It may be suggested that during the Żebbuġ phase individual identity was expressed and enhanced through a broader collective identity. It is likely that there were multiple identities based upon the strength and solidarity of kin groups who actively competed with one another. By this time, the islanders seem to have forgotten their link to their ancestral homeland with the forging of a unique cultural identity expressed through the individuality of the material remains (Evans 1971, 1953; Trump 1966).

During the following Mġarr phase, decoration again consists of incision before firing, although it becomes much broader and more assured. The incised triangles of Żebbuġ ware are replaced by delicate fringes of lightly scratched lines which held a white paste inlay. This was sometimes covered in an additional red ochre wash that anticipates the exclusive use of red ochre during the following Ġgantija phase. Decoration commonly comprises curvilinear patterns and there are the first hints of the 'comet' pattern which became characteristic of the following phase. The comparatively little pottery of Mġarr-type recovered from the islands, along with the lack of distinct remains, suggests that Mġarr was a short transitional phase with little to indicate that close contacts were maintained between the islanders and their neighbours. As Evans notes, 'With the Mġarr phase the culture of the Maltese Temple Period develops an even more distinctly insular personality, a process which was to go even further later' (1971, 215). The same can be said for Malta's island identity.

The Full Temple Period (*c.* 3600–2400 BC): elaborating

The archaeological context
It is during the Ġgantija phase (3600–3100 BC) that the earliest datable temples were constructed in a unique, architecturally complex and sophisticated style, the monumentality of which would have symbolic meaning across the landscape for millennia. From this time the islands enter a period of prolonged stylistic phases which suggest a strong element of stability. They also experience a cycle of cultural and possibly physical isolation from the wider Mediterranean, although the extent of this isolation has recently been contested (*e.g.* Rainbird 2007; Robb 2001; Skeates 2010). The Tarxien and Saflieni phases (3100–2400 BC) mark the apogee of the Temple civilisation when the islands become highly structured into distinct zones of the temples, funerary hypogea and domestic sites. This may have driven intra-community rivalry, although the coherent use of common architectural forms and portable objects may be a reflection of solidarity and cooperation. The collective focus of the community is provided by the burial hypogea where the deceased were incorporated in repetitive multi-stage rituals that accentuated the apparent unity of the islands' communities in death. By the end of the Temple Period the architecture of the temples becomes more complex and access may have been restricted to a ritual elite. Such changes, alongside the possibility of environmental degradation, may have contributed to the demise of the Temple Culture at *c.* 2400 BC when all traces of this complex society disappear (Malone *et al.* 1999; Pace 2004; Stoddart 1999; Trump 2010).

The pottery styles

The Ġgantija phase is the point at which the inhabitants of the Maltese Islands really begin to surpass their neighbours in terms of style and technical expertise. The pottery of this and the following Tarxien phase is 'the most insular and shows the least sign of outside influence of them all' (Evans 1959, 67) and fabric and form clearly derive from the pottery of preceding phases. A new decorative technique, of lightly scratching the pattern onto the surface after firing, is associated with Ġgantija pottery and continues throughout the Temple Period. The scratched lines were intended to hold blocks of red ochre paste which comprised the actual visible pattern. All decoration was executed in 'sweeping scratched curves with both assurance and exuberance' (Trump 2008, 223) and falls into two broad stylistic groups: free-field curvilinear 'comet' motifs, sometimes ending with a terminal circle or 'cherry'; and rectilinear 'chequerboard' motifs. Few parallels can be found outside for pottery of the Ġgantija phase with the 'comet' motifs a purely insular development, although general patterns have been noted between the 'chequerboard' motifs and chessboard patterns of scratched wares of southeast Sicily and French Chassey (Evans 1953, 73).

Pottery of the following Tarxien phase survives in greater quantity than material from all other phases put together. The pottery assemblage displays greater variety in form and style and there is evidence of internal development over time, although this subdivision has yet to be determined. What is known, thanks to the excavation of the Brochtorff Circle (Malone *et al.* 2009), is that a separate funerary style developed during the Tarxien phase, known as the Saflieni-style. The majority of decoration follows the same technique employed during the Ġgantija phase, that of scratched decoration followed by red ochre incrustation. The decorative patterns, however, are very different, more varied and closely related to vessel type. The most common decoration is the graceful volute pattern which is of a very stereotyped form. There were elaborate variations of this design, with volutes forming branched patterns of extreme complexity, some bearing projected 'thorns', others ending in 'fishtails'. Such motifs echo those found on relief carving from the temples themselves (Evans 1971, 1959; Trump 2008, 1966).

Such advances in pottery design imply an aspect of change within the Tarxien phase which still needs to be further defined. As Trump (2008, 232) ponders, 'was the experimentation a conscious breaking away from the convention-bound rut, an attempt to revivify a failing tradition, or a sign of degeneracy, a collapse of accepted norms?' We may never fully know the answer since the Temple Period was brought to a somewhat abrupt end and replaced by a completely different, and in many ways inferior, tradition during the Bronze Age. What we can infer from the available evidence is that the islanders' unique cultural identity became reinforced through the elaboration of a standardised style, whose basic elements remained fixed, although their design became increasingly complex. It seems that the identity of the individual, hinted at during the Żebbuġ phase, had been lost and at the same time replaced by the dominance of a standardised collective.

The Bronze Age (*c.* 2000–700 BC): redefining and assimilating

The archaeological context

After a cultural break of approximately 400 years the Tarxien Cemetery phase (2000–1500 BC) marks the beginning of the Maltese Bronze Age. Changes in the archaeological record are so diverse and distinct as to suggest a complete break from the preceding Temple Period as the complex elements of the Temple Culture were replaced by cremation burials, metal weaponry and the construction of dolmens and menhirs. Whatever the reason behind such change, it is clear that the islands were re-integrated into the wider Mediterranean. This is evidenced by the occurrence of Tarxien Cemetery material on the Isola d'Ognina, south of Syracuse in Sicily and the stylistic similarities found between the Maltese dolmens and those of the Otranto region of Apulia in southern Italy (Leighton 1999; Malone *et al.* 2009; Pace 2004; Stoddart 1999). The following Borġ in-Nadur phase (1500–700 BC) marks the second major period of development of the Maltese Bronze Age when the archaeological evidence becomes more domestic in character. It is during this phase that fortified townships first make their appearance on the islands such as Borġ in-Nadur on Malta and In-Nuffara on Gozo. The final phase of prehistory, Baħrija (900–700 BC), is a minor one with Baħrija itself the only important site. Here the pottery has clear connections with Iron Age Calabria which may imply population movement from southern Italy to Malta at around 900 BC. By the eighth century BC Malta enters the historic era with the Phoenician colonisation of the islands, leaving the legacies of prehistory as a distant memory (Bonanno 1990; Pace 2004; Trump 2010).

The pottery styles
The pottery of the Tarxien Cemetery phase is completely different in every respect from the previous eras. Decoration is of a strictly rectilinear style made up of bands of parallel lines, deeply incised into the surface and arranged in horizontal and zigzag formations. The resultant triangles are hatched or divided into alternating plain and hatched chequer motifs. Domestic vessels, named 'Thermi' bowls, have been associated with the Tarxien Cemetery phase. Evans (1956) notes the similarity between Thermi vases and material from Thermi on Lesbos in the Aegean, while Bernabò Brea (1966) discovered similar sherds on the Isola d'Ognina, south of Sicily. Other parallels with Tarxien Cemetery pottery are found in the Capo Graziano culture of Lipari, although subtle differences suggest a 'cousinship [rather] than a direct affiliation of one to the other, or even direct descent from the same parent group' (Evans 1971, 224).

The pottery of the Borġ in-Nadur phase is again of a completely different form and could suggest a further immigration to the Maltese Islands. This time, however, there is some evidence for the survival of the earlier Tarxien Cemetery tradition, if only for a short while, as evidenced at Borġ in-Nadur itself (Trump 1961b). Decoration consists of cut-out bands of parallel lines and inverted chevrons, occasionally interrupted by a single crossbar with a dot at either end, deep-incised lines with applied pellets, and multiple zigzags between dash-filled bands. Painted decoration is also present, although more rare, and has been named 'dribbled ware' (*ibid.*, 259). The change to red-slipped bowls and pedestalled vessels with cut-out decoration in the Borġ in-Nadur phase has been noted as similar to that of the contemporary Thapsos culture of southeast Sicily (Evans 1971; Leighton 1999). Pottery of the final phase of Maltese prehistory, Baħrija, is technically similar to Borġ in-Nadur ware, although decoration is of an elaborate form, consisting of square-sectioned furrows combined with the technique of chip-carving to create raised patterns on the surface. Motifs generally comprise zigzags, meanders and triangles. A 'foreign' ware, which cannot be typologically derived from local Borġ in-Nadur ware, has been linked to the Fossa Grave

Culture of Calabria and may suggest further population movement to the Maltese Islands during this phase (Trump 1961b).

A review of both the archaeological context and the pottery styles suggests that during the Maltese Bronze Age the unique cultural identity of the Temple Culture had been lost and in its place came a multiplicity of identities that were inherently linked with the wider Mediterranean. Distinctiveness and individuality were replaced by a coherent pan-Mediterranean ideology that was expressed within a multitude of identities. Whether the identities of the Borġ in-Nadur and Baħrija cultures of the Maltese Islands were conflicting or concurring is yet to be fully determined.

Conclusions

The aim of this chapter was to explore the identities of prehistoric Malta's inhabitants through a contextual analysis of the changing styles of their prehistoric pottery sequence. The islands' bounded, relatively isolated and insular nature was considered to be an ideal setting to explore aspects of identity which have been forged, forgotten, contested, and reinvented during its long and colourful history. The Maltese Neolithic period was a time when the islanders remembered their ancestral roots and expressed an identity which was very much linked to their origins. At the same time they were also beginning to forge their own identity. By the Early Temple Period, the islands' inhabitants seem to have forgotten this link with their ancestral homeland. They forged a unique cultural identity which expressed the importance of the individual within a broader collective identity. By the Full Temple Period, the identity of the individual had been lost and at the same time replaced by the dominance of the collective. The islands' unique cultural identity became reinforced through the elaboration of a standardised style, whose basic elements remained fixed although their design became increasingly complex. Finally, by the Bronze Age this unique identity had been replaced by a multiplicity of identities which were inherently linked with the wider Mediterranean and the enforcement of a pan-Mediterranean ideology. It is hoped that this investigation has shown the potential that explorations of identity have to provide a greater understanding of Maltese prehistory. With further research, such an approach could consider ritual versus domestic identities, inter-island identities and the role of the artisan in the construction of island identities (Budden and Sofaer 2009; Costin and Wright 1998).

Acknowledgements

I would like to acknowledge and thank the following persons who have provided valuable guidance and assistance throughout my research and have helped make this chapter possible: my supervisor Dr Caroline Malone for her vital encouragement and support; Dr Simon Stoddart for his continued help and advice; Mr Joseph Attard Tabone for his invaluable local insight; Heritage Malta, and in particular, Ms Sharon Sultana, Mr George Azzopardi, and Ms Vanessa Ciantar, for their crucial assistance; and the Department of Classics and Archaeology at the University of Malta for their help and support. I would also like to thank my funding body, DEL, for making this research possible.

References

Bernabò Brea, L. (1966) *Sicily before the Greeks*. New York, F.A. Praeger.

Blake, E. (1999) Identity-mapping in the Sardinian Bronze Age. *European Journal of Archaeology* 2(1), 35–55.

Bonanno, A. (1990) The archaeology of Gozo. In C. Cini (ed.) *Gozo: the roots of an island*, 11–45. Valletta, Said International.

Budden, S. and Sofaer, J. (2009) Non-discursive knowledge and the construction of identity. Potters, potting and performance at the Bronze Age Tell of Szazhalombatta, Hungary. *Cambridge Archaeological Journal* 19(2), 1–18.

Casella, E. C. and Fowler, C. (eds) (2005) *The archaeology of plural and changing identities*. New York, Kluwer Academic/Plenum Publishers.

Conkey, M. and Hastorf, C. (eds) (1990) *Uses of style in archaeology*. Cambridge, Cambridge University Press.

Costin, C. L. and Wright, R. P. (eds) (1998) *Craft and social identity* (Archaeological Papers of the American Anthropological Association 8). Arlington, American Anthropological Association.

Evans, J. D. (1953) The prehistoric culture-sequence in the Maltese archipelago. *Proceedings of the Prehistoric Society* 19, 41–94.

Evans, J. D. (1959) *Malta*. London, Thames and Hudson.

Evans, J. D. (1971) *The prehistoric antiquities of the Maltese islands*. London, Athlone Press.

Fletcher, A. (2004) Ceramic styles at Domuztepe: evidence for social interaction in the Late Neolithic. In H. Kuhne, R. M. Czichon and F. J. Kreppner (eds) *Proceedings of the Fourth International Congress of the Archaeology of the Near East. Volume 2. Social and cultural transformation: the archaeology of transitional periods and Dark Ages*, 111–24. Berlin, Harrasswitz Verlag.

Hegmon, M. (1992) Archaeological research on style. *Annual Review of Anthropology* 21, 517–36.

Hodos, T. (2010) Local and global perspectives in the study of social and cultural identities. In S. Hales and T. Hodos (eds) *Material culture and social identities in the ancient world*, 3–31. Cambridge, Cambridge University Press.

Leighton, R. (1999) *Sicily before history. An archaeological survey from the Palaeolithic to the Iron Age*. London, Gerald Duckworth & Co. Ltd.

Lucy, S. (2005) Ethnic and cultural identities. In M. Diaz-Andreu, S. Lucy, S. Babic and D. N. Edwards (eds) *The archaeology of identity: approaches to gender, age, status, ethnicity and religion*, 86–109. New York, Routledge.

Malone, C. (2008) Metaphor and Maltese Art: explorations in the Temple Period. *Journal of Mediterranean Archaeology* 21(1), 81–109.

Malone, C., Stoddart, S., Bonanno, A., Gouder, T., and Trump, D. (1995) Mortuary ritual of the fourth millennium BC in Malta: the Żebbuġ Period chambered tomb from the Brochtorff Circle at Xagħra (Gozo). *Proceedings of the Prehistoric Society* 61, 303–45.

Malone, C., Stoddart, S., Bonanno, A., and Trump, D. (2009) *Mortuary customs in prehistoric Malta. Excavations at the Brochtorff Circle at Xagħra (1987–94)*. Cambridge, McDonald Institute of Archaeological Research.

Pace, A. (2004) Malta during prehistory. In K. Gambin (ed.) *Malta: roots of a nation*, 25–44. Malta, Midsea Books.

Rainbird, P. (2007) *The archaeology of islands*. Cambridge, Cambridge University Press.

Robb, J. (2001) Island identities: ritual, travel and the creation of difference in Neolithic Malta. *European Journal of Archaeology* 4(2), 175–202.

Sackett, J. R. (1977) The meaning of style: a general model. *American Antiquity* 42, 369–80.

Skeates, R. (2010) *An archaeology of the senses. Prehistoric Malta*. Oxford, Oxford University Press.

Stoddart, S. (1999) Long-term dynamics of an island community: Malta 5500 BC–AD 2000. In R. H. Tykot, J. Morter and J. E. Robb (eds) *Social dynamics of the prehistoric central Mediterranean*, 137–47. London, Accordia Research Institute.

Tilley, C. (2004) *The materiality of stone. Explorations in landscape phenomenology*. Oxford, Berg.

Trump, D. H. (1961a) Skorba, Malta and the Mediterranean. *Antiquity* 35, 300–3.

Trump, D. H. (1961b) The later prehistory of Malta. *Proceedings of the Prehistoric Society* 27, 253–62.
Trump, D. H. (1966) *Skorba and the prehistory of Malta*. London, Society of Antiquaries.
Trump, D. H. (ed.) (2008) *Malta: prehistory and temples* (3rd Edition). Malta, Midsea Books.
Trump, D. H. (ed.) (2010) *Malta: an archaeological guide* (Revised 2nd Edition). Malta, Progress Press.

9

THE BRONZE AGE SMITH
AS INDIVIDUAL

Heide Wrobel Nørgaard

Introduction

This chapter draws upon the personal observations of a trained goldsmith to detail how individual markers in working sequences can be interpreted, and also examines the motivation behind technological choices. Every step in a working sequence leaves 'traces' behind. These signatures of individuality can be the result of mistakes during crafting, the imprint of tools or the result of individual 'motor habits'. Today's research concentrates on the individual in prehistory. However, the archaeologist's only tool to investigate these individuals is the material culture they have used. The traces documented on bronze ornaments in the area of the Nordic Bronze Age can reveal much more than just the sequence of the tasks involved in their crafting: they can show the individuality of the metalworker. The residues of the crafting process of high quality objects can be used as a tool to investigate such intimate individual characteristics as the thoughts and ideas of the craftsman, the way in which they used their tools or transferred specific ideas onto objects. In this chapter, the different traces and their related actions are summarised under specific headlines in relation to diverse aspects of individuality. When several items with identical individual traces appear it might be possible to sketch out the craftsman behind them, or, in a broader sense, to define the characteristics of a singular workshop.

Actions of the mind

A working sequence is the thought process which accompanies the crafting of a piece. Knowledge about the specific order of steps is fundamental to the successful completion of the object. This knowledge is developed through experience, and is in many cases learned and adapted. On many prehistoric metal objects, single steps of a complete sequence can be documented by means of traces. The collar from Weitgendorf, Kr. Priegnitz in Mecklenburg

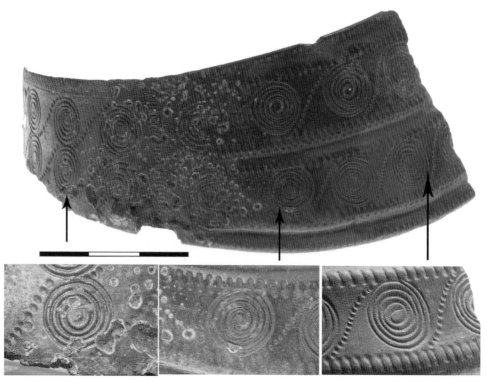

Figure 9.1: The neck collar from Weitgendorf I, Kr. Priegnitz (MM II8269) in Mecklenburg shows a recognizable sequence of crafting steps. (A colour plate of this figure is at the back of the volume.)

dated to 1550–1300 BC and crafted by lost-wax casting[1] reveals at least two successive working steps. When interpreting the marks left in the wax model, it can be assumed that the decoration on the ribs was placed following that of the spirals and that the connecting dot-lines are punched after the spirals (Figure 9.1). However, the best means of creating repetitive patterns is exemplified by the collar from Annebjerg Skov, Holbæk Amt (Aner and Kersten 1976; Nørgaard 2011a) dated to 1300–1100 BC. The technique for the creation of recurrent patterns is still under debate (Berger *et al.* 2010; Rønne 1989). However, this collar shows traces which can be connected to a starting point in the punch line or the recurring imprint of a stamp.

Actions of a specific hand

In research the term 'hand' is occasionally used as a synonym for a person when talking about technique and technology. However, the fact that the physical and chemical requirements of crafting today are similar to those in prehistory (*i.e.* the melting point of copper alloys) allows us the possibility to correlate specific traces with specific hand actions. Here it is possible to determine the hand as a part of the body of an individual that actually held the

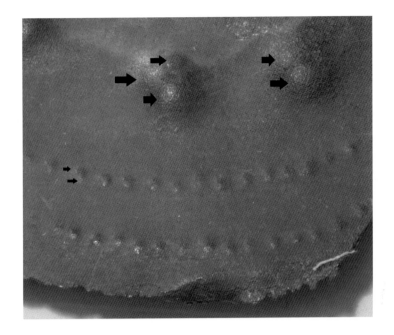

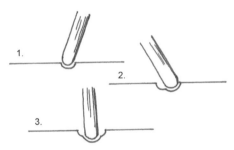

Figure 9.2: The disc-pin from Heinrichswalde, Kr. Neubrandenburg (ALM 7236b) with the multiple light bulges and the reconstruction of the crafting technique.

tool or struck the punch. These individual traces mainly show a possibility (*i.e.* right or left hand action) interpreted from today's craftsman's perspective.

The semi-circular imprints which were added in the wax model of the collar from Lübz, Kr. Parchim can be interpreted as a specific hand action. Due to the fact that the right side is set deeper into the wax one could conclude that the craftsman used his left hand to hold the tool and his right hand to place the punch ('punch' being a generalised term for the tool, most likely wood or metal, which made the described imprint). Another example to prove individual hand action is aptly illustrated by the disc-pin from Heinrichswalde, Kr. Neubrandenburg (Schubart 1972) in Mecklenburg. The bulges on the disc-pin show distinct, repeated punches and the resulting destruction in strike direction (Figure 9.2). The orientation of the crack in the bulge suggests that the direction of the punch came from the right side, which would mean therefore that the tool was handled with the left hand.

Intuitive and unconscious actions

High quality craftsmanship is based on a complex interaction of skills, material properties, timing, and experience. Therefore, it is possible that working sequences cannot be executed due to mistakes in the material or actions, as well as insufficient experience. These unexpected situations are common in the crafting process and require intuitive action. The result of such actions in material culture can be traced in unique patterns. The investigation of the Mecklenburg material reveals new traces, like rib-waves. These clearly visible waves in the rib-decoration of the Pisede type neck collar from Lubmin in Ostvorpommern (dated to 1550–1300 BC) are the result of a mistake concerning the material and the tool used which took place during the crafting process. While cutting the decoration in the ribs (a working step done in the wax-model), too much material was moved, requiring subsequent smoothing (Figure 9.3). The diagonal cuts are too deep and the following process would not have been necessary had the decoration been placed after casting. This smoothing happened to be in the opposite direction, and resulted in the spreading of the surplus material. Other intuitive and unconscious actions could be documented as well. The spirals on a Mecklenburg type neck collar (Nørgaard 2011b) from 1550–1300 BC are of a vastly different sort. Due to the limited space at the sides of the piece, the shape of the spirals had to be reduced. For this reason, the end-spirals close differently than those more towards the middle of the pattern. As mentioned by Lechtman, the activities used to produce an object are stylistic and the choices made accordingly form part of the package that creates style (Lechtman 1975, 5–7).

Learned and adopted actions

It can be assumed that the technical way of constructing specific ornamental details like spirals is a learned behaviour. The modern example of master and apprentice cannot be calqued directly onto prehistory. However, it shows one possible way in which acquired knowledge is shared. Most commonly, the learned working sequences were adopted and were subsequently developed and improved. In this case, technical patterns can be related to the same hand or to the same source.

The extensions at the end of the spiral decoration from the Mecklenburg type neck collar from Weitgendorf II, Kr. Priegnitz, are clearly visible. These characteristic traces only occur within a specific region. A further clear indication of the techniques employed is the presence of the smooth grooves between spike and plate of the belt disc from Dabel, Kr. Sternberg (Schubart 1972). They are explicable through a technique also used in ceramics. The uniformity of the spiral centre on the belt disc from Lavø, Frederiksborg Amt on Zealand (Aner and Kersten 1973, 53) is clear evidence for the stamping method (Rønne 1989) and would therefore be a mediated methodology.

On the other hand, similar recurrent patterns or symbols cannot be explained as simple, adopted actions. They should be seen rather as internalised behaviour dictated by society and mindset. Spirals were a commonly used decoration in 1550–1100 BC. More than 90% of the investigated ornaments have spirals which turned counter-clockwise; an overall turning direction typical for the Nordic Bronze Age (Herner 1987). They are connected with various lines, most often from the left bottom side to the right top side.

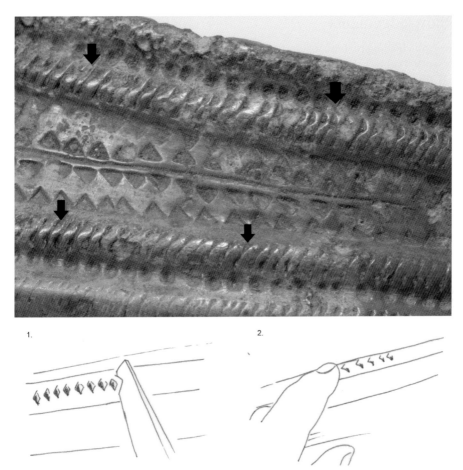

Figure 9.3: The collar from Lubmin, Kr. Ostvorpommern (ALM 1994/3/1) with the clearly visible waves in the rib-decoration and the reconstruction of its crafting technique.

Summary

Various prehistoric craftsmen's traces are visible on prehistoric bronze ornaments. They can be used and interpreted to gain more knowledge about the craftsman as an individual. The most common traces can be seen as intuitive reactions on errors through crafting and especially these errors can be used to identify workshops due to the fact that they point out the hand that crafted. The intensive study of technical details on bronze ornaments during the Early and Middle Bronze Age in northern Europe will lead to several individual traces like the ones mentioned above. Similar traces on different objects lead to the assumption that one individual was involved in the crafting process. Given that it is probable that Bronze Age workshops would most likely have been small family-like institutions (Lüning 2005), conducive to the sharing of techniques and (possibly) even tools, the results of the investigation can characterise and locate possible workshops.

Acknowledgements

The research leading to these results has received funding from the European Union Seventh Framework Program (FP7/2007–2013) under Grant Agreement no. 212402. Additional special thanks to Samantha Reiter for continuing to develop my English and to Helle Vandkilde and Svend Hansen for motivating me during my work.

Note

1   The lost-wax technique also known as 'cire perdue' is one of the most commonly used casting techniques in Bronze Age Europe. The object was almost completely created in wax (mostly a mix of beeswax, talc, rosin and fat). The model was then packed in a clay form consisting of different layers. After the wax melted and the mould dried – now hollow because of the lost wax – the liquid metal is cast in the mould. Once the cast cooled, the mould was destroyed to reveal the item (Born and Hansen 2001, 182; Drescher 1953; Hundt 1980: 63–79).

References

Aner, E. and Kersten, K. (1973) Frederiksborg und København Amt. Die Funde der älteren Bronzezeit des nordischen Kreises in Dänemark, Schleswig-Holstein und Niedersachsen. Neumünster.

Aner, R. and Kersten, K. (1976) Holbæk, Sorø und Præstø Amter Die Funde der älteren Bronzezeit des nordischen Kreises in Dänemark, Schleswig-Holstein und Niedersachsen. Neumünster.

Berger, D., Schwab, R. and Wunderlich, C. H. (2010) Technologische Untersuchungen zu bronzezeitlichen Metallziertechniken nördlich der Alpen vor dem Hintergrund des Hortfundes von Nebra. In H. Meller (ed.) *Der Griff nach den Sternen. Wie Europas Eliten zu Macht und Reichtum kamen.* Internationales Symposium in Halle (Saale), 16–21. Februar 2005. Halle, Saale.

Born, H. and Hansen, S. (2001) *Helme und Waffen Alteuropas.* Mainz, Zabern.

Drescher, H. (1953) Eine technische Betrachtung bronzezeitlicher Halskragen. *Offa* 12, 67–72.

Herner, E. (1987) *Profession med tradition: teknisk-kvalitativ analys av den äldre bronsålderns spiralornamentik, dess central- och lokalproduktion.* Lundensia, Almqvist och Wiksell.

Hundt, L. (1980) The long history of Lost Wax casting. *Gold Bulletin* 12, 63–79.

Lechtman, H. (1975) Style in technology – some early thoughts. In H. Lechtman and R. Merrill (eds) *Material culture. styles, organisation, and dynamics of technology*, 3–20. New York, West Publishing Co.

Lüning, J. (2005) Zwischen Alltagswissen und Wissenschaft im Neolithikum. In T. L. Kienlin (ed.) *Die Dinge als Zeichen. Kulturelles Wissen und materielle Kultur*, 53–80. Bonn, Dr. Rudolf Habelt GmbH.

Nørgaard, H. W. (2011a) Die Halskragen der Bronzezeit im nördlichen Mitteleuropa und Südskandinavien. Bonn, Dr. Rudolf Habelt GmbH.

Nørgaard, H. W. (2011b) Workshops in Mecklenburg. In A. Hauptmann, D. Modarressi-Therani and M. Prange (eds) *Archaeometallurgy in Europe III*. Abstracts. 4, 248–9. Sonderheft ed. Bochum, Deutsches Bergbaumuseum Bochum.

Rønne, P. (1989) Early Bronze Age spiral ornament – the technical background. *Journal of Danish Archaeology* 8, 126–43.

Schubart, H. (1972) *Die Funde der älteren Bronzezeit in Mecklenburg.* Neumünster.

Architectural and
ritual expressions

Introduction

Dirk Brandherm

Gazing at the sky, ground, and navel

Identity is a multifaceted concept, its study open to a variety of diverse approaches. This holds true not only for exploring identity in contemporary communities or in societies of the fairly recent past, but also for any attempt at reconstructing and understanding prehistoric identities. As we move back in time, however, lines of inquiry which to some degree rely on emic testimony or even more generally on verbal testimonials, sooner or later will inevitably run out of suitable source material. Hence, prehistoric archaeology has to rely on etic and non-verbal evidence entirely, *i.e.* on the fossilised expression of communal or individual behaviour. As both architecture and ritual contain a strong element of consolidated behavioural patterns, it makes good sense for case studies from both domains to be presented together in this section.

Fittingly the first of the three contributions in this section deals with one of the most emblematic types of ritual architecture known from prehistoric Ireland. Here MacDonagh examines some peculiar features characterizing a group of stone circles centred on the Sperrin Mountains. He makes a convincing case for a reading of their unusual design as mirror images of the lunar surface. The limited distribution of their design clearly reveals shared beliefs at a regional level, and thus more than likely also incorporates some element of a shared ritual identity.

In contrast to stone circles, rock art may perhaps not qualify as architecture in the narrow sense of the term, but like the former it certainly forms part of the built environment. It is also a product of very much place-bound ritual expression and hence offers considerable potential to gain some rare insight into specifically localised aspects of ritually encoded identity. In her study of rock-art traditions in the north of Ireland Enlander endeavours to unlock some of this potential, exploring subtle differences both in the conscious choice of specific sites and rock types, as well as in human interaction with the surface scape of particular rock-art panels. This interaction is seen as establishing a long-term relationship between local communities and their surrounding landscape, with rock art shaped by, and at the same time feeding back into, the social memory of these very communities. Against the background of this mutual relationship, Enlander discusses the potential role of distinctive local geologies in the building of equally distinctive local identities.

We are given an insight into the identity of place as a functioning 'think tank' with Sapwell's analysis of rock art in northern Sweden. Sapwell concentrates on a particularly dense concentration of rock art at Nämforsen. The Nämforsen region was associated with seasonal movement, large gatherings of people, and exchange: all of which were facilitated by its position within a wide-reaching network of waterways. The rock art in this region is notable for the frequency of motifs compared to other rock-art landscapes. Sapwell uses

GIS and spatial statistics to map the alterations in certain motifs. These alterations, notably observed through the boat and the elk motifs, are linked back to changes in the wider landscape and forms of material culture. The author suggests that the act of inscribing these motifs on the rock-art panels facilitated the creation and maintenance of changing and converging identities in this important region.

It would probably be difficult to find anyone willing to dispute that megalithic monuments, as prominent and symbolically charged elements in the prehistoric landscape, must have played a significant role in shaping the identity of Neolithic communities throughout much of northwest Europe. The potential impact of bodily experience of the building process of such monuments on prehistoric identities is less frequently examined. In her contribution to this volume, Meegan tries to remedy this and explores new ways to fathom the effects this very physical experience might have had on the identity of Neolithic people. By discussing the role of the design process of a 3D virtual model (of the Knowth megalithic complex) in fostering reflexive awareness and acting as a stimulus for speculation on the bodily experience of the builders, Meegan also argues for a re-conceptualization of phenomenological reasoning more generally.

UNDER THE SAME NIGHT SKY – THE ARCHITECTURE AND MEANING OF BRONZE AGE STONE CIRCLES IN MID-ULSTER

Michael MacDonagh

Introduction

There are over 100 stone circle sites in Ulster spread right across the province, but mostly concentrated in the foothills of the Sperrin Mountains in Counties Tyrone and Londonderry (Figure 10.1). They are evidence of a thriving Bronze Age presence in the upland landscape prior to a decline in soil fertility and eventual advancement of blanketing bog cover *c.* 500 BC (Pilcher 1969). Their wide distribution clearly indicates connections, links and shared beliefs between the scattered local communities of circle builders. This chapter highlights similarities in the design and layout of various stone circle sites in mid-Ulster and proposes that a specific design template was followed in their construction. Finally, a possible origin of the template is revealed.

The architecture of the mid-Ulster stone circles

At a general level, the architecture of the circles across the region is relatively homogenous. At the core of the design of every stone circle site lay the main intent of its builders: the construction of a circle (or circles), defined by a perimeter of stones. There is considerable variation in the detail of their construction across the sites. For example, at some sites, the perimeters are walled constructs, with stones tightly set against each other as at Copney, County Tyrone [NISMR[1] Tyr 027:033] (Figures 10.5–10.6), while at other sites, the perimeter stones are spaced with gaps between them, as at Beaghmore, County Tyrone [Tyr 020:004] (Figure 10.4). While the detail of circle design and construction was not rigid across the region, architectural similarities certainly outweigh the differences.

Most of the stone circles of the mid-Ulster family are small, with diameters of no more than 15m. Many are found as single circles, but some are accompanied by others in paired or triplet groupings. A few sites, such as Copney and Beaghmore, discussed further below, are impressive groupings of circles set out across wide landscapes, the design and layout of which can only be fully appreciated when seen from the air or in plan (Figure 10.2).

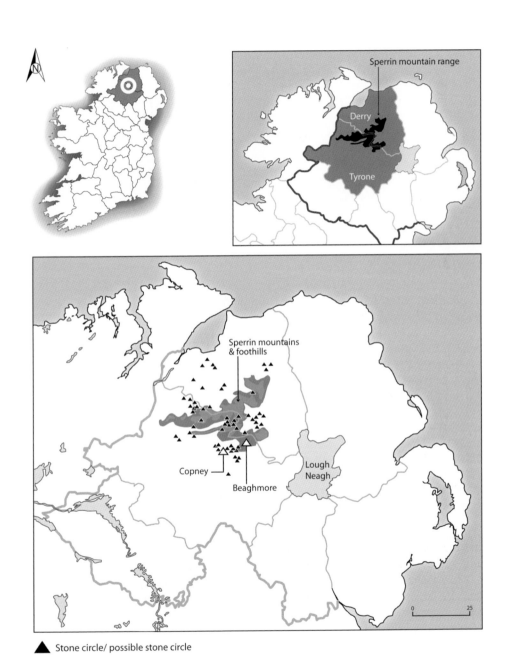

Stone circle/ possible stone circle

Figure 10.1: Distribution of stone circles across the Sperrin Mountains and foothills (after McConkey 1987).

Figure 10.2: Aerial view of Beaghmore stone circle complex, County Tyrone (Tyr 020:004) (Courtesy of the Northern Ireland Environment Agency). (A colour plate of this figure is at the back of the volume.)

Whether simple, single circles or grander tableaux, the mid-Ulster circles are all somewhat diminutive. The towering orthostats that characterise some brooding Scottish circles, such as Brodgar and Stenness and to a lesser extent other Irish examples from Counties Cork and Kerry, such as Drombeg, are nowhere to be seen. Instead, relatively small stones were used to construct the Ulster circles. At the Beaghmore complex the stones are rarely more than 1m in height; its builders were using what was readily available and with the minimum requirement of quarrying, moving and block-raising technology. Stone rows are also present at many Ulster sites; these are often double-rowed, with one row being constructed from relatively much smaller stones (*e.g.* Copney, see Figure 10.3). The presence of double-rowed alignments at many of the sites is one clear common design trait of the mid-Ulster circles, and more are discussed below. Evidence of shared design traits is most clear in the multi-circle complexes, suggesting that each of these complexes did not develop randomly but followed clear design templates.

Figure 10.3: Copney stone circle complex, County Tyrone (Tyr 027:033): double-rowed stone alignment from east, Circle B in background (Courtesy of the Northern Ireland Environment Agency).

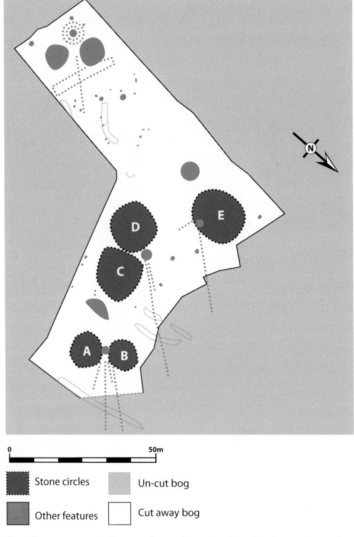

Figure 10.4: Beaghmore stone circle complex: schematic plan showing main circle complex (after Pilcher 1969).

The stone circle complexes of Beaghmore and Copney

The stone circle complex of Beaghmore lies about 12km northwest of Cookstown in County Tyrone. As a State Care monument, conserved and easily accessible by the public, it is the most well-known of the mid-Ulster stone circle sites and is also one of the largest identified complexes. It was discovered through turf cutting in the 1930s and partly excavated in the 1940s and 1960s (McL. May 1953; Pilcher 1969). The removal of the blanket bogland that

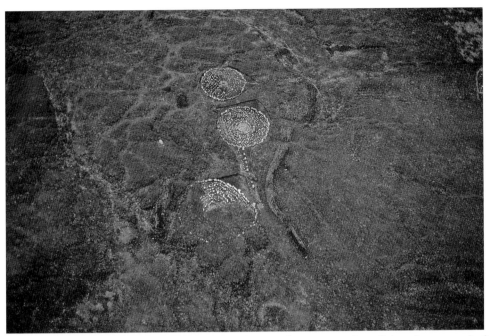

Figure 10.5: Copney stone circle complex: aerial view of western portion of site after removal of bogland in 1995, showing, from top: Circles A and B and the double stone row alignment leading to Circle C. (Courtesy of the Northern Ireland Environment Agency).

had grown to cover the site revealed seven circles and various stone rows, cairns and traces of earlier field banks (Pilcher 1969). Uncut bogland still surrounds the site in most directions, almost certainly concealing further associated features. At present, dating evidence is still derived from Picher's analysis which indicates a pre-construction date of 1550 BC and a post-construction date of 800 BC enveloping the construction of the circles (*ibid.*). The main part of the site is dominated by five circles, Circles A–E, with two smaller circles to the south, Circles F and G, somewhat removed from the others, and various stone rows that extend out from the circles in a general north-easterly direction (Figures 10.2 and 10.4).

Since the site was discovered, the stone row alignments at Beaghmore have been the focus of much attention, with research focusing on whether they align with key points on the horizon, such as those associated with the movements of the sun or moon on notable calendar events, such as solstices. Following his excavations in the 1940s, Beaghmore's first excavator pondered whether we could ever truly know of such associations (Mc L. May 1953, 193). Several decades later A. S. Thom tried to prove such links, compiling masses of data on 'megalithic yards' altitudes, azimuths and declinations of the sun and moon and applying them to the Beaghmore alignments (Thom 1980). While the general north-easterly alignment was noted as being generally directed towards the summer solstice sunrise, nothing was conclusively proven regarding the stone alignments' celestial orientations, in that no key calendar date was noted for their orientation. Hayes, among others, has argued against our

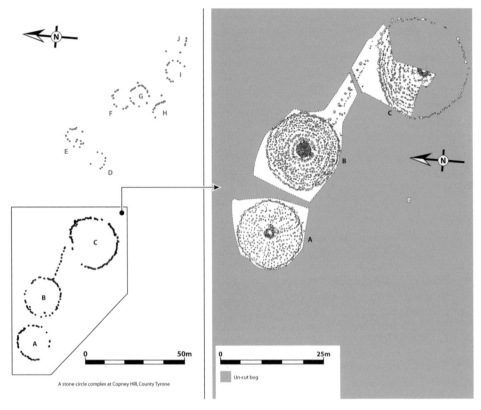

Figure 10.6: Copney Stone Circle Complex, County Tyrone: overall site plan left: overall site plan (left) and detail of Circles A–C after removal of bogland (right) (after Foley 1983 and MacDonagh 1998).

modern quest for ancient astronomical accuracy (Hayes 1999). He adjudges that in relation to the field of archaeoastronomy and our understanding of the influence of the skies on the monument building of prehistoric peoples, the views of the mathematical sophisticates had brought scorn upon a field that could provide genuine help in our understanding of prehistoric societies (*ibid.,* 32) to whom heavenly associations may have played a more symbolic and ritual role.

On Copney hill, 11 km southwest of Beaghmore, up to 10 circles form a complex on its northern slope. First recorded by Claire Foley in the 1980s (Foley 1983), blanket bog was excavated from the three largest circles and the stone row alignment at the highest eastern end of the site in 1995 by the author (Foley and MacDonagh 1998). This work revealed complex arrangements of stones within each of the three large circles (Circles A–C), each with a robbed-out burial cairn and cist at its centre (Figures 10.5–10.6). A standing stone and seven smaller circles (Circles D–J) on the lower slope to the east complete the known complex, although blanket bogland on the hillside may well conceal other features.

A design template for the stone circles?

Wandering through the mid-Ulster circle sites offers a different experience than visiting the enormous sentinel-stoned circles of the Scottish Isles. The Scottish circles demand questions pertaining to the technology of raising such large blocks. The Ulster circles are in stark contrast as the stones used are small. The impression of Beaghmore is of a designed landscape, a themed park if you will, or – in archaeological terms – a ritualised landscape (Tilley 1994). Elements of design are everywhere: groups of circles and stone row alignments extending out from them at tangents orientated in certain directions, and small cairns positioned on circle perimeters. These complex sites are best viewed in plan or from the air, allowing the viewer to fully appreciate the layout of and interrelationship between the various features (*e.g.* Figures 10.2 and 10.5). It is not fanciful to assume that there may have been purpose and meaning in how the various circles were laid out in relation to each other. This notion of a 'grand design', as opposed to any random and meaningless development of the complexes, is strengthened by the architectural similarities that exist between a number of the Ulster sites: double-rowed alignments, deliberate construction of irregular circles and specific configurations in their layout.

Double-rowed stone alignments

As mentioned above, double-rowed stone alignments are present at many of the mid-Ulster circles, comprising two parallel rows of stones, one with large and one with smaller stones, as at Copney (Figure 10.3). While some rows may well be associated with the rising or setting of the sun or moon at certain calendar dates, the meaning of the double row is not fully clear and is not explored in depth here, although it is evident that some common design trait was present at a number of sites.

Lack of circularity to the circles

At Beaghmore and Copney a majority of the 'circles' are in fact rather irregular in plan. The three largest circles at the eastern end of the Beaghmore complex (Circles C–E) deviate from circularity to the greatest degree (Figure 10.4). While displacement of some perimeter stones, due to bog growth and accidental dislodgement during turf cutting, can account for some deviation from the round, this is not enough to explain the overall lack of circularity in their construction. Circles A and B at Beaghmore are much more circular in design than Circles C–E, indicating that their builders could achieve regularity when desired (Figure 10.4). This raises the intriguing question as to why some 'circles' would be deliberately constructed as non-circular.

At Copney, Circles A and B are as circular as stone circles can be, providing evidence that their builders had mastered that simple technique (Figures 10.5 and 10.6). However, Circle C at Copney bulges egg-like at the northeast to make a seemingly desperate reach for the stone row alignment. Did the builders of Circle C miscalculate, and did they only notice late on that the perimeter was not going to reach the stone row alignment, and hence were they compelled to clumsily stretch the perimeter of Circle C so that the two could meet? Error on the part of the Copney circle builders is surely an unsatisfactory conclusion

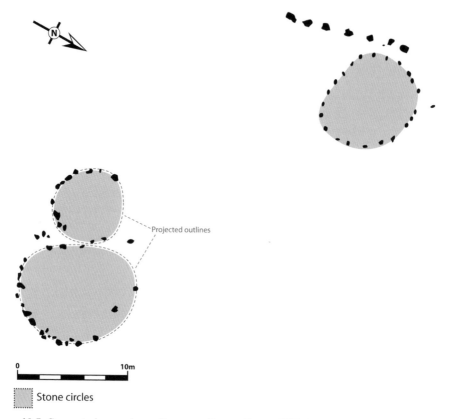

Figure 10.7: Stone circle complex at Tremoge, County Tyrone (TYR 037:021) (after McConkey 1987).

to reach when at the same site Circles A and B *are* circular (Figure 10.5), and when other sites, such as Beaghmore, also show clear non-circularity in the building of some circles and good circularity in others. The evidence suggests that the Bronze Age stone circle builders clearly had adequate precision when it was required, but that in some cases they chose not to use it.

This lack of regularity to many of the circles must be seen as another shared design trait in the Ulster sites, clearly evident at the two excavated complexes of Copney and Beaghmore, and also at other unexcavated examples, including Tremoge, County Tyrone (Tyr 037:021), 10km south of Beaghmore (Figure 10.7) and at Ballybriest, County Londonderry (Ldy 045:019), discovered by the author in 1995.

Configuration of the circles

Did the circle complexes develop randomly or were they positioned in deliberate and meaningful positions in juxtaposition to each other? If any repeated pattern in the layout

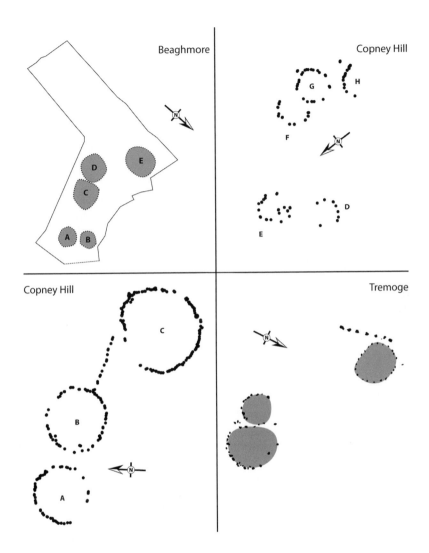

Figure 10.8: Composite illustration showing similarities in layout of stone circle complexes. Clockwise from top left: Beaghmore, Circles A–E (after Pilcher 1969); Copney, Circles D–H (after Foley 1983); Tremoge (after McConkey 1987); Copney, Circles A–C.

of the circles can be discerned, this could be seen, on top of the evidence for shared design traits already established, as further evidence that the builders of the various sites were following some form of template.

Little attention has been paid to the overall layout of the individual circles in the multi-circle complexes of mid-Ulster. Mc L. May noted that 'the grouping of the structures apparently conform to some plan' (McL. May 1953, 191) but did not explore that theme further with regard to the circles *per se*, rather he focussed his attention on the orientation of the stone rows, as have so many researchers since, largely ignoring the design and layout of the circles themselves.

Both the Beaghmore and Copney complexes are dominated by three large circles: Circles C, D and E at Beaghmore (Figure 10.4) and Circles A, B and C at Copney (Figure 10.6). At both sites the three large circles are laid out in a similar juxtaposition to each other: two of the three large circles are adjacent to each other (C and D at Beaghmore and A and B at Copney) with the third circle at each site (E at Beaghmore and C at Copney) slightly offset to the side of a long axis drawn through the centres of the other two. At Copney this pattern is repeated with Circles F, G and H which are set out in exactly the same manner as the three larger circles upslope to the west, although on a different orientation: Circles F and G are positioned next to each other with Circle H offset (Figure 10.6).

The three circles at Tremoge, mentioned above, are also laid out in a similar pattern (Figure 10.7) as they are also at Culvacullion, County Tyrone [Tyr 018:003] (although at the latter site, the third circle is set to the other side of the long axis through the other two circles).

This startling similarity in the layout of some of the circles at a number of the multi-circle complexes strongly supports the idea that the stone circle builders across the region were adhering to a deliberate design template when constructing their sites (Figure 10.8).

The origin of the design template

If we were to accept the evidence that a design template was followed by the circle builders in constructing some of the stone circle sites, then we need to explore what the origin of such a design was, and ask specifically what the builders may have been trying to represent? In 1999 an idea was put to the author by Mr Laurence Weir regarding the origin of the layout of the circles at Beaghmore: that the circles were laid out to reflect a mirror image of the surface of the moon. It is that marvellous idea that was the starting point for this research presented here.

To an observer from earth the face of the moon is dominated by the lunar *maria*. The *maria*, called such by the17th-century astronomer Giovanni Battista Riccioli (who thought they were analogous with the earth's oceans), are circular impact sites filled with volcanic magma that has cooled into various basaltic formations (Wlasuk 2000, 19). They appear darker due to less reflective iron-rich geology and are visible to the naked human eye, known to children of course as the *Man in the Moon*. To the naked eye they have vague borders, spilling into each other forming an indistinct dark shape, although some appear more distinct and individual at times (Figure 10.9).

Telescopic images show more defined elements of globularity but even unaided the human eye still perceives shape and form to them, if not circularity. The drawings of nine year olds Aoife Casey and Heather Eogan (whose grandfather Professor George Eogan incidentally excavated at Beaghmore in the 1960s) testify to the human eye seeing the *maria* as having distinctive globular forms (Figure 10.10). One's observed level of definition of the *maria* varies according to the phasing of the moon, the relative shadow effect of the sun on the moon's surface topography, the amount of artificial light and air pollution, and, of course, one's eyesight. The relative size of the moon to the observer plays a part too. For reasons of optical illusion, the moon often appears larger on the horizon to some observers (Ross

Figure 10.9: Telescopic photograph of the nearside of the moon as we see it from earth, the lunar maria and other features visible.

Figure 10.10: Sketches of the surface of a full moon (Aoife Casey and Heather Eogan, aged 9, 2012).

1.

2.   3.

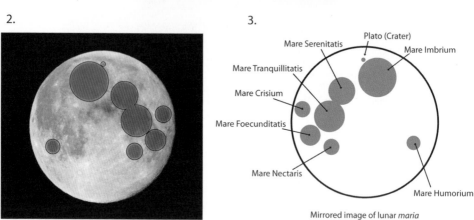

Figure 10.11: 1) is a telescopic photographic image of the lunar surface as we see it, upon which are visible the lunar maria; *2) is the same image with various lunar* maria *highlighted giving them definition; 3) is a mirror image plan of these lunar* maria, *with their respective astronomical names.*

and Plug 2002) – the so-called *moon illusion* – and at those times when its elliptical orbit brings it 50000km closer to the earth (perigree), a mere 356577km distant, it appears larger still (Wlasuk 2000, 4). The coincidence of a full moon at its perigree orbit point happens irregularly. It occurred on 19 March 2011, the first time since 1993. Those who witnessed it with clear skies (as it was across Ireland that evening) shall recall its larger than normal size (14%), greater brightness (30%) and better definition of its surface features (NASA 2011).

> 'the dark spots in the moon do not appear as one but having something like isthmuses between them, the brilliance dividing and delimiting the shadow. Hence, since each part is separated and has its own boundary, the layers of light upon shadow'
>
> Appolonides to Lamprias in *Concerning the Face Which Appears in the Orb of the Moon (De facie quae in orbe lunae apparet)* Plutarch's *Moralia 1st century AD* (translation by Cherniss 1957, 45).

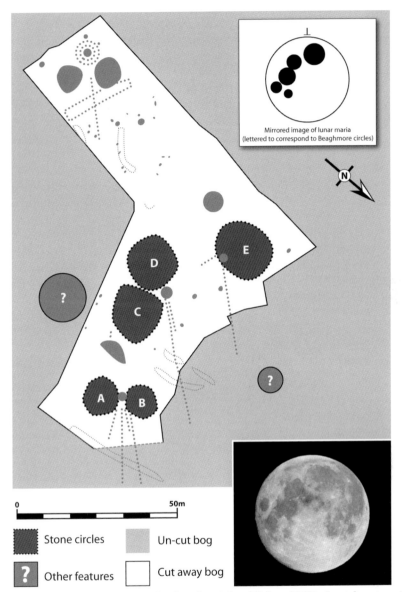

Figure 10.12: Beaghmore Stone Circle Complex (after Pilcher, 1969). Inset box top right marks the defined lunar maria *as per Figure 10.11. Inset bottom right shows a mirror image of the moon.*

Beaghmore, Copney, stone circles and the moon

The layout of the circle group comprising Circles A–E at Beaghmore is displayed in Figure 10.12. It is proposed here that in laying out these five circles at Beaghmore, the builders set them out to correspond in mirror-image form with the layout of various lunar *maria*, as

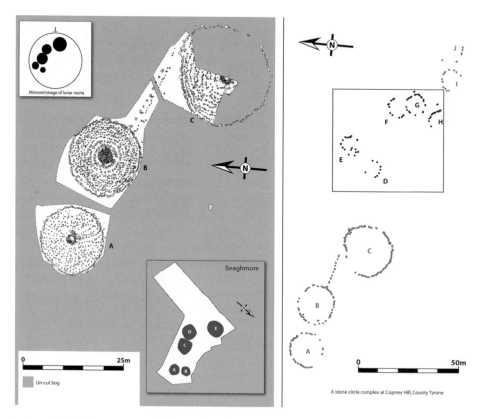

Figure 10.13: Copney stone circle complex, Co. Tyrone (right: overall site plan; left: detail of Circles A–C after bog removal). Inset bottom shows Beaghmore circle layout and top left insert shows plan of defined lunar maria *(main site plan after Foley 1983).*

shown in inset box in right-hand corner (also refer back to Figure 10.11). It is proposed that at Beaghmore, Circle A represents *Mare Foecunditatis*, Circle B *Mare Nectaris,* Circle C *Mare Tranquilitatis,* Circle D *Mare Serenitatis*, and that Circle E represents *Mare Imbrium*.

The two circle symbols marked with '?' in Figure 10.12 are in areas of blanket bogland that have not been cut away. According to the mirrored-lunar image theory being put forward here, their positions are placed to correspond to *Mare Humorium* and *Mare Crisium* (see Figure 10.11(3)). Should bogland ever be removed from these areas, it would be interesting to see if there were stone circles in these locations. While absence of circles in either of these two locations would not disprove this lunar connection theory, discovery of circles here would certainly lend further credence to it.

At Copney the three largest circles (A, B and C) are laid out in a similar configuration as the three largest circles at Beaghmore: two circles adjacent to each other with the third offset some distant removed. According to the lunar *maria* theory, Circles A–C at Copney were laid out to correspond to *Mare Imbrium, Mare Serenitatis* and *Mare Tranquilitatis* respectively, the same as circles E, D and C at Beaghmore (Figure 10.13).

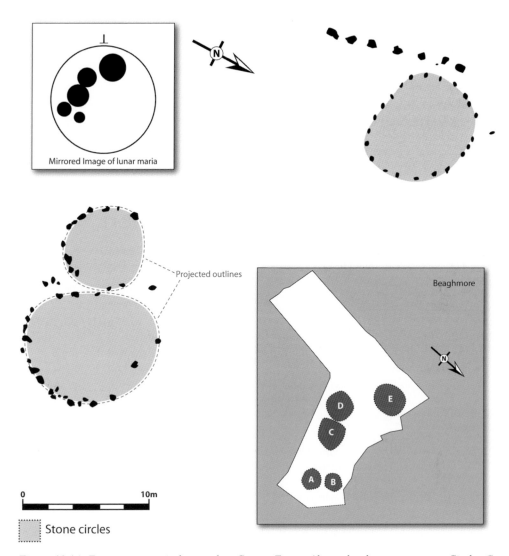

Figure 10.14: Tremoge stone circle complex, County Tyrone (deemed to be set out as per Circles C, D and E at Beaghmore: bottom right insert) (site plan after McConkey 1987).

The smaller Circles D–H at Copney, just downslope from the three large circles mentioned above, display a remarkable overall similarity to the layout of Circles A–E at Beaghmore, as seen earlier (Figure 10.8). It is proposed that Circles D–H at Copney were laid out to correspond to the *maria*, just as Circles A–E at Beaghmore (Figure 10.13).

At Tremoge the three circles are laid out as per Circles A–C at Copney and Circles D–F at Beaghmore (Figure 10.14), corresponding to *Mare Imbrium, Mare Serenitatis* and *Mare Tranquilitatis.*

As has been shown, the lunar *maria* are seen with the human eye as globular, not circular. If, as suggested here, the *maria* were the design template used by the circle builders, this could help explain the deliberate lack of circularity to many of the circles. (The author offers no theory on the stone rows deriving from this lunar reflection hypothesis: telescopic images of the moon do show 'ray craters' with lines emanating out from the impact points (see Figure 10.9) but these are not visible to the unaided human eye (the author's anyway) and it is not posited that the stone rows are copies of these.)

The moon as a mirror

'The man, you see, asserts that what is called the face consists of mirrored likenesses, that is images of the great ocean reflected in the moon, for the visual ray when reflected naturally reaches from many points objects which are not directly visible and the full moon is itself in uniformity and lustre the finest and clearest of all mirrors'

Lamprias' mocking of Clearchus to Appolonides in '*Concerning the Face Which Appears in the Orb of the Moon*' from Plutarch's *Moralia, 1st century AD* (translation by Cherniss 1957, 41).

We know it as an orbiting satellite of earth-derived material created from a collision many millions of years ago, and we understand the dynamics of its presence in our lives, gravitational law and its influence on our tides. We do *not* know what prehistoric people thought the moon to be, but we do know that, quite naturally, it was of great interest to thinkers in the historical world and their thoughts may be seen as representing some of the those of earlier societies.

Concerning the Face Which Appears in the Orb of the Moon, the writings of the first-century AD Graeco-Roman historian Plutarch (*c.* AD 46–120) highlights the cosmological and scientific questions of that age that surrounded the moon. In his Platonic rejection of the moon being a mirror of the earth, he evidently illustrates that at the time, the notion was held by some at least. In the 10th and 11th century the great Arabic astronomer Ibn AlHaitham also rejected the moon-mirror notion, which obviously still persisted in the minds of some (Schoy 1923). As late as the 19th century, Alexander von Humboldt tells of a Persian from Ispahan (in modern day Iran) who assured him that what we see in the moon is the map of our earth (Von Humboldt 1850, 544).

Conclusions

There are monuments built by ancient societies across the globe, the designs of which appear to pay homage to celestial objects and astronomical dynamics. From Stonehenge to the Neolithic megalithic tomb at Maes Howe in Scotland, to elements of the Mayan city of Chichen Itza and the Pyramids of Giza, ideas abound as to the role of the sun and moon and planetary movements in their designs. There are also, of course, the concomitant doubters of such ideas. In Ireland, the Winter solstice appears to be prominent in prehistoric monumental architecture, with the sunrise lighting the back of the chamber at the Newgrange passage tomb (County Meath) and displaying a seeming level of accuracy that is to be admired, and as is also present that same morning at the Maes Howe tomb on Orkney. Astronomical precision in designing ancient monuments, which may be gained simply from many years of observation, is also evident at the Neolithic site of Callanish on the Outer Hebrides, Scotland, where the moon plays a prominent role at its lunar minor standstill every 18.6 years (McHardy 2010).

There is enough evidence to support some claims of astronomical precision in some prehistoric architecture. Whether the Bronze Age builders of the mid-Ulster circles possessed that precision or not is unknown, but in any case the author suggests it played no part in the design of the circles. He simply suggests here that the circles were built to represent the moon. Single circle sites may have been built to represent the moon itself. The more complex multi-circle sites contain various layouts of circles that represent what the builders saw in the face of the moon. There are variations from site to site, local differences in interpretation, as the detail of what people saw in the face of the moon varied according to the observer(s), as it still does, and artistic licence is allowed in any depiction. At some sites, circles are regular circles, while at others, notably Beaghmore, the circles are far from circular, suggesting that its builders adopted a realistic style of depicting the globular shaped lunar *maria*. While there are variations in detail, the very strong similarity in the layout of the circles at a number of complex sites suggests that a template may have been followed, perhaps copying from one original site – was Beaghmore the template, with other sites being imitations of it?

We do not know what role the moon played in the cosmology, ritual and religion of the Bronze Age communities who built the circles. However, the mirror representations of the lunar *maria*, as suggested at Beaghmore and Copney, indicate that the circle builders, like some people many centuries after them, saw the moon as a mirror in the sky, reflecting their 'world'. The 'moon circle' sites of Ulster were inspired by a process of moon staring, of mirror-gazing. Perception of oneself through reflection is important, as psychology tells us. The Lacanian 'mirror stage' in infancy is a developmental milestone, one of jubilation at first seeing one's reflection and the understanding with it of one's individuality as separate from others, the comprehension of seeing oneself as a unified entity and self (Murray 2010). Could such individuation have applied to the various circle building communities? Were they each making their mark in wider society that held similar beliefs of the moon, each defining themselves in that society by constructing a depiction of their known 'world' as seen reflected in the big mirror in the sky? In modern terms is it not simply the same grounding imperative as having a globe on your desk, a tourist map in the backpack, a star chart on the wall, seeing your town on a map, knowing where you are and where you fit in to your wider world? Whatever psychological imperatives of identity and definition played into the circle builder's belief that the moon contained a reflected image of their world, the links between the various circle building communities are clear, shown by the architectural similarities that exist between various circle sites. And as the soil got poorer and wetter, and as bogland conditions started to envelop the mid-Ulster circle sites half a millennium before the birth of Plutarch, the perception of the reflected image of their world in the lunar mirror would have become steadily darker.

Acknowledgements

The notion that the Beaghmore stone circles may have been laid out to represent a mirrored reflection of the face of the moon comes from Mr Laurence Weir, of Castledawson, County

Londonderry who I met by arrangement at Beaghmore in 1999. After many years of my own moon gazing I finally try to offer some credence to his marvellous lunar theory and thank him for allowing me to expand on it with my apologies for my procrastination. I thank Fergus Niland for his talent in providing me with the illustrations necessary to put forward this most visual of theories and also Bill Thayer at the University of Chicago for his fantastic work on Plutarch (http://penelope.uchicago.edu/Thayer/E/Roman/Texts/Plutarch/ Moralia/The_Face_in_the_Moon*/home.html) and finally to Paul Logue and Tony Corry of the Northern Ireland Historic Monuments Unit for photographs.

Note
1   NISMR- Northern Ireland Sites and Monument Record Site Reference Number

References

Cherniss, H. (1957) (with W. C. Helmbold) *Plutarch's Moralia*, Vol. 12, 43. Loeb Classical Library, Cambridge, Mass., Harvard University Press.

Foley, C. (1983) A stone circle complex at Copney Hill, County Tyrone. *Ulster Journal of Archaeology* 46, 146–8.

Foley, C. and MacDonagh, M. (1998) Copney stone circles: a County Tyrone enigma. *Archaeology Ireland* 12, No. 1 (Spring), 24–8.

Hayes, T. D. (1999) Using astronomy in archaeology with a look at the Beaghmore alignments. *Ulster Journal of Archaeology* 58, 32–42.

McConkey, R. (1987) *Stone circles of Ulster*. Unpublished MA Thesis. Belfast, Queen's University Belfast.

McHardy, I. (2010) *Callanish: monument, moon and mountain*. Scotland, Island Books Trust.

McL. May, A. (1953) Neolithic habitation site, stone circles and alignments at Beaghmore, Co. Tyrone. *Journal of the Royal Society of Antiquaries of Ireland* 83, 174–93.

Murray, M. (2010) *Holding up a mirror to ourselves*, The Irish Times, Dublin. *https://www.irishtimes.com/newspaper/health/2010/1224272508427.html Marie Murray http://www.highbeam.com/doc/1P2-22200065.html [Accessed 2012].*

NASA (2011) http://science.nasa.gov/science-news/science-at-nasa/2011/16mar_supermoon/ [Accessed 2012].

Pilcher, J. R. (1969) Archaeology, palaeoecology and 14C dating of the Beaghmore stone circle site. *Ulster Journal of Archaeology* 32, 73–91.

Ross, H. E. and Plug, C. (2002) *The mystery of the moon illusion*, 180. USA, Oxford University Press.

Schoy, K. (1923) *Uber den Gnomonschatten und die Schattentafeln der Arabischen Astronomie*. Hannover, Hannover H. Lafaire.

Thom, A. S. (1980) The stone rings of Beaghmore: geometry and astronomy. *Ulster Journal of Archaeology* 43, 15–19.

Tilley, C. (1994) *A phenomenology of landscape*. Oxford, Berg.

Von Humboldt, A. (1850) *Kosmos*: Entwurf einer physischen Weltschreibung III, 544. Stuttgart, Gotta.

Wlasuk, P. (2000) *Observing the moon*. In P. Moore (ed.) *Practical Astronomy* Series, 4. London, Springer-Verlag.

11

REFERENCE, REPETITION AND RE-USE: DEFINING 'IDENTITIES' THROUGH CARVED LANDSCAPES IN THE NORTH OF IRELAND

Rebecca Enlander

Introduction

Material culture is not a mute appendage of society: it actively acquires its own biography through social interactions with people. Through time and space these biographies are in a perpetual process of creation and redefinition (Gosden and Marshall 1999). If social identities are fundamentally linked to the physical remnants of material culture, and the biographies of both human and construct are allied through social interactions, then the visual and non-visual consumption of material qualities could be seen as identity forming in itself. With reference to the socially constituted meanings of both object and place, this chapter will explore the rock art tradition in the north of Ireland, and its role in the creation and maintenance of social identity. Rock art sites can dually be classified as material construct and natural place, and so reference to both of these spheres within the culturally constituted world are beneficial when approaching the identity potential of these carved locations.

While it is largely recognised here that, as a human construct, rock art belongs to a stylistic tradition, this belonging neither implies a single, coherent practice through space and time, nor the collective identity of rock art producing societies. Rather, it is the variability encountered within the practice, the recognition of carving events and site use which may reveal social agents and facets of their collective identities. The extensive petrologies encountered across Ireland (see below) ultimately inform the distinct nature of both stone surface and topography at a local level. Therefore, by considering geological variability of rock art localities, the presence of regional rock art 'identities' may be drawn out. Although a variety of rituals may have taken place at these sites, given the lack of site-specific excavation and the ephemeral traces that ritual may leave in the archaeological record, it is stone and the practice of inscribing the rock surface that will be explored here.

Rocky foundations

The carved rock surfaces of Ireland form a branch of a wider art tradition encountered across Atlantic Europe: a broad geographical area frequently defined by an emphasis on (largely coastal) cultural connections. These connections are attested to by the exclusive distribution of passage graves and their associated megalithic or passage grave art, and the tradition of abstract cup-and-ring art during the Neolithic and Early Bronze Age (Bradley 2009; 1997). The rock art tradition draws upon a basic repertoire of largely curvilinear motifs which include cupmarks, and cups surrounded by concentric rings, with the occasional addition of radiating grooves or tails. These motifs may occur in isolation, or form dense clustered or interlinked designs. Additionally, the landscape contexts where many sites are carved *in situ* upon 'living' rock surfaces are broadly similar, with an emphasis on landscape positions which relate to movement and visibility across the wider terrain (Bradley 1997).

A limited number of rock art excavations in Ireland, Britain and Norway also hints at the common use of at least some rock art localities. There are several shared traits which can be demonstrated at a limited number of sites across this extensive region. These comprise the use of quartz in the carving process; comparable remains of clay or stone platforms and boundaries; and the insertion of quartz and other stone debris into natural cracks at rock art panels (see Coles 2005, 97–9; Goldhahn 2008, 18; Jones *et al.* 2011; Jones and O'Connor 2007; O'Connor 2003, and below).

However, at a more localised scale, regional expressions of rock art frequently reference subtle characteristics of their localities. In many ways the individual stone surfaces have sensitively influenced the very motifs carved upon them. Although the importance of distinct, regional scales of carving activity have been explored more recently in northern England (Sharpe 2007), Scotland (Jones *et al.* 2011) and Ireland (O'Connor 2006), serious consideration of local variability and subtleties, in both the setting and form of rock art sites, are lacking (Evans and Dowson 2004, 103; Sharpe 2007, 2). There is a tendency to identify similarities in the material presented in the archaeological record in order to create nationally applicable cultural narratives (drawing on Jones 2011). However, such narratives regularly ignore local variation and impose a common acceptance of cultural and aesthetic values across disparate geographical regions. The external physical attributes of material culture, including visual cues or symbols, are traditionally thought to merely signify shared meanings and organisation of social relations characterising a particular audience (see critique of this approach by *e.g.* Jones 2007; Tilley 2000). Specifically universal ideals or explicit cultural connections are still supported using the stylistic distribution of rock art 'behaviour', while there remains little insight into the cultural context of rock art sites. The results of recent excavations suggest that these sites were far from isolated points in the landscape (Jones *et al.* 2011; Jones and O'Connor 2007; O'Connor 2003).

By no means novel to more general studies of the European Neolithic, the social significance of themes such as experiential qualities of process or materiality of surfaces have not been explored in regards to the open-air rock art localities of northwest Europe (although see Jones *et al.* 2011 regarding the character of carved rock surfaces in Kilmartin, Argyll). By considering the geological variability of rock art localities in the north of Ireland, it is hoped that the presence of discrete regional interactions – perhaps indicative of the assertion of local identities – can be established. Furthermore, the degree to which interaction with stone surfaces in regionally specific ways may be considered as identify forming, both in reference to the social individual and also the rock surface, will be explored. To this end, rock art sites will be approached as both natural places of 'difference' and products of human process, even if these meanings were only ever enforced periodically. The notion of life-biographies, applicable to both object and place, will be explored before variability and the identity potential of several rock art localities in the north of Ireland will be considered in terms of their geological and anthropogenic character.

Stone agents and place

As touched upon, rock art is at once a cultural product and a natural 'living' surface. As an element of the natural landscape, regional manifestations of rock art display sensitivity to both the rock surfaces they inhabit, and the characteristic topographies they dwell in. A range of emotive features concerning place and social memory must have been informative in the selection of rock art localities. Landscape itself may be argued to begin with places, the locations of which may include physically unmodified natural features (or equally features of past human origin). Landscape is then formed through a web of interactions between people and places (Zedeno 2000, 106–8). Equally, the stone surfaces selected in the production of rock art did not necessarily *become* important with the addition of carving (Bradley 1997, 213). Local topography and the particularities of available stone surfaces constitute just two of these defining elements. Díaz-Andreu (2001), for instance, identified distinct geological choices in two rock art regions of the Iberian Peninsula, the selection of which were further synthesised through the depth of landscape ritualization and the role of individuals' identity. So distinct geologies form a layer of ritual focus within this landscape, the depth and identity of which is defined and manipulated through the use of rock art motifs (*ibid.*, 160–7).

In this way, natural spaces are defined through identity-forming events which begin with the inclusion of distinct landscape features into the meaningfully constituted world. Particularly, in regards to rock art localities, these places are frequently characterised by distinctive geologies (see case studies below). The character of space then becomes recognised as part of the observed world. Through repeated interaction with these places, layers of deposited meaning further heighten the perceived importance of place which may be formalised or 'socialised' (Taçon 1994) through the production of rock art. To generalise regarding all elements of the social landscape, we see the gradual development of cultural hubs over time, rather than being predetermined as sacred or ritual (drawing on O'Connor 2006, 245–6; van Dommelen 1999), and so their identities are always in the process of redefinition.

Rock art sites are more than place alone, even if their cultural meaning is recognised only periodically by society: these sites have been physically marked, and thus a convergence of social meanings shrouds them. This is more than simply difference in the perception of space, where the social identity of an audience may affect both recognition and interpretation of socially constituted places. Rather, the production and consumption of both motif and surface allowed social beings to physically inscribe at least an element of their perceived identity upon the landscape. Through site re-use, these carved surfaces became indicators of their own lengthy biographies and testaments of past human interaction.

Stone objects and identity

The recognition that cultural objects obtain dynamic biographies through their explicit link to people, and consequential social interactions has been well attested by Gosden and Marshall (1999). Both human and object then share 'mutual biographies' (*ibid.*, 173) and processes or means of 'value creation' (*ibid.*, 170). Furthermore, such a process ultimately sees 'persons and things com[ing] to mutually constitute each other's identities' (Thomas 1996, 82). A very tangible example of the way objects can collect significance and meaning comes from the *tabua*, or whale's teeth, strung and worn around the neck in Fiji. Darkening with age through successive handling and exchange, 'its many owners become incorporated into the ivory, and the power of successive chiefly owners accumulates within the substance of the tooth' (Gosden and Marshall 1999, 171). So, as a ritualised commodity, their value is based on the longevity of exchange which is indicated through their colouration (despite the fact that through time, these biographies become generalised, as few have 'remembered histories' (*ibid.*, 170–2)). If rock art (like the *tabua*) indexes past human interaction, then interaction with these surfaces allowed the carver to constitute themselves in the present, while resonating deeply with those agents of the past.

However, without the means of exploring those interactions or processes of value which define and redefine an object's meaning, it is difficult to both establish the accumulation of social biographies, and to explore the ways in which material culture may contribute to social knowledge and identity. Given that addressing *in situ* rock art as a cultural object is unsatisfactory, the powerful association between cultural stone and place will be considered in order to further this narrative. Engagement with stone, from source identification and acquisition, to working, use and exchange was bound by social traditions, the knowledge of which was passed down through the generations. Places imbued with a history of stone acquisition or production then form integral elements of the perceived world; such places may have been the subject of social narratives which resonated deeply with ancestral identity in specific communities (Edmonds 1999, 36–41). With reference to megalithic building materials in Western Europe, Scarre (2004a; 2004b) has emphasised the potency and significance of stone prior to its acquisition, incorporation and display in such monuments, whereby meaning associated with place (both local and distant) is embodied in these materials (also see Cooney 2000, 136; Jones 2007, 182). Through engagement with their specific materiality or characteristics, materials are active in their own transformation into material culture. With regards to megaliths, the potency of materials (both visual and tactile qualities) must have been socially mediated, as collaborative action was required to transport and position such stones (Scarre 2004b, 141–2, 151) and so '[human] agents both engage with material culture and are the product of that engagement' (*ibid.*, 141).

The selection of distinctive surfaces or places in the production of rock art suggests that these were points of significance, even veneration in the landscape, which no doubt gradually developed into cultural hubs through time. The physicality of production must have reinforced very personal relationships with place and, through the process of creating rock art at these locations, both material and carver were transformed through this engagement. Specifically, rock art production (as with all such interactions with stone, clay and other materials), must have been a highly tangible undertaking, even a deeply sensory encounter (Ouzman 2001). In light of this convergence of values, the remainder of this chapter will explore the citation of local geologies through the manifestation of rock art in several regions of the north of

Ireland, and consider the reference, repetition, and re-use of sites and motifs as a means of multi-vocal identities being constituted.

Geology as landscape

The diversity of rock types encountered in Ireland's geology reflects the variability of environment and the distinct regions which form the various landscapes of this island. The current scenery has also undergone natural and cultural modification, due to the climatic extremes of the Palaeogene and Quaternary, and millennia of human influence. Ireland's topography is much like a saucer, with its mountainous rim and comparatively flat interior, which is punctuated by infrequent islands of sandstone, and is underlain by Carboniferous limestones and blanketed in more recent peat. From the stark, windswept terrain of County Donegal to the rolling drumlin landscape of Counties Down and Armagh, pierced by the peaks of the Mourne Mountains, Ireland is a land of contrasts (Mitchell *et al.* 2010). By exploring geological variability, as reflected in the surfaces selected in the production of rock art, and by considering both the geological and anthropological character of carved surfaces, it is hoped that regionally specific trends can be established.

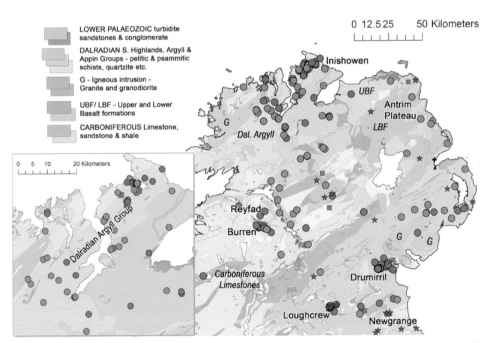

Figure 11.1: General map for the north of Ireland indicating individual rock art and passage grave art localities, plotted onto solid geology 1:500,000 © gsi.ie using ArcMap 10. Legend indicates significant geological formations. Inset map: the Inishowen region where rock art predominantly falls on the Dalradian Argyll Group, most commonly within the Termon Formation. (A colour plate of this figure is at the back of the volume.)

If the distribution of rock art clusters in the north of Ireland is explored in relation to the solid geology of each locality (Figure 11.1), certain preferences can be observed. The main clusters of rock art occur across the Dalradian Argyll and Appin Groups, particularly in areas of outcropping quartzite, schistose psammites and pelitics[1] (Donegal: Doagh Island and Inishowen, and the broad Letterkenny area), and across the area characterised by the Lower Palaeozoic Down-Longford Terrain which is broadly sandstones and shales.

The concentration of rock art sites at the Monaghan/Louth border regions also occur within this broad formation on an open plain to the southwest of the Carlingford Mountains, and south of Slieve Gullion (both topographically conspicuous igneous complexes). Outside of these groups, there are very few rock art sites which employ naturally outcropping stone in the north of Ireland; generally sandstone or psammite erratic boulders and slabs are selected. Another cluster of rock art in the Burren/Marlbanks townlands of the Fermanagh/Cavan border is situated where a broad limestone and shale formation meets the sandstones of Cuilcagh Mountain, close to the Marble Arch Caves. The rock art itself occurs on large erratic sandstone boulders and slabs, often sitting directly on the limestone pavement.[2] For the purposes of this chapter, three distinct clusters of rock art will be discussed (Figure 11.2), including the carved sandstone outcrops of Drumirril, County Monaghan, the distinct metamorphic surfaces of Doagh Island, County Donegal, and the elaborately carved glacial erratics at Reyfad, and its surrounding region, in County Fermanagh. All three localities demonstrate considerable variability in their geologic and topographic choice, preference for stone type and form, and the character of rock art encountered. The exploration of these regional traditions will examine the unity of natural and cultural values, and consider to what extent regionally specific carving practices reflect and maintain social identity.

Local geologies: local identities?

Drumirril

The site of Drumirril, County Monaghan, occupies the land of a former deer park and the localised extent of rock outcrop is essentially limited to these walled grounds, an area comprising around 40 acres. The rock art of Drumirril has recently been examined by the late Blaze O'Connor and, although bedrock distribution and the incorporation of natural features and carved motifs was discussed, the geological character of the surfaces themselves did not form a major part of her work (2006, 91–2). However, the presence of an earthen enclosure, pits and postholes, and possible burning events associated with rock art was demonstrated by her small-scale excavation (see O'Connor 2006; 2003), and suggests that the prehistoric significance of this area extends beyond the production of rock art panels.

The site is dominated by distinct linear ridges typically orientated northeast–southwest and, where visible, surface outcrop is dominated by Silurian sandstone, often exhibiting marked dissolution hollows (which are caused by natural weathering). Many of these natural hollows are striking in appearance due to their distinctly elongated form, while cleavage lines result in block-like units of outcrop. The undulating nature of the land is emphasised by the location of the decorated surfaces, most of which occupy the higher ground, warranting subdued views across the surrounding area.

The motifs employed at Drumirril are characterised by multi-ringed cups which range from the use of single to seven concentric circles. The use of radiating grooves is also

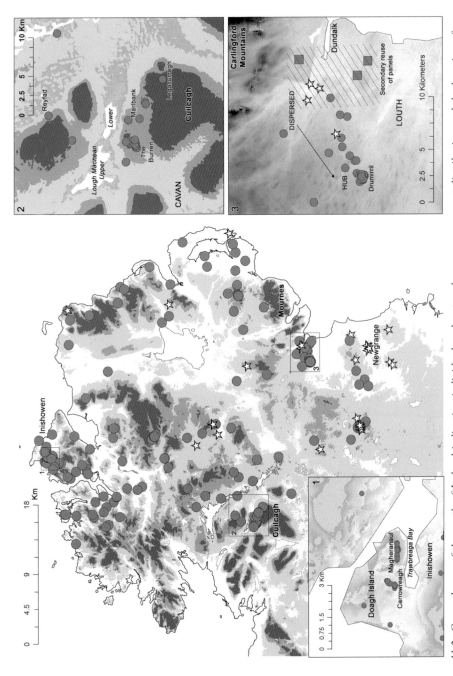

Figure 11.2: General map of the north of Ireland indicating individual rock art and passage grave art distribution and the location of case-study areas referred to in text: 1 – Doagh Island and Inishowen; 2 – the Burren and the wider Fermanagh and Cavan border region; 3 – Drumirril and the wider Dundalk region.

common, and while isolated cups do occur, these always occupy the same surface as other devices, suggesting repeated use of this locality (Nolan 1999; O'Connor 2006). Of the 35 surfaces identified, it was observed that in 33 cases natural features bore some influence on the carving present; this influence most commonly took the form of the incorporation of natural dissolution hollows into carved motifs. Hollows formed central cups in cup-and-ring motifs, and were employed as orbiting cups in several multi-ringed designs. Naturally occurring joints in the rock were transformed into radial grooves or tails with the addition of a cup and enclosing ring (Figure 11.3).

At a regional level, aspects such as topography and particular geological formations played a role in structuring the distribution of rock art. The dense cluster of carvings at Drumirril dwells on the periphery of surrounding rock art panels and constitutes the most complex use of motifs in the region (see Figure 11.2(3)). Furthermore, the site remains relatively hidden due to the undulating topography of the immediate landscape, indicating that it is not just visually prominent locations which are the focus of ritual decoration (Bradley 1997, 119–20; O'Connor 2006, 245–7). Carved motifs frequently respond to the characteristic, naturally occurring hollows and fissures of the rock surface through their placement and design, while the clustering and (infrequent) superimposition of subsequent motifs, demonstrates the longevity of carving events at this site. The significance of place is emphasised both through inscription in the first instance, and explicit reference to the naturally occurring forms through the positioning and appearance of the rock art. As a rock art hub, such carving events and related performances at Drumirril may have been separated by generations, and it is through this repetition of ritual that social identities and notions of belonging are legitimised.

Doagh Island
Doagh Island is a small peninsula at the northern end of Inishowen, County Donegal, which is isolated from the mainland by a narrow sound, Trawbreaga Bay. The rock art on Doagh Island was meticulously recorded by Martin van Hoek (1987) and subsequently analysed by Blaze O'Connor, although as with the Drumirril sites, the geological character of the surfaces themselves did not form a major part of these works (2006, 90). Two large clusters of carved surfaces dominate the southern part of the isle and, although close, each cluster is distinct in its use of outcropping stone and in the motifs employed. The most westerly of these clusters, Carrowreagh, occupies a low-lying landscape dominated by extensive, ice-smoothed outcrops of the Termon Pelites, which all dip gently to the southeast. Despite its low topography, the area warrants good views southwards, across the sound to the mainland and its rugged interior. The carvings employed at Carrowreagh are dominated by cup and disc-marks, with limited use of enclosing rings (frequently single) and radiating tails. As the carved surfaces were smooth, only negligible evidence of the incorporation of natural features was apparent; radial motifs follow the direction of surface slope.[3]

At the site of Magheranaul, the most easterly of these clusters, a total of 64 areas of decorated outcrop occur in a roughly linear arrangement. These surfaces are most frequently flat, heavily fissured outcrops of pelite and schistose pelite, which gently mimic the natural topography of the local terrain and are difficult to pick out from any great distance. As observed at Carrowreagh, the low topography of Magheranaul provides surprising wide views across the sound and to the mountainous mainland beyond, and the southern slope of the

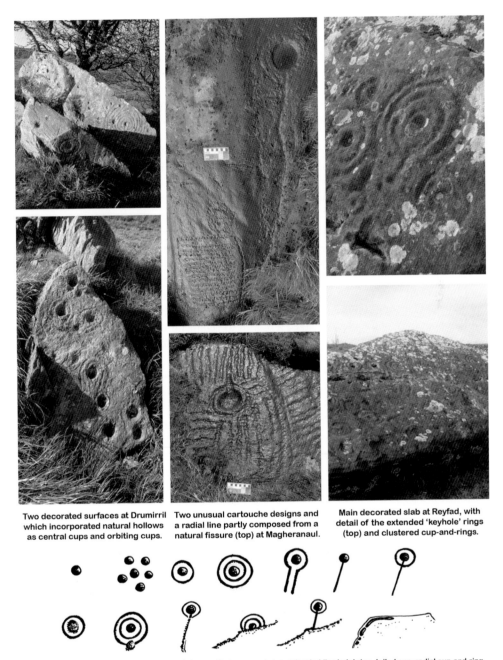

Two decorated surfaces at Drumirril which incorporated natural hollows as central cups and orbiting cups.

Two unusual cartouche designs and a radial line partly composed from a natural fissure (top) at Magheranaul.

Main decorated slab at Reyfad, with detail of the extended 'keyhole' rings (top) and clustered cup-and-rings.

Common motifs: single cup, rosette, cup-and-ring, multiple cup-and-ring, extended 'keyhole' ring, tailed cup, radial cup-and-ring.

Common uses of natural features: natural depression as central cupmark, natural depression as orbiting cupmark, fissure employed as tail, fissure truncates motif, radial motif converges with fissure, lip (edge) enhanced with cups/ gutter.

Figure 11.3: Rock art motifs encountered at the study sites of Drumirril, Magheranaul and Reyfad, and common motifs and incorporation of natural features into designs. (A colour plate of this figure is at the back of the volume.)

landscape affords the outcrops an elevated view of the water. The carvings employed range greatly, from isolated cupmarks and discs to much more elaborate radial, grid and cartouche designs (see Figure 11.3), the latter of which have not been observed at any other site in Ireland (although an association with passage tomb art has been suggested by Bradley (1997, 134) and Johnston (1993, 271–4)). Where the outcrops occur as linear, almost horizontal surfaces, a greater density and variety of motifs can be observed.

A total of 15 sites incorporate natural features, including the incorporation of natural hollows and the use of fissures to truncate, elaborate or divide motifs. The incorporation of natural features is most striking at surfaces which incorporate these cartouche or grid-like motifs. Both smoother and heavily folded surfaces are readily available throughout this landscape, but seem to have been disregarded in favour of fissured surfaces for composing rock art. Natural jointing often acts to frame certain motifs, and the elaborate cartouches and tailed discs which characterise the rock art of Magheranual frequently link to, or incorporate, natural grooves, perhaps in an effort to demarcate or formalise the components of surfaces. Obviously it cannot be assumed that all surfaces were exposed equally during the past, but a selection process of sorts is certainly apparent when surfaces used are considered.

The restricted nature of Doagh Island, essentially a modest parcel of fertile-land removed from Inishowen by a narrow sound, has been interpreted as significant by Bradley (1997, 134) and O'Connor (2006, 247), precisely because of this liminal or 'bounded' quality. While topography undoubtedly played a role in the concentration of carvings, the contrast between these two clusters of rock art is stark, and it is the dissimilarity in geology which may have informed the appearance of these distinct rock art hubs. From the ice-smoothed surfaces employed at Carrowreagh, to the sheet-like surfaces of Magheranaul, geological form certainly informed the use and arrangement of individual motifs and more complex compositions at these localities; imagery was literally drawn-out of these surfaces and accumulated through time. As implied at Drumirril, the repeated use of these sites on Doagh Island and the repetition of distinct motifs which become characteristic of place, serve to legitimise the definition of space and mediate social ideologies. Due to the tentative nature of rock art, it is difficult to establish if Carrowreagh and Magheranaul were in use simultaneously, but the characteristic nature of the rock art implies a separation between these two places.

Reyfad

The final site to be considered is that of Reyfad, County Fermanagh, which occupies an elevated position in the landscape with excellent views across the Lower Erne Basin. The site consists of six large sandstone glacial erratics, of which five bear rather extensive carvings which range from single cupmarks, to multi-ringed cups, extended or keyhole rings, and dished motifs (Figure 11.3). Hard limestones are a notable feature in the landscape, characterised by karst terrain features, including sinkholes and caves. Frequently, sizable sandstone boulders can be seen resting on the limestone pavement, often creating a pedestal effect produced by the differential erosion between the protected limestone under the boulder and that of the wider countryside. This peculiar effect can be observed at Reyfad, where the largest erratic once sat upon such a pedestal but an attempt to split the stone during the 19th century (see Wakeman 1875, 452) has resulted in it slipping forward from its original position. In this respect, the Reyfad stones are comparable with the recently documented rock art on sandstone erratics identified in the Burren and Marlbank areas of the Cavan/ Fermanagh border, a number of which also exhibits limestone pedestals.

The longevity of carving at Reyfad is evidenced by the principal stone, where a jumble of conjoined and superimposed motifs dominates the main surface, while the sides also bear further devices. There is nothing to suggest the deliberate composition of a single design here; rather, the accumulation of repeated figures, which reference both the surfaces' natural form and pre-existing motifs, is indicative of separate carving events. If considered as an element of regional rock art patterns (see Figure 11.2(2)), then the physical topography of the locality serves to delimit the main area of rock art from its southern through to its northern extent. This serves to create a narrow pass accessible from the east between the northern slopes of Cuilcagh, and the southern shore of Lough Macnean Upper and Lower. At the fringe of this entrance is Legacurragh to the southeast and, perhaps mirroring it, is Reyfad to the northeast, while a concentration of carved erratics along the northern slopes of the Cuilcagh Mountains also protected limestone pedestals. Many also exhibit other forms of rock sculpting, including the definition of a lip along the boulders edge (Burns and Nolan 2011; 2007; Gaby Burns and Jim Nolan pers. comm.; Kytmannow *et al.* 2008). It is proposed that the local geological and topographic character of this locality was a drawing point for prehistoric communities in the production of rock art. The performance of creating art acted as a tool in the orchestration and preservation of social ideology while strengthening social affiliations with that specific place, if such a distinction can be made.

Reference, repetition and re-use

The case studies presented here have sought to demonstrate the ways in which humans interacted with stone surfaces in an animated way through the production of rock art in the north of Ireland. From natural jointing to hollows, the utilization, redefinition and formalising of geological features is a recurrent theme. Regionally specific traditions, manifested in surface selection and treatment have also been tentatively explored. As socially mediated place, the landscape of both locality and rock surface itself was interacted with through reference and inscription. Through the development of distinct hubs, complete with characteristic geologies and carved forms, the assertion of local identities could be negotiated. At a collective level at least, the identity potential of rock art can be established through the exploration of often subtle differences in the tradition.

This chapter began by considering the concepts of material culture, place and cultural stone, and the colourful biographies they acquire through their interactions with people: these are worth reconsidering here. Rock art cannot be defined as any one of these concepts alone and site manifestation is defined in regionally specific ways, with variable emphasis on natural topography, geological form and abstract imagery. The incorporation of culturally significant stone into megalithic architecture embodied and redefined potent places in the perceived world. This narrative could be developed in regards to rock art sites, where inscription itself acted as a medium to draw meaning from the natural world, and perhaps even formalising this significance. At its basic level, the rock art motifs encountered were at the very least informed by naturally occurring features on the rock surface; through time, reference to both natural and cultural form was significant in the creation and maintenance of regionally specific traditions. Just like the *tabua* of Fiji, successive interactions were indexed on the rock surface acting as physical indicators of their own biographies. In the absence of historical documentation, individual biographies cannot be explored in any depth, but it is the repetition and re-use of these distinct sites in distinct ways that allows us to come within reach of a tangible identity of the past. Agents imparted an element of their social identity onto the exposed surface of the world, an identity of belonging and perceived-self which constituted themselves in space and time.

Acknowledgements

I am very grateful to the following people for their comments on an earlier version of this chapter: Rebecca Crozier, Victoria Ginn, Dr Caroline Malone, and Dr Alastair Ruffell, and to Ian Enlander for all of his help and advice with all things geological. Thanks are also due to Gaby Burns and Jim Nolan, whose enthusiastic surveying of the Burren and Marlbank over the last decade have led to the discovery of a wealth of prehistoric remains, and who have generously shared their findings with me. My research is kindly supported by the DEL and I would also like to thank all of the organisations who supported our original conference and the publication of this work.

Notes

1 The Dalradian Argyll and Appin Groups of Donegal consist of a range of metamorphic rocks including quartzite (metamorphosed quartz sandstone), psammites (metamorphosed sandstone) and pelite (metamorphosed mudstone and siltstone) which range considerably in colour, texture and surface form. The Lower Palaeozoic Down-Longford formation is characterised by Silurian sandstones and shales of coarse to fine bedding. O'Connor points out that rock art sites in the Monaghan/ Louth border region consistently fall on turbidite sandstone (formally referred to as greywacke), and this stone's role in the construction of the Boyne Valley Passage tombs (2006, 91; also Cooney 2000). The passage grave cemetery of Loughcrew and surrounding open-air rock art sites also fall within an envelope of this bedrock type.

2 The Burren and Marlbank townlands are characterised by Carboniferous limestone bedrock. Superficial (primarily glacial) deposits are of particular interest as many non-limestone erratics, especially large sandstone boulders seem to have been incorporated into a variety of monuments (see Kytmannow *et al.* 2008), and form the focus of rock art and other modification in the region.

3 The Carrowreagh and Magheranaul sites, Donegal have been variously documented (Lacy 1983; O'Connor 2006; van Hoek 1987) and several of the surfaces detailed have now been lost or destroyed. During the course of this research, only 20 of the possible 34 surfaces at Carrowreagh could be accounted for, while all of the proposed 64 surfaces at Magheranaul remain accessible or have been well documented (surface must have had a full description and/or drawing or photograph, or have been identified in the field by the present author to be considered in this research).

References

Bradley, R. (1997) *Rock art and the prehistory of Atlantic Europe: signing the land.* London, Routledge.

Bradley, R. (2009) Image *and audience: rethinking prehistoric art.* Oxford, Oxford University Press.

Burns, G. and Nolan, J. (2007) Prehistoric rock art in the Burren / Marlbank area. *Archaeology Ireland* 21 (2), 26–30.

Burns, G. and Nolan, J. (2011) *Burren – Marlbank modified boulder monuments and rock sculptings.* Unpublished report.

Coles, J. (2005) *Shadows of a northern past: rock carvings of Bohuslän and Østfold*. Oxford, Oxbow.

Cooney, G. (2000) *Landscapes of Neolithic Ireland*. London, Routledge.

Díaz-Andreu, M. (2001) Marking the landscape: Iberian post-Palaeolithic art, identities and the sacred. In G. Nash and C. Chippindale (eds) *European landscapes of rock-art*, 158–75. London, Routledge.

Edmonds, M. (1999) *Ancestral geographies of the Neolithic: landscape, monuments and memory*. London, Routledge.

Evans, E. and Dowson, T. A. (2004) Rock art, identity and death in the Early Bronze Age of Ireland and Britain. In V. Cummings and C. Fowler (eds) *The Neolithic of the Irish Sea: materiality and traditions of practice*, 103–12. Oxford, Oxbow.

Goldhahn, J. (2008) Rock art studies in northernmost Europe, 2000-2004. In P. G. Bahn, N. Franklin and M. Strecker (eds) *Rock art studies: news of the world III*, 16–36. Oxford, Oxbow.

Gosden, C. and Marshall, Y. (1999) The cultural biography of objects. *World Archaeology* 31(2), 169–78.

Johnston, S. (1993) The relationship between prehistoric Irish rock art and Irish passage tomb art. *Oxford Journal of Archaeology* 12(3), 257–79.

Jones, A. (2007) *Memory and material culture*. Cambridge, Cambridge University Press.

Jones, A. (2011) Regionality in prehistory: some thoughts from the periphery. In A. Jones and G. Kirkham (eds) *Beyond the core: reflections on regionality in prehistory*, 1–4. Oxford, Oxbow.

Jones, A. and O'Connor, B. (2007) Excavating art: recent excavations at the rock art sites at Torbhlaren, near Kilmartin, Mid-Argyll, Scotland. *PAST* 57, 1–3.

Jones, A., Freedman, D., O'Connor, B., Lamdin-Whymark, H., Tipping, R., and Watson, A. (eds) (2011) *An animate landscape: rock art and the prehistory of Kilmartin, Argyll, Scotland*. Oxford, Windgather Press, Oxbow.

Kytmannow, T., Mens, E., Kerdivel, G., and Gunn, J (2008) *'Creating sacred and secular spaces': a study of the glacial erratics and early human settlement in the Cavan Burren landscape*. Unpublished report for Cavan County Council.

Lacy, B. (1983) *Archaeological survey of County Donegal*. Lifford, Donegal County Council.

Mitchell, I., Cooper, M., McKeever, P., and McConnell, B. (2010) *The classic geology of the north of Ireland*. Belfast, Geological Survey of Northern Ireland.

Nolan, M. L. (1999) *North Atlantic rock art: a study of the Louth/ Monaghan region*. Unpublished MA Thesis. Cork, University College Cork, School of Archaeology.

O'Connor, B. (2003) Recent excavations in a rock art landscape. *Archaeology Ireland* 17(4), 14–6.

O'Connor, B. (2006) *Inscribed landscapes: contextualising prehistoric rock art in Ireland*. Unpublished PhD Thesis. Dublin, University College Dublin, School of Archaeology.

Ouzman, S. (2001) Seeing is deceiving: rock art and the non-visual. *World Archaeology* 32(2), 237–56.

Scarre, C. (2004a) Choosing stones, remembering places: geology and intention in the megalithic monuments of Western Europe. In N. Boivin and M. Owoc (eds) *Soils, stones and symbols: cultural perceptions of the mineral world*. 187–202. London, University College London Press.

Scarre, C. (2004b) Displaying the stones: the materiality of 'megalithic' monuments. In E. DeMarrais, C. Gosden and C. Renfrew (eds) *Rethinking materiality: the engagement of mind with the material world*, 141–52. Cambridge, Cambridge University Press.

Sharpe, K. (2007) *Motifs, monuments and mountains: prehistoric rock art in the Cumbrian landscape*. Unpublished PhD Thesis. Durham, Durham University.

Taçon, P. (1994) Socialising landscapes: the long-term implications of signs, symbols and marks on the land. *Archaeology in Oceania* 29, 117–29.

Thomas, J. (1996) *Time, culture and identity*. London, Routledge.

Tilley, C. (2000) Interpreting material culture. In J. Thomas (ed.) *Interpretive archaeology: a reader*, 418–26. London, Leicester University Press.

van Dommelen, P. (1999) Exploring everyday places and cosmologies. In W. Ashmore and B. Knapp (eds) *Archaeologies of landscape: contemporary perspectives*, 277–85. Oxford, Blackwell.

van Hoek, M. (1987) The prehistoric rock art of County Donegal (part 1). *Ulster Journal of Archaeology* 18, 11–32.

Wakeman. W. F. (1875) On certain markings on rocks, pillar-stones and other monuments, observed chiefly in the County Fermanagh. *The Journal of the Royal Historical and Archaeological Association of Ireland* 3(23), 445–74.

Zedeno, M. N. (2000) On what people make of places: a behavioural cartography. In M. B. Schiffer (ed.) *Social theory in archaeology*, 97–111. Salt Lake City, University of Utah Press.

'THINK TANKS' IN PREHISTORY: PROBLEM SOLVING AND SUBJECTIVITY AT NÄMFORSEN, NORTHERN SWEDEN

Mark Sapwell

Introduction

Many places embody multiple identities and tangles of differing ideas and experiences. People of dissimilar traditions or expectations may understand a place in contrasting ways. The subjectivity of understanding a landscape has been afforded rich anthropological and archaeological attention, in exploring the interrelations of prejudice, habit (Tilley 1997) and bodily experience (Hamilakis and Tarlow 2002) when engaging with the world. While understanding the identity of any place necessarily involves subjectivities of experience, in some cases subjectivity itself constitutes the identity of place. These are locations where the meeting and mixing of ambitions and objectives form a major part of its understood status. A modern example used in this chapter is the think tank, which describes both a place and community set with a task to solve problems and to develop new ideas and solutions. In the case of the think tank, the mixing of perspectives and the working out of ideas is primary to its identity. The content of this problem solving is secondary to the act of discussion itself in forming its character. Highlighting places which specifically involved the mixing and working out of ideas has important consequences for archaeology. In modern examples, think tanks are commonly loci for the development of new ideas, which may ultimately motivate social change. If similar types of place were present in prehistory, they would serve as windows into how new experiences of the world were realised in the past and contributed to changes in social knowledge.

This chapter examines the rock art palimpsest of Nämforsen in northern Sweden and argues how this landscape may be understood as a place where ideas were worked out, shared and evaluated. In examining how rock art motifs are added over time and how these trends of addition change, it is possible to trace shifts in attitude towards particular images and ideas. By linking these shifts back into the wider landscape and to other forms of material culture, this chapter ends by inferring how ideas developing at Nämforsen are involved in wider cultural trajectories of northernmost Europe from the fifth to the second millennium BC.

Nämforsen: a think tank in the present

The Nämforsen rock art palimpsest is named after a series of rapids flowing between a small collection of islands in the Ångerman River in Ångermanland, Sweden (Figure 12.1). It includes outcrops of gneiss granite rock on two islands (Brådön and Notön) and the surrounding shoreline (Laxön and southern shore). Within an area of c. 2500m^2 there are presently recorded over 2100 carvings (Larsson and Broström 2011; Larsson and Engelmark 2005), which were pecked into the rock. The corpus of motif types is relatively strict, and include predominantly elk (34%), boats (17%), anthropomorphic (4%), footsoles (2%), and fish (1%) images, though most are nonfigurative lines and shapes (42%)[1]. This range of imagery is also common on other rock art sites in northern Sweden, such as Stornorrfors in Västerbotten and Fångsjön in Jämtland. However, among the 55 examples of rock art landscapes in northern Sweden, Nämforsen is peculiar in that it contains almost 39 times more motifs than the next largest rock art landscape (*e.g.* Stornorrfors at c. 54 figures), and 260 times more than the average rock art landscape in northern Sweden (c. 7–8 figures). From a combination of land uplift chronologies, stylistic analysis and surrounding archaeology, the Nämforsen rock art palimpsest has been dated from c. 4200 BC, with the youngest carvings dated to c. 1800 BC (Baudou 1993; Forsberg 1993).

Nämforsen has been widely interpreted and each approach possessed its own focus, theoretical motivation and lifespan. The tangles of its research history provide a template for examining the subjectivities of the rock art landscape in prehistory. The Nämforsen rock art palimpsest was first introduced to the archaeological community in the mid-19th century by N. J. Ekdal and later Karl Sidenbladh. It was originally comprehensively documented by Gustaf Hallström from 1934, culminating in his 1960 publication which remains a

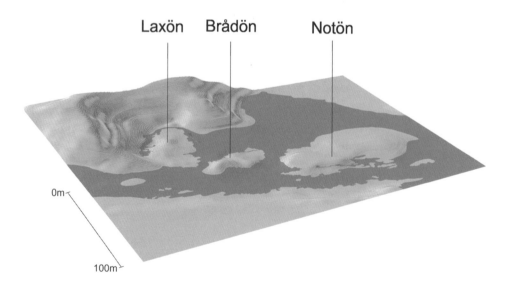

Figure 12.1: Map of Ångermanälven River with Nämforsen islands: Laxön, Brådön and Notön (after Hallström 1960).

foundation in rock art research today. Inspired by James Frazer (1993 [1922]) and Gutorm Gjessing (1936; 1932), Hallström suggested the Nämforsen carvings were involved in sympathetic hunting magic, where fortune or control may be achieved through the creation of a prey's image. Hunting magic lost favour in rock art research from the 1980s, but is being readdressed more recently (Goldhahn 2008; Huggert 1996) in connection with animic and shamanic models (Bolin 2000; Guther 2009).

From the 1970s to 1990s, interpretations increasingly focused on Nämforsen's connection to the south Scandinavian Bronze Age. Mats Malmer (1981, 97; 1975, 44) argues that many of the images were derivations of the Bronze Age rock art tradition in southern Sweden, such as those at Bohuslän and Skåne. In contrast, Baudou (1989, 29) and Forsberg (1990, 195) argue that, based on land uplift chronologies, the carvings of northern Sweden pre-date those in south Scandinavia and therefore likely comprised an autochthonic northern tradition. This argument contributed to a wider debate involving the distinctiveness and complexity of prehistoric arctic communities.

In 1991, Christopher Tilley's *Material Culture and Text* brought Nämforsen into the wider discussion of the role of linguistics in archaeological interpretation. Inspired by de Saussure (1983) and Lévi-Strauss (1969; 1963), Tilley's post-structural approach interpreted the motifs as constituting rules of opposition which expressed differences between social groups. In an effort to assign content to the images, Tilley drew on ethnographic parallels with the Siberian Evenki to relate the use of imagery and the landscape to shamanic practice. During this time of postprocessual debate in Britain, Nämforsen became a platform for demonstrating both the possibilities and failings of a linguistic approach. While its use was important to the postprocessual debate, its extent was generally limited to the theoretical community. In less theoretically focused research, Tilley's affect was less felt. For example, Christian Lindqvist's (1999; 1994) studies on the distribution of images at Nämforsen barely references linguistic approaches.

Later interpretations re-emphasized ethnographic parallels, partly in an attempt to address the failings of a post-structural method in exploring the content of an image. These often focused on strengthening the shamanic associations of Nämforsen (Bolin 2000; 1999; Lahelma 2007). This emphasis was accompanied by nuanced approaches to landscape, such as considerations of multi-sensory experiences, introduced to Nämforsen by Joakim Goldhahn (2002). In the mid-2000s there was a renewed interest in contextualising Nämforsen further into surrounding material culture. This can be noted from new excavation projects (George 2005), Lindqvist's (2000) zoo-osteological study, Per Ramqvist's (2002) large-scale analyses of rock art and settlement in Sweden, and later Jenny Käck's (2009) comprehensive thesis of the 'Switchgear' settlement material. This theme continues into the most recent research which emphasizes the relationship between landscape and art (Gjerde 2010) and shared associations between rock art and other forms of practice (Sjöstrand 2010a; 2010b).

The narrative of research outlined above helps illustrate how, since its first documentation, Nämforsen has been deeply involved in the mixing and interchange of ideas. Some concepts drift in and out of research fashions (*e.g.* hunting magic), and some endure across the majority of its research lifetime (*e.g.* land uplift chronologies). Some new developments are widely known and referenced (*e.g.* new excavation and survey material) while others are relevant only to a limited community (*e.g.* postprocessual interpretations). Not only is the understanding of Nämforsen highly subjective, but there also occur periods of its research where discussion and testing of ideas become more important than the content of Nämforsen itself. The clearest example is its role in the postprocessual debate, where it became an important platform for evaluating linguistic models. To describe present-day Nämforsen therefore involves a complex story of mixing and interchanging interpretations, covering varying scales, influential extents and emphases, and fluid shifts of its status between research object and discursive forum. The remainder of this chapter asks whether a similar situation was present at Nämforsen during its use in prehistory. More specifically, it asks whether at times the Nämforsen landscape could be considered a place where discussion and the exchange of ideas was a primary part of its identity as place.

Affordances of the Nämforsen landscape and its role in exchange

Before exploring how Nämforsen enabled the development and evaluation of ideas, it is important to first examine how this rock art landscape was likely involved in the meeting and exchange of differing traditions. The location of Nämforsen in the northern Sweden landscape affords an important role in communication between communities. Baudou (1993) and Malmer (1975, 43), and more recently Gjerde (2010, 358) note that from *c.* 4500–4000 BC, the Baltic coast reached far closer to Nämforsen and comprised a fjord between the sea and the upland river systems. During the Neolithic, these rivers would have been heavily used as a method of transportation (Janson and Hvarfner 1966, 42), and Nämforsen would have been located at an important node of these water networks, between the sea and the Ångerman River and its tributaries. Importantly, the Nämforsen rapids would have obstructed a journey through this river system. When meeting this part of the river, the traveller would have had to pick up his or her boat, and carry it by land, and so actively engage with this landscape. Like a prehistoric toll booth, the impeding rapids would have broken up the tacit habit of river travel and motivated specific attention and action in the journey. By nature of its position between the sea and upland rivers, and its rapids, the Nämforsen region afforded an important role in the use of the rivers and in travel between regions.

The affordances inferred from the Nämforsen landscape may be supported further by examining the archaeological material of this small region. Nämforsen holds one of the largest occupation sites in northern Sweden: the Ställverkboplatsen, or 'Switchgear' settlement consisting of over 1400 lithics of many varieties and 6kg of various types of ceramic. The settlement does not contain house impressions as is typical of other parts of northern Sweden (Lundberg 1997; 1985), and was probably occupied only partially through the year. The sheer size of this settlement has led many researchers (Baudou 1993, Gjerde 2010; Janson and Hvarfner 1996) to suggest Nämforsen as a place where people gathered in large numbers. The scale, timing and reason for this aggregation differs between studies. Forsberg (1993) and Ramqvist (2002; 1992) argue that Nämforsen was largely visited for its salmon that spawned in the summer season. Lindqvist (1999), Hagen (1976) and Goldhahn (2010, 2002) all focus on its role as a place of communal activity and exchange. Throughout its long lifetime, it is likely that Nämforsen was the subject of multiple occupations throughout the year (Käck 2009) and was used in differing ways. Importantly, the overall consensus is that through both its position in the landscape and its surrounding material culture, Nämforsen and its rock art were closely involved in the seasonal movement and gathering of people.

Nämforsen was not only involved in the meeting of people but also in exchange. This activity may be inferred from the lithics at the 'Switchgear' settlement, especially 700 examples of worked slate. From the fifth to the second millennium BC, northern Scandinavia was involved in an intense exchange network of slate. Similar forms of slate points and arrowheads are found in northern Sweden, Norway, Finnmark and Finland, and connect these regions from the very beginning of the Neolithic (Bakka 1974). Slate is first used regularly in the Late Mesolithic, but its production intensifies from *c.* 4000 BC in the form of blades and arrowheads. Across northern Scandinavia, slate objects are distributed unevenly, and tend to cluster at particular sites, such as Överveda in Ångermanland (Baudou and Selinge 1977). The exchange of slate is therefore grounded on the distribution between exchange or production centres. As Nämforsen involves one of the largest collections of slate objects in northern Sweden (Käck 2009, 60–2), Baudou (1992) describes the rock art landscape as one of these centres, and as being heavily involved in this complex and extensive network of slate exchange.

Goldhahn (2010, 2002) similarly assigns Nämforsen a powerful role in exchange, particularly in the movement of red slate; a material largely specific to the Caledonian mountain range along the Nordingrå area in Ångermanland[2]. Objects of this slate type are found as far afield as coastal Finland, and Uppland in south east Sweden. Both Goldhahn and Jacqueline Taffinder (1998) describe red slate as an important exchange object in Scandinavia. In both local and foreign contexts, its exchange draws value through the material's traceability to its unique origin. In containing over 50 examples of this material, Nämforsen was involved in this specific form of exchange which involved an emphasis on locality and origin.

The discussion has so far gathered current research in framing Nämforsen as a distinctive place of cross-communication in northernmost Europe. In a world where river travel was prevalent, Nämforsen would have acted as a cataract or toll booth in communication networks that required the traveller to take notice and actively engage in this particular landscape. Its large 'Switchgear' settlement site demonstrates that Nämforsen was visited repeatedly and by many people throughout its lifetime. Finally, the large amount of slate recovered within this settlement strongly connects Nämforsen to an intense and extensive exchange network that was characteristic of northern Scandinavia from *c.* 4000 BC. Even before its famous rock art is examined, Nämforsen may already be described as a significant location for meeting, communication and exchange. The final section of this chapter explores how, within this setting of aggregation and exchange, Nämforsen may have served as a place where ideas were tested and developed. To address this possibility, the discussion turns to the rock art.

The art of accumulation: Nämforsen as think tank in the past

One of the most distinctive aspects of Nämforsen is the sheer number of rock art motifs it contains. Considering the large number of motifs and the large date ranges of its associated settlement site (*c.* 4200 to the Iron Age), it is reasonable to suppose that the motifs at Nämforsen were added over time. The rock art that is seen today is therefore the result of repeated acts of image making: a long-term, open-ended project performed by many people over a long period of time. The importance of accumulation in rock art has been noted in research throughout the world (Taçon and Chippendale 2008, 74), and has been reiterated recently for Nämforsen (Sjöstrand 2010c). If rock art was produced over time at Nämforsen, the accumulation of images came about through a sequence of artists that reacted to each other's work. An artist would contribute images to the rock, having been affected by the carvings that already exist and attracted to those he or she felt were most appropriate for addition. Through this process of continual addition and accumulation, the rock art at Nämforsen is far from static (Jordan 2004), but traces long-term dialogues between people over time.

To unpick the rock art dialogues, an ideal method is to date each motif separately and trace trends of image making through time. However, when examining rock carvings, it is very difficult to directly date the sequences of accumulation. A widely used chronological method in Scandinavia is to date a rock carving by noting when a receding waterline first made the rock itself accessible to carve (Forsberg 1993; Sognnes 2003). This has generated dated sequences of rock art clusters at Nämforsen where rock art of higher elevations are considered generally earlier than those of lower elevations. While a useful guideline, the focus of the land uplift method on the rock and not the image, and its low resolution, make it difficult to date separate motifs within a cluster (Ling 2004, 134). This study therefore relies on this method only in comparing clusters and regions of the landscape.

The *c*. 2100 motifs at Nämforsen are arranged in localised clusters across the rock landscape. The size of these clusters range from singular images to groups of over 400 motifs. While it is difficult to know the exact sequence of image making, we may accept that the larger rock art clusters involved denser or more extensive work and a traceably greater degree of attention in the past. For example, the rock art cluster Lillforshällan is one of the largest rock art clusters at Laxön in Nämforsen, and, therefore, may be seen to represent a far more extensive or intensive degree of dialogue between artists. The image makers regarded it appropriate to add to this panel and not to other areas. In contrast, areas of Nämforsen with only one or two images may represent artistic events that did not encourage further contribution. While the larger carving clusters involved qualities that inspired addition and continued attention, the smaller involved qualities that dissuaded further action.

Describing the Nämforsen rock art palimpsest in terms of selective accumulation enables the questioning of how particular images and ideas may have inspired continued attention and addition more than others. Importantly, by examining how particular images move in and out of these clusters through time, it may be possible to trace how ideas move in and out of attention and extended dialogue. The following sections of this chapter offer cases in exploring this approach. First, a contrast between two types of motif of very different clustering trends is suggested. Then, by seeing how these trends change across the Nämforsen landscape, the discussion offers a narrative where a particular way of thinking changes its status in rock art practice.

Traditions of repetition and experimentation

A key aspect of the following case study works on the assumption that larger clusters are more likely to have involved continued or intense attention and artistic dialogue in the past. This argument assumes that images which are more often involved in larger clusters reflect more substantial acts of accumulation and dialogue and that these clusters would have likely been more consistently relevant to people in the past. The study below examines which

Figure 12.2: Photograph of elk figures of the silhouette/scooped style, which cluster together, and with other types of motif. Scooped elks are more likely to cluster than any other motif. This image is from Lillforshällan, Laxön, Nämforsen. Accompanied by a 3D reconstruction of the Lillforshällan panel. (A colour plate of this figure is at the back of the volume.)

images are most likely to be involved in larger clusters and continued accumulative acts, and whether these trends seem to differ across the landscape.

To measure and compare the degree of clustering between types of motif, 875 motifs[3] were tested from Laxön, Nämforsen, using Geographic Information System (GIS) modelling and spatial statistics. Using the ArcMap10 '*Near Distance*' tool, a matrix was generated which recorded the Euclidean distance between each motif. These distances (totalling *c.* 882,000) were classed according to the types of motif involved (*e.g.* distance from Elk to Human) and summarised into various averages for comparison. By comparing these it is possible to gauge general likelihoods for how far particular types of motif occur from another.

The spatial tests highlight that a particular type of elk motif, the scooped (*uthuggna*) or silhouetted elk (Figure 12.2) is far more likely to be involved in rock art clusters than any other type of image. Compared to other types of motif, scooped elk figures are on average situated closer to other rock art figures by up to 1m (Figure 12.3). They are far less likely to be seen in isolated groups and more in larger rock art clusters. As well as the most likely to cluster with other images, the scooped elk motif is one of the most standardized images at Nämforsen. Compared to the other styles of elk, or the boat or fish motif, the scooped elk demonstrates the most regular size, shape and proportion. As an image, the scooped elk's distinctive aesthetic is grounded in non-variance. This standardization would have been best realised when seeing a number of these motifs at once, so repetition of the scooped elk motif may be seen as closely associated with its character of regularity. As forming parts of the scooped elk's unique aesthetic, regularity and non-variance would have been bound in the motifs tendency to inspire continued attention and artistic addition.

In contrast to the regular, repetitive and compositionally engaged scooped elk, one of the most isolated motifs at Laxön are unusual images, or figurative motifs that cannot be placed into a specific motif category (*e.g.* boat and elk). These often involve either the deformation of a common motif (*e.g.* unusual additions to elk figures), or the hybridisation of common motifs (*e.g.* the merging of elk and human, or human and fish in Figure 12.4). Generally, unusual figures like these are, on mean average, 2–3m further from other figures than elk, boats and humans. These unusual motifs are either entirely unique or very rare within Nämforsen, and

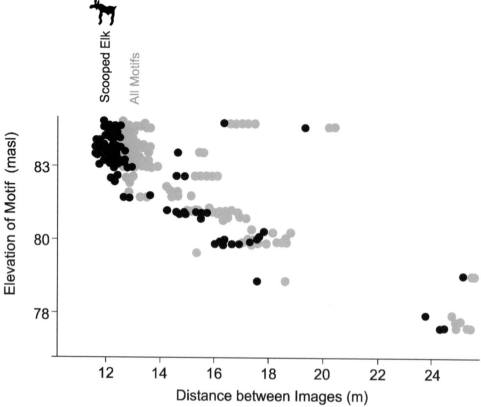

Figure 12.3: Graph plotting average proximity of scooped elks to other motifs, compared to the average motif. Each point represents a separate motif. The leftward shift of the scooped elks demonstrates that this type of motif is generally more clustered than other motifs.

this contrasts dramatically with the scooped elk tradition of repetition. As rare occasions of abnormal mixing of categories, many of the unusual motifs appear to be experimental in nature: a mixing of subjects that was tried and not repeated. This experimentation is not as involved in continued attention and addition at Nämforsen as other motif types. The contrast is very interesting as it demonstrates two very different ways of treating images at Laxön. Here, there is a distinct distancing between standardised action which warrants continued attention and response, and more experimental attitudes of mixing and warping common images, which rarely inspire further addition and continued dialogue.

Past interpretations of the warped and hybridised images tend to associate artistic acts of merging with forms of shamanic practice. For example, Antti Lahelma (2007, 119) suggests that two examples of elk images at Laxön with boats merging into their antlers (Laxön, F1:1 and Figure 12.4), refer to a general sense of co-essence between elk, human, and his or her mode of travel. This interpretation is drawn from Saami accounts of the *noaidi*, or shamanic personage who, by attaining trance, works to merge with and transform into particular animal guides. For Lahelma, depictions of merging imagery are an interesting

*Figure 12.4: Examples of unusual, experimental motifs at Laxön, Nämforsen. a) human-elk 'centaur'
on DX, b) human-fish 'mermaid' hybrid on DX, c) boat merging into antlers of elk on F1. These motifs
are often more isolated than other types of motif, though this alters across elevation. (A colour plate
of this figure is at the back of the volume.)*

allusion to more contemporary accounts of shamanic trance, which may have existed in
some form also in prehistory. While this is an interesting approach which makes use of the
rich ethnography available in northernmost Europe, it is important to ensure that pressing
a shamanic interpretation does not overlook other possibilities for the act of hybridisation.
For example, Dušan Borić (2007) and Aperecida Vilaça (2005) suggest that, more generally,
hybridisation is often involved in both questioning and maintaining categories between
subjects. This may be involved in shamanic practice, or may instead be totally removed from
any institutionalised achievement of trance. While the possibility of shamanic practice at
Nämforsen is not rejected here, it is safer to stop short at Borić and Vilaça's association, that

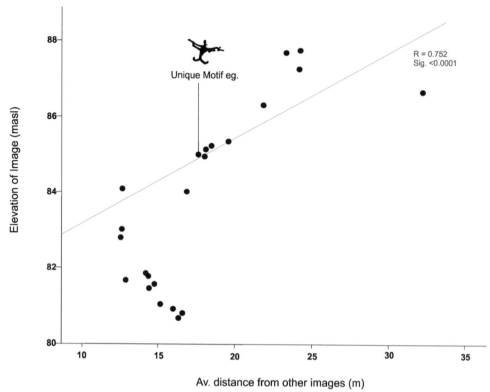

Figure 12.5: Graph plotting the average proximity between unusual motifs and all other motifs, against elevation. Each point represents a separate motif. The positive gradient demonstrates that as the elevation of the motif increases, it generally becomes more isolated.

hybridisation involves an active negotiation and maintenance of held categories. The unusual warped and merging motifs found at Laxön may be described in this way, as experiments which test the capacity for particular subjects and categories to co-blend.

The story of the 'experimental motif' becomes still more compelling when its proximity to other images is compared across the Nämforsen landscape. Generally, when the rock art occurs at lower elevations, the unusual motifs become less isolated and creep closer to other images. This correlation may be seen when the rock motifs are plotted on a graph comparing its average proximity to its elevation (Figure 12.5). The significance of this pattern depends greatly on what meaning is assigned to elevation. If a land uplift chronology is followed, then this change by elevation represents a changing trend through time. In earlier periods of Nämforsen (*c.* 4200 BC) acts of experimentation with categories appears to have been distinctively separated from continued dialogues of image making. Instead, more standardised images inspired addition and continued attention. However, as time passed (*c.* 4200–4000 BC), the unusual elaboration and merging of categories became increasingly relevant, and more integrated into intensive or extensive dialogue through images.

A similar pattern is seen in the use of boat imagery at Laxön. While boat motifs may be divided into many styles and categories (Kaul 1998; Lindqvist 1984), a very general

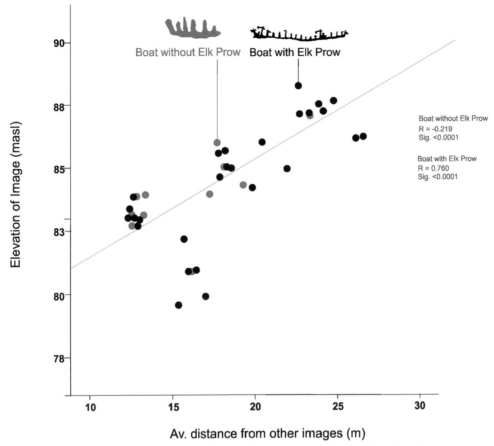

Figure 12.6: Graph plotting the average minimum distance between boat motifs with elk prows against elevation. This is compared to the average minimum distance between boat motifs without elk prows. Each point represents a separate motif. The graph shows that while boats with elk prows demonstrate a correlation between elevation and proximity, boats without elk prows do not.

distinction at Nämforsen are those with elk head prows, and those without. Those with elk prows tend to be either of double lined style or single lined with a thick triangular bow, similar to those at Zalavruga in western Russia. Boat motifs without elk headed prows tend to comprise a single line, often with long crewstrokes. Generally, boats without elk heads tend to be more isolated from other images than those with elk heads, though the variation of this trend is very high. What is interesting here is that, as the elevation of the rock surfaces decrease, boat motifs with elk head prows tend to become more integrated into rock art clusters, in a similar way as unusual motifs. Boats without elk prows do not increase or decrease their proximity to other motifs with elevation (Figure 12.6). If elevation is linked to chronology, this shows that opinions towards the elk prow become increasingly integrated into more continued and repeated practices, while those boat motifs without elk prows seem unchanged.

The elk prow represents a particular form of merging between categories: between the elk and the boat. This specific format of merging is relatively common at Laxön, and would seem to be a more agreed way that the elk and boat categories meet and combine. The boat without elk head is also often involved in merging, though often in irregular ways, such as merging with elk antlers, or with nonfigurative lines. It would seem that during *c.* 4000 BC, consensus favoured one way of understanding how the boat connects with other categories over another.

The timing of these two changes (integration of experimenting with categories and integration of the elk headed prow) closely parallel a period in northern Scandinavia when the slate exchange network is beginning to gain momentum. The increasing intensity of slate exchange between regions of Norway and northern Sweden would have opened up regions to newly discovered communities with presumably differing traditions and ways of experiencing the world. As the contacts became more prominent with the increasing use and exchange of slate objects, it would have been advantageous to become more open to new ways of thinking about the world, and to integrate unusual ways of conceptualising categories into more everyday, and popular practices.

As new lines of contact were established between Finland, Norway, and northern and southern Sweden, the role of the rivers would have become increasingly important and associated with the act of travel and communication. If again land uplift chronology is followed, from *c.* 4100 BC, the rock art at Laxön marks a generally increasing consideration of the role between elk and boat. The elk prow becomes more incorporated into continued discussion while attention to other concepts of merging boat categories remains unchanged. The gradual incorporation of the elk prow into more extended dialogue through rock art may refer to an attempt to combine new increasing emphases on water travel with more traditional attitudes of the elk. The rock art here therefore becomes involved in working through the relationships between particular artistic traditions.

Conclusions

The two rock art stories above demonstrate that through following how images differentially belong to patterns of addition, particular ideas are seen to move in and out of focus in prehistoric rock carving practice. At Laxön, the making of rock art was entangled in the formation of new attitudes towards the combination of categories. This involved changing and increasing attention towards unusual or experimental merging and a developing convergence between the boat and elk. The rock art imagery traced these shifting attitudes. Positioned in a key node for meeting and exchange in the landscape, the imagery enabled people to trace for themselves the development of new ideas. A key identity of the Nämforsen rock art palimpsest is therefore its 'think tank' character, in enabling the converging of traditions and developing of ideas.

Many questions remain open in considering the 'think tank' status of Nämforsen. First, the study above focuses on the act of adding images as inferences of continuing attention and activity. However, continued attention may have also occurred around images without any material act of adding images. For example, Hauptman Wahlgren (2000) suggests that the southern Scandinavian, Bronze Age rock carvings are occasionally re-carved and renewed as a means of re-instigating attention to a rock surface. This form of continued activity differs from the kind presented above; by emphasizing single images, the artist does not interact with the surface as a whole, or the motifs placement within larger image clusters. While it is suggested that the act of accumulation was a powerful technique at Nämforsen, it would be beneficial in further research to explore whether renewal of images was undertaken also at this rock art palimpsest, and to compare the two techniques. Also, the narratives of shifting attitudes outlined above draw from the land uplift theory that rock art at higher elevations tend to be of an earlier date. While past and present research solidifies this theory by using cross-comparisons with stylistic and compositional chronologies (Forsberg 1993; Sapwell forthcoming), we should also consider models which assign different associations to elevation, such as the importance of varying distances from the river shoreline, or the movement of the rapids (Ramqvist 2002).

Finally, it is important to iterate that interpretations which emphasize acts of testing and developing ideas at Nämforsen do not exclude other possible activities within the rock art landscape. For example, the importance of recreating landscapes in the rock art (Gjerde 2010), or communicating with ancestors (Bolin 2010; 2000) may have also been important to the occupiers of Nämforsen. Rather, by exploring how the art is composed through the landscape, this chapter has argued that Nämforsen was likely involved in *multiple* associations. At least at Laxön and involving the subject of merging categories, any singular or universal interpretation is best understood within a framework that acknowledges Nämforsen as a place for the meeting and development of different traditions, as a prehistoric think tank.

Acknowledgements

This chapter draws from part of a PhD thesis funded by the Cambridge Domestic Research Scholarship and St. John's Learning and Research fund. My thanks to Liliana Janik for her enthusiasm and support, to Sheila Kohring for her ideas, and to attendees of the Europa Postgraduate Conference 2012 for their suggestions. Also, my sincere thanks to Rebecca Enlander, Victoria Ginn and Rebecca Crozier for inviting me to contribute this chapter.

Notes

1   These percentages are inferred from Larsson and Broström's 2003–2005 re-survey of Nämforsen, published in 2011.

2   Sources of red slate were originally thought to occur only in Ångermanland, such as Tåsjö and Storbäck (Becker 1952) This led a number of archaeologists to automatically source any lithics of red slate to this northern Swedish region. Red slate is, however, also known in parts of Lappland, northern Norway and Finnmark. Magnusson *et al.* (1963) also mention the presence of small deposits in Småland in middle Sweden.

3   In the compositional test, a motif was defined in two ways. First, a motif was considered as any artificial disturbance on the rock, which included all nonfigurative shapes. Second, a motif was considered as any image that was iconically identifiable, which meant dividing carvings into smaller singular motifs. Within Laxön, this generated the number of 875 motifs.

152   *Mark Sapwell*

References

Bakka, E. (1974) *Geologically dated rock carvings at Hammer near Steinkjaer in Nord-Trøndelag*. Bergen, Universitet i Bergen.
Baudou, E. (1989) *Stability and long term changes in north Swedish prehistory and example of centre-periphery relations*. British Archaeological Report. Oxford, Archaeopress.
Baudou, E. (1992) Boplatsen vid Nämforsen. *Arkeologi i Norr* 3, 71–82.
Baudou, E. (1993) Hallristingarna vid Namforsen, datering och kultumiljo. In L. Forsberg, T. B. Larsson, (eds) *Ekonomi och Näringsformer i Nordisk Bronsålder: Rapport från det 6: e Nordiska Bronsålderssymposiet, Nämforsen 1990*, 247–61. Umeå, Studia Archaeologica Universitatis Umensis.
Baudou, E. and Selinge, K. G. (1977) *Västernorrlands Förhistoria*. Motala, Borgströms Tryckeri AB.
Becker, C. J. (1952) 'Die nordschwedischen Flintedepots', *Acta Archaeologica* XXIII, 37–79.
Bolin, H. (1999) Crossroads of culture: Aspects of the social and cultural setting in northern Sweden during the last two millennia BC. In H. Bolin (ed.) *Kultur-landskapets korsvägar: Mellersta Norrland under de två sista årtusendena f Kr*, 97–138. Stockholm, Stockholm Studies in Archaeology.
Bolin, H. (2000) Animal magic: the mythological significance of elks, boats and humans in north Swedish rock art. *Journal of Material Culture* 5, 153–76.
Bolin, H. (2010) The re-generation of mythical messages: rock art and storytelling in northern Fennoscandia. *Fennoscandia Archaeologica* XXVII, 21–34.
Borić, D. (2007) Images of animality: hybrid bodies and memesis in early prehistory. In C. Renfrew and I. Morley (eds) *Material beginnings: a global prehistory of figurative representation*, 89–105. Cambridge, The McDonald Institute for Archaeological Research.
Forsberg, L. (1990) De Norrländskam hällristningarnas sociala kontext: Alternativa tolkningar. *Arkeologi i Norr* 2, 55–70.
Forsberg, L. (1993) En Kronologisk analys av ristningarna vid Nämforsen. In L. Forsberg, T. Larsson (eds) *Ekonomi och Näringsformer i Nordisk Bronsålder: Rapport från det 6: e Nordiska Bronsålderssymposiet, Nämforsen 1990*, 175–246. Umeå, Studia Archaeologica Universitatis Umensis.
Frazer, J. (1993) [1922] *The golden bough*. Ware, Wordsworth Editions Ltd.
George, O. (2005) *Rapport 2005: 4. Arkeologisk Kursundersökning av Raä 158 Ådals-Lidens sn. Boplats och Lämningar Från Stenålder-historisk Tid*. Länsmuseet Västernorrland.
Gjerde, J. M. (2010) *Rock art and landscapes: studies of Stone Age rock art from northern Fennoscandia*. Department of Archaeology and Social Anthropology. Tromsø, University of Tromsø.
Gjessing, G. (1932) *Artiske Helleristninger i Nord-Norge*. Oslo, Aschehoug.
Gjessing, G. (1936) *Nordenfjelske Ristninger of Malinger av den Artiske Gruppe*. Aschehoug, Oslo.
Goldhahn, J. (2002) Roaring rocks: an audio-visual perspective on hunter-gatherer engravings in northern Sweden and Scandinavia. *Norwegian Archaeological Review* 35, 29–61.
Goldhahn, J. (2008) Rock art studies in northernmost Europe, 2000–2004. In P. Bahn, N. Franklin, M. Strecker (eds) *Rock art studies, News of the World III*, 16–32. Oxford, Oxbow Books.
Goldhahn, J. (2010) Emplacement and the hau of rock art. In J. Goldhahn, I., Fuglestvedt, A., Jones (eds) *Changing pictures: rock art traditions and visions in northern Europe*, 106–127. Oxford,, Oxbow Books.
Guther, H. (2009) Problem med Schamanistiska Tolkningar av de Nordfennoskandiska Hällbilderna. *Fornvännen* 104, 18–32.
Hagen, A. (1976) Begkunst: Jegerfolkets helleristninger og malninger i norsk steinalder. Oslo, Cappelen.
Hallström, G. (1960) *Monumental art of northern Sweden from the Stone Age: Nämforsen and other Localities*. Stockholm, Almqvist & Wiksell.
Hamilakis, Y. and Tarlow, S. (2002) *Thinking through the body: archaeologies of corporeality*. New York, Kluwer Academic Plenum Publishers.
Hauptman Wahgren, K. (2000) The lonesome sailing ship: reflections on rock-carvings of Sweden and their interpreters. *Cambridge Archaeology Journal* 8, 67–96.
Huggert, A. (1996) Human, fish and snake engravings on an animal headed dagger from Torvsjön, Åsele, Northern Sweden. *PACT* 51, 441–56.
Janson, S. and Hvarfner, H. (1966) *Ancient hunters and settlements in the mountains of Sweden*. Stockholm, Riksantikvarieämbete.

Jordan, P. (2004) Examining the role of agency in hunter gatherer cultural transmission. In A. Gardner (ed.) *Agency uncovered: archaeological perspectives on social agency, power and being human*, 107–34. London, UCL Press.

Käck, J. (2009) *Samlingsboplatser? En diskussion om människors möten i norr 7000 f Kr - Kr f med särskild utgångspunkt i data från Ställverksboplatsen vid Nämforsen*. Umeå, Umeå University.

Kaul, F. (1998) *Ships on bronzes: a study in Bronze Age religion and iconography*. Publications from the National Museum Studies in Archaeology and History, Copenhagen.

Lahelma, A. (2007) 'On the back of a blue elk': recent ethnohistorical sources and 'ambiguous' stone age rock art at Pyhänpää, Central Finland. *Norwegian Archaeological Review* 40, 113–37.

Larsson, T. and Broström, S. G. (2011) *The rock art of Nämforsen, Sweden: the survey 2001–2003*. Umeå, Umark.

Larsson, T. and Engelmark, R. (2005) Nämforsens ristningar är nu fler än tvåtusen. *Populär Arkeologi* 4, 12–3.

Lévi-Strauss, C. (1963) *Structural anthropology*. Indiana, Basic Books.

Lévi-Strauss, C. (1969) *The elementary structures of kinship*. Boston, Beacon Press.

Lindqvist, C. (1984) *Arktiska hällristningsbåtar och den marina anpassningen*. Meddelanden från Marinarkeologiska Sällskapet 2.

Lindqvist, C. (1994) *Fångstfolkets Bilder: En studie av de nordfennoskandiska kustanknutna jägarhällristningarna*. Stockholm, Institutionen för arkeologi och antikens kultur.

Lindqvist, C. (1999) *Nämforsenristningarna: En återspegling av jägarnas liv och världsbild*. Tidsspår, 105–36.

Lindqvist, C. (2000) *Osteologisk analys och tolkning av Faunamaterialet från utgrävningarna vid Nämforsen*. Raä nr. 158, Näsåker 12;1, Ådalsliden sn., Ångermanland åren 1996–97. Nämforsenprojektet 2000.

Ling, J. (2004) Beyond transgressive lands and forgotten seas: towards a maritime understanding of rock art in Bohuslän. *Current Swedish Archaeology* 12, 121–40.

Lundberg, Å. (1985) "Villages" in the inland of Northern Sweden 5000 years ago. In E. Baudou and M. Backe (eds) *Archaeology and environment*, 293–301. Umeå.

Lundberg, Å. (1997) *Vinterbyar- ett bandsamhälles territorier i Norrlands inland 4500–2500 f.Kr.* Umeå.

Magnusson, N. H., Lundqvist, G., and Regnéll, G. (1963) *Sveriges Geologi*, Stockholm.

Malmer, M. (1975) The rock carvings at Nämforsen, Ångermanland, Sweden, as a problem of maritime adaption and circumpolar interrelations. In W. Fitzhugh (ed.) *Prehistoric maritime adaption of the circumpolar zone*, 42–9. Paris, Mouton Publishers.

Malmer, M. (1981) *A chronological study of north European art*. Stockholm, Almqvist & Wiskell Internation.

Ramqvist, P. (2002) Rock-art and settlement: issues of spatial order in the prehistoric rock-art of Fenno-Scandinavia. In G. Nash and C. Chippendale (eds) *European landscape of rock-art*, 144–57. London, Routledge.

Ramqvist, P. H. (1992) Hällbilder som utgångspunkt vid tolkningar av jägarsamhället. *Arkeologi i Norr* 3, 31–54.

Sapwell, M. (forthcoming) *Thinking through pictures: the role of rock art palimpsests in forming knowledge in northernmost Europe, Division of Archaeology*. Cambridge, University of Cambridge.

Saussure, de, F. (1983) *Course in general linguistics*. London, Duckworth.

Sjöstrand, Y. (2010a) Raka eller böjda ben? Om variation bland älgarna på Nämforsen hällristningar. *Fornvännen* 105, 9–18.

Sjöstrand, Y. (2010b) 'Should I stay or should I go?': on the meaning of variations among mobile and stable elk motifs at Nämforsen, Sweden. In J. Goldhahn, I., Fuglestvedt, and A. Jones (eds) *Changing pictures: rock art traditions and visions in northern Europe*, 139–53. Oxford, Oxbow Books.

Sjöstrand, Y. (2010c) Product or production: on the accumulative aspect of rock art at Nämforsen, northern Sweden. *Current Swedish Archaeology* 18, 251–69.

Sognnes, K. (2003) On shoreline dating of rock art. *Acta Archaeologica* 74, 189–209.

Taçon, P. and Chippendale, C. (2008) Changing places: ten thousand years of north Australian rock-art transformation. In D. Papagianni, R., Layton, and H. Maschner (eds) *Time and change: archaeological and anthropological perspectives on the long term in hunter-gatherer societies*, 73–94. Oxford, Oxbow Books.

Taffinder, J. (1998) *The allure of the exotic: the social use of non-local raw materials during the Stone Age in Sweden*. Uppsala, Uppsala University Press.

Tilley, C. (1991) *Material culture and text: the art of ambiguity*. London and New York, Routledge.
Tilley, C. (1997) *A phenomenology of landscape: places, path and monuments*. London, Berg.
Vilaça, A. (2005) Chronically unstable bodies: reflections on Amazonian corporalities. *Journal of Royal Anthropological Institute* 11, 445–64.

13

GOING THROUGH THE MOTIONS: USING PHENOMENOLOGY AND THREE DIMENSIONAL MODELLING TO EXPLORE IDENTITY AT KNOWTH, COUNTY MEATH, DURING THE MIDDLE NEOLITHIC

Eimear Meegan

Introduction

Today, the concept of identity as both fluid and relative almost goes without saying within the study of prehistory. Long gone are the somewhat one-dimensional interpretations of prehistoric identity as a rigid set of cultural habits and norms acquired at birth (Shanks and Tilley 1987, 29). Instead, people in prehistory are now generally regarded as having been actively involved in the formation of their own personhood, which was both multifaceted and a lifelong work-in-progress (Shanks and Tilley 1992). This approach, in recognising the entanglement of endless threads of social and cultural life, has sought to populate the past with a cacophony of voices and perspectives (Shanks and Tilley 1987). While it has certainly brought a greater depth to our understanding of prehistoric societies, adding shades of light and dark to the pictures we paint, it has also brought a fresh challenge: how do we ensure that we allow these different voices to be heard, and avoid simply putting words in their mouths?

Reflexivity is essential in this respect, as a means of bringing the inherent bias of our interpretations to the surface, and allowing us to recognise the echoes of our own experience (Hodder 2000; 1997; 1982). Nevertheless, while an awareness of the impact of the present on the interpretation of the past is paramount, there is also the equally important task of adopting a complimentary set of principles, which serve to create conditions whereby past voices can indeed be heard. It is argued here that such principles are perhaps to be found in phenomenological philosophy. Furthermore, three-dimensional modelling techniques have much to offer in terms of applying these principles to the analysis of the material record in a way that is transparent and open to enquiry. To illustrate this approach, this short chapter will focus on Middle Neolithic (*c.* 3200–2600 BC) passage tomb construction at Knowth, County Meath (Eogan 1984), where at least 20 smaller tombs surround the grandiose Site

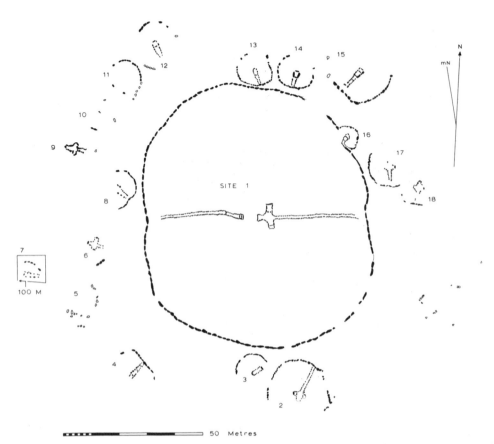

Figure 13.1: The ground plan from Knowth (after Eogan 1984, 14). Sites 19 and 20 are not represented here as they were identified after this survey had been completed.

1, which contains two tombs back to back (Figure 13.1). Before making a case for its interpretive potential and the role three-dimensional modelling might play within this, a brief overview of the fundamentals of phenomenological reasoning will first be explored.

Cogito ergo sum?

Phenomenology emerged very much as a reaction to the subject/object dichotomy of Cartesian worldview. At its heart is the fact that we are always already in the world. We cannot reduce ourselves to mere cerebral existence as Descartes' 'I think therefore I am' suggests. Rather, our thoughts and actions are anchored firmly within the body, which is both spatially and temporally located within the world. Phenomenological theory argues, therefore, that it is only by engaging with this bodily encounter with the world that we can gain insight into the nature of existence (Husserl 1970[1900], 252; Sartre 1969[1943], 351). Given this foregrounding of material engagement, it is hardly surprising that this philosophical framework has proven popular with some of those working within post-processual landscape archaeology. This appropriation has been characterised by the use of contemporary bodily experience to shed light on past experiences of prehistoric landscapes, an approach first applied by Chris Tilley (2008; 2004; 1994) but which initially gained a wealth of followers (Brophy 1999; Cummings 2002; Frazer 1998; Watson 2001). Its popularity was relatively short lived though, as the methodological cracks inherent in the use of the body in this way were duly noted (Brück 2005; 1998; Fleming 1999), and serious doubts were expressed regarding the compatibility of phenomenology and archaeology.

However, a re-reading of the primary philosophical texts suggests that Tilley's methodology is perhaps based on a misinterpretation of phenomenological principles. The potential value of phenomenology lies not in the mistaken support it was thought to lend the use of the body to recreate past experience, but in its exploration of the way in which people's understanding of their own existence, and the possibilities of that existence, arises out of a *pre-reflective reciprocal* exchange between their physical form and their material surroundings (Merleau-Ponty 2004[1945], xi). It is this interpretation that offers the possibility of exploring the emergence of identity through the material exchanges embodied by material culture. Using three-dimensional modelling to work through such exchanges further offers the possibility of engaging with this co-constitutive discourse in a way that privileges process over product, in an environment in which the overall flow of this process can be recognised and demonstrated. Putting this theory into practice at Knowth, the overriding aim is thus not to produce a photorealistic prehistoric world into which people in the present day can simply enter in order to simulate past experience, but to use the modelling process as a means of thinking through the various exchanges between the tomb builders and the materials they used.

The real in the virtual

The tombs at Knowth, as in the rest of the Boyne Valley, were built predominantly from greywacke (Corcoran and Sevastopulo forthcoming), a local, poorly sorted sandstone the likely source of which is between 10km and 16km away, in an area that stretches from Piperstown to Clogherhead, County Louth (*ibid.*). Though some of these stones appear to have been loose, most of the greywacke from Knowth seems to have been quarried from bedrock (*ibid.*). Once removed from the parent outcrop, the stones are thought to have been strapped to the underside of a raft or a log boat, and brought by sea to the mouth of the River Boyne. From here, they would then have been sailed along the Boyne, and dragged up the steep river terraces to the site (*ibid.*), where they were probably raised into position using a combination of wooden leavers and cairn material for support.

The approach advocated here is one that draws and builds on extensive research that has explored the methods of extraction and transportation of specific stone types used by the tomb builders, and both the architectural and engineering devices employed (Corcoran and Sevastopulo forthcoming; Eogan 1986). Although this research has provided a backdrop of rigorous data, it fails to provide any meaningful insight into what it was like to live through the construction process, and how this may have shaped those builders' understanding of their world. Though, as argued above, the modelling process might be used to help fill this gap, it must be informed by the more practical research described for any significant

Figure 13.2: The so-called Guradian Stone from the western passage of Site 1.

contribution to be achieved. To this end, the models produced as part of this project have been largely created using the extensive plans, elevations and drawings made during the excavation of the site. Additional free-hand sculpting and texturing of the finer details of the megaliths was also done using photographs taken in the field as a guide (Figures 13.2–13.3). This latter work of course involves a far greater degree of interpretation but, as previously explained, the purpose of modelling the passage tombs is not to produce the most 'realistic' models possible; rather, these models are intended to aid exploration of the interweaving of materials throughout the construction process.

Bodies of flesh and stone

Bringing the evidence for these often compartmentalised aspects of construction together within a single, three-dimensional space, has allowed the various strands of data to be considered not merely as discreet categories, but as materialities that flow into, and make sense of each other. As the form, texture and decoration of each of the stones at Knowth gradually emerged in three dimensions, the very intense nature of the contact that would have existed between the builders and the stone they were encountering became increasingly apparent. From beginning to end, there would have been a constant friction between the bodies of the builders and the body of the stone they were extracting, moving, shaping and decorating; just as the stone's physical form bears the effects of this, so too must the bodies of the builders. If this friction is considered in the context of phenomenological philosophy, and in particular the reciprocal discourse between people and materials that is described by Merleau-Ponty, it could perhaps be seen as a communion of flesh and stone, a choreographed performance in which they become locked together in a kind of embrace, melding into a

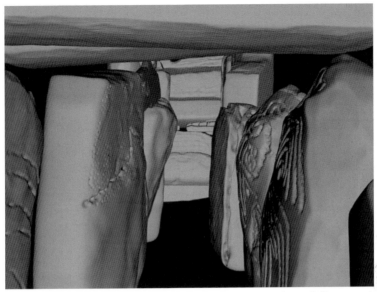

Figure 13.3: A view down the modelled western passageway into the undifferentiated chamber.

single form (MacFadyen 2006, 127 for a discussion on the blurring of material boundaries). If we then consider, the fact that most of the megaliths in question were quarried from bedrock – the very core of the landscape – it is perhaps possible that through the construction of the tombs at Knowth, the builders came to embody their environment, at least in part. This would have made for a strongly rooted and widely shared local identity. Furthermore, working at such close quarters for such prolonged periods of time, the builders are likely to have been almost as in tune with the movements and rhythms of each other's bodies as they were with their own, perhaps to the extent that they may have considered each other as extensions of themselves. As well as tying the builders to the landscape therefore, the construction process may well have worked to bind them to each other, reinforcing even further their sense of community and belonging.

Conclusion

The use of three-dimensional models is by no means new or innovative within archaeological research. In the past though, when modelling has been used, the emphasis has tended to fall heavily on the finished product, with little attention being paid to the actual modelling stage, other than in relation to technical execution. By turning this approach on its head, and focusing instead on the processes involved, it is possible to use three-dimensional techniques to work through material exchanges in a very visceral way which, informed by a re-conceptualisation of phenomenological reasoning as exploring the material reciprocity of subject and object can be used to explore how identities emerged and how voices were made in prehistory.

Acknowledgements

Many thanks to my supervisor Professor Gabriel Cooney and to Dr Joanna Brück for their comments, and to Professor George Eogan and Dr Kerri Cleary for access to the Knowth archive. My research is kindly supported by the University College Dublin John Hume Institute for Global Irish Studies.

References

Brophy, K. (1999) Seeing the cursus as a symbolic river. *British Archaeology* 44, 6–7.
Brück, J. (1998) In the footsteps of the ancestors: a review of Christopher Tilley's 'A Phenomenology of Landscape'. *Archaeological Review from Cambridge* 15, 23–36.
Brück, J. (2005) Experiencing the past? The development of a phenomenological archaeology in British prehistory. *Archaeological Dialogues* 12, 45–72.
Corcoran, M. and Sevastopulo, G. (forthcoming) The provenance of the stones used in construction and decoration of the passage tomb at Knowth. In G. Eogan (ed.) *Excavations at Knowth 6: The Archaeology of the large passage tomb at Knowth, Co. Meath*. Dublin, Royal Irish Academy.
Cummings, V. (2002) Between mountains and sea: a reconsideration of the Neolithic monument of south-west Scotland. *Proceedings of the Prehistoric Society* 68, 1254–6.
Eogan, G. (1984) *Excavations at Knowth 1*. Dublin, Royal Irish Academy.
Eogan, G. (1986) *Knowth and the passage tombs of Ireland*. London, Thames and Hudson.
Fleming, A. (1999) Phenomenology and the megaliths of Wales: a dreaming too far. *Oxford Journal of Archaeology* 18, 119–25.
Fraser, S. M. (1998) The public forum and the space between. The materiality of social strategy in the Irish Neolithic. *Proceedings of the Prehistoric Society* 64, 203–24.
Hodder, I. (1982) *The present past: an introduction to anthropology for archaeologists*. London, B.T. Batsford.
Hodder, I. (1997) Always momentary, fluid and flexible: towards a reflexive excavation methodology. *Antiquity* 71, 691–700.
Hodder, I. (ed.) (2000) *Towards reflexive method in archaeology: the example at Çatalhöyük*. Cambridge, McDonald Institute for Archaeological Research and British Institute of Archaeology at Ankara.
Husserl, E. (1970[1900]) *Logical investigations*. Translated by J. N. Findlay. New York, Humanities Press.
MacFadyen, L. (2006) Building technologies, quick architecture and Early Neolithic long barrow sites in southern Britain. *Archaeological Review from Cambridge*, 117–34.
Merleau-Ponty, M. (2004[1945]) *A phenomenology of perception*. London & New York, Routledge.
Sartre, J. P. (1969[1943]) *Being and nothingness*. Translated by Hazel E. Barnes. London, Methuen.
Shanks, M. and Tilley, C. (1987) *Social theory and archaeology*. Cambridge, Polity Press.
Shanks, M. and Tilley, C. (1992) *Re-constructing archaeology. Theory and practice*. London and New York, Routledge.
Tilley, C. (1994) *A phenomenology of landscape*. Oxford, Berg.
Tilley, C. (2004) *The materiality of stone: explorations in landscape phenomenology*. Oxford Berg.
Tilley, C. (2008) *Body and image: explorations in landscape phenomenology* 2. California Left Coast Press.
Watson, A. (2001) Composing Avebury. *World Archaeology* 33, 296–314.

Our construct or theirs?

Introduction

Audrey Horning

If archaeologists agree on anything about the slippery concept of identity, it is that identity is seldom fixed. Individuals and groups can possess multiple, often situational identities that at times may be defined by circumstances of birth, gender, race, ethnicity, class, religion, political affiliation, occupation, economic and social status, prestige, age, health, physical condition, and even geographical location. Identity is dynamic, multifaceted, and easily misunderstood or simplified by observers, be they contemporaries or archaeologists gazing back through the centuries. The chapters in this section, by Cătălin Nicolae Popa and Nicole Taylor, directly address this dilemma: how do we discuss and understand the complexities of past identities without imposing our modern constructs of identity upon a malleable, if at times unwilling, past?

This is no mere esoteric or academic debate. As Popa makes abundantly clear in considering the contemporary construction of Dacian identity in relation to Romanian nationalist politics, who 'they' were is central to who 'we' are. Romania, of course, is hardly anomalous in framing archaeology through the lens of nationalism. There is no nation that does not, one way or another, employ the past to understand and explain the present. Does this render archaeology impotent or irrelevant when it comes to telling us something about past human experiences? Of course not. But if we are to ever critically appreciate and analyse the legacy of existing understandings about archaeology, we must recognise the context of the production of those archaeologies and take seriously our own ethical position.

Since the early antiquarian inquiries of the 15th century, archaeological remains have been used to support nationalist claims. While Renaissance scholars used antiquities to provide classical precedents for political change for a more secular society, the Tudor elite employed their understandings of the process of Romanisation in Britain to construct the colonial ideologies that justified expansion into Ireland and the Americas. Similarly, the 19th-century emergence of western imperial nationalism was closely linked with the excavation of major sites of the classical world. In the midst of this activity emerged the nation of Romania in 1881, consciously setting out to anchor itself in the pre-Roman pasts of its new territory.

Romanian identity then and now, as explained by Popa, rests upon the belief in an historical process of ethnogenesis that combined the best elements of indigenous, or 'Dacian', society with that of the invading Romans in the first centuries AD. Iron Age archaeological assemblages have long been employed and implicated in the construction of a seemingly uniform and materially bounded Dacian identity. But would the Late Iron Age inhabitants of the region between the Danube and the Balkans ever have conceived of themselves as part of any sort of heroic Dacian proto-nation as envisioned in the present? Popa thinks not, but rightly worries about the implications of an outright rejection of a narrative that is central to contemporary social and political cohesion.

Arguably, seeking unity in the present through re-imagining the past is not always an insidious process. Strategic essentialism, as defined by Gayatri Spivak, has been empowering for many indigenous groups seeking to reclaim their histories and identities. So is it inherently bad to emphasise a heroic Dacian past if it fosters cohesion today? Or do our responsibilities lie more with the people of the past, whom we have elected through our role as archaeologists to represent without consultation? On the other hand, if challenges to simplistic constructions of the past open scholars up to personal risk in the present through opposing powerful political elites, is it not understandable for scholars to avoid the issue entirely and to seek, in Popa's words, the 'safety of positivist research'?

Taylor approaches the issues of positionality from a rather different angle, noting the paradox between the intimacies of osteoarchaeological examination of individual bodily remains with the impossibility of ever knowing the person that once animated those remains. Taylor is fully cognizant that we cannot assume that what it means to be a woman, child, or man in our society today necessarily bears any relation to the experience of people in the past, nor even that such socially meaningful categories in our society had the same, or indeed, any meaning in the past. Rather she calls for a more honest awareness of our own understandings of identity and attitudes towards death, and advocates employing those perspectives towards humanising the past.

In studying Late Bronze Age mortuary behaviour, Taylor aligns herself with scholars like Sarah Tarlow who have reminded archaeologists that emotion is core to human life and cannot be left out of archaeological interpretation. Such a reminder should never have been necessary. To deny past people the ability to feel sadness and grief as well as joy and anger is as much a challenge to our own humanity as it constitutes a denial of theirs. Just because we can never escape our own subjectivities does not mean that we cannot seek meaning from and in the past through the judicious employment of our own understandings and experiences even if we can do no more than widen the range of interpretative possibilities.

While addressing the fraught relationship between past and present in relation to the archaeological study of identity in very different ways, both authors fundamentally agree that understanding our own positionality and the manner in which our research may be received and [mis]understood is core to furthering the archaeological study of identity. Like Taylor, we may choose to embrace the interpretive power of our own subjectivities. Alternatively, we may share Popa's unease over the disconnect between politically expedient conceptions of archaeological identities and the actual ambiguities of what we conventionally term the archaeological record. Either way, past and present cannot be easily disentangled. And perhaps they should not be.

THE TROWEL AS CHISEL: SHAPING MODERN ROMANIAN IDENTITY THROUGH THE IRON AGE

Cătălin Nicolae Popa

Introduction

The idea that the past is actively constructed in the present is no longer a novelty. Archaeologists like Hodder (1986) and others (Miller and Tilley 1984; Shanks and Tilley 1987a) have pointed out all too clearly that our own subjectivity, social context, and experience come into play to a great extent during archaeological interpretation. This chapter will illustrate how the lack of understanding and acknowledgement of these important factors can lead to the manipulation of archaeological results and determine a fundamental shift in the identity of an entire nation.

Romania is a modern country located in southeastern Europe which, despite its important variation in geographical forms, presents a remarkable cultural and linguistic unity. It is thought that an explanation of this phenomenon lies in the common ancestry of the population. This can be expressed through the genealogical equation: Dacians + Romans = Romanians. This chapter will focus on the Dacian component, investigating what it stands for, the processes that led to its integration in the Romanian ethnogenesis[1], and the role played by archaeology and politics in this operation.

Who were the Dacians?

Archaeologists employ the terms Dacians, Getai and Geto-Dacians when dealing with the population that inhabited the modern territory of Romania in the period dated between the middle of the 1st millennium BC to AD 106 after which the land was incorporated into the Roman Empire. The labels Getai and Dacians were first used by Latin and Greek writers, respectively, when referring to some of the indigenous people of the Middle Danube and the river mouth. Romanian archaeologists have taken more or less for granted that they designated the same population and have joined them together to create the modern name Geto-Dacians.[2] In academic publications all three terms are employed and there is no generalised rule for when a scholar uses Geto-Dacian, Getai or Dacian (Dana and Matei-Popescu 2006, 203–4). Nevertheless, if one considers the geographical spread, it is possible to observe that overall the term Dacian is preferred to refer to the Late Iron Age finds coming from within the Carpathian Arch (*e.g.* Berciu and Popa 1971; Florea *et al.* 2000; Gheorghiu 2005; Glodariu 1989; Macrea and Glodariu 1976), while Getai is usually utilised when speaking about those coming from the south and east of the mountains (*e.g.* Sîrbu 1996).[3] Geto-Dacians can be employed in any of the two situations and remains the most widely used name, thus emphasising the ethnical unity of the Late Iron Age people (*e.g.* Babeş 1999; Babeş 1979; Căpitanu & Ursachi 1972; Ciugudean and Ciugudean 1993; Gostar and Lica 1984; Măndescu 2006; Pescaru and Ferencz 2004; Preda 1986). As for the non-academic publications, the three terms seem to be interchangeable and all of them are used on a large scale, although the name Dacians seems to be especially popular (Crainicu 2009; Oltean 2008; Petan 2007).

Discovering the Dacians

The construct of the Geto-Dacians can be traced back to the 19th century and its birth was parallel to, and partly motivated by, the emergence of the modern Romanian state, with political events reverberating in archaeological research (Table 14.1). The first steps in the

Table 14.1: The main political and archaeological (Late Iron Age) events in Romania between 1850 and 1944.

Romania – political events	Romanian archaeology
1859 Wallachia and Moldova unite in one state	
1866 a prince of German origin is brought to the throne of the new country which gets the name of Romania	
	1874 Alexandru Odobescu introduces the first course of archaeology at the University of Bucharest
	1877 Tocilescu finishes his monumental work *Dacia before the Romans*
1877–1878 Romania joins a Russian-Turkish war to obtain its independence; recognized in 1881	
	1913 *Prehistoric Dacia* of Densuşianu is published after his death
1916 Romania joins World War I against its ally Austro-Hungary because of the claims to Transylvania and Bucovina	
1918 Greater Romania (*Romania Mare*) is formed (the maximum expansion of the modern state	
	1924 *Dacia* journal is established
	1926 Pârvan publishes *Getica*
1944 the communists comes to power after the loss of important territories	
	after 1944 Romanian archaeological discourse becomes invaded with Marxist terms ; nationalist inferences are suppressed

formation of the country were made in 1859 when the provinces of Moldavia and Wallachia were united under one prince, Alexandru Ioan Cuza. In 1866, a new prince was brought to the throne, Carol I Hohenzollern-Sigmaringen, coming from a noble family closely related to the Prussian king. The new state was only released from Turkish suzerainty (*i.e.* gained independence) in 1881, following the war of 1877–1878 when Romania found itself allied with Russia against the Ottoman Empire (Hitchins 1992). In archaeology this was parallel with the introduction of the first archaeology course at the newly formed University of Bucharest and the publication of Grigore Tocilescu's monographic work *Dacia înainte de Romani* (*Dacia before the Romans*) (Tocilescu 1877).[4] In the time that followed until the First World War, Romania consolidated itself internally and searched for opportunities to lay claim to the adjacent territories inhabited by Romanians. This process already had a major impact on Romanian archaeology, as seen in the work of Nicolae Denusușianu (1986), published originally in 1913, who believed that the ancestors of the Romanians, whom he identified with the Pelasgians[5], represented the cradle of all civilization. However, his views are considered extreme, for which reason many would argue that his volume cannot be considered as the outcome of serious scholarly work.

After the First World War, when Romania almost tripled its size by incorporating nearly all of the claimed territories, there was a need to give historical legitimacy to this much enlarged state. The time of the Dacian kingdom become a 'Golden Age' (Lockyear 2004, 33–5), since that was the only period when a political structure which incorporated the same territories as inter-war Romania existed, thus providing legitimacy for the newly formed multi-ethnic Romanian state (Hitchins 1992, 1069–70). In archaeology this can be seen in the establishment of *Dacia*, the most important archaeology journal of the country to this date. Additionally, in 1926 Vasile Pârvan published *Getica* (Pârvan 1926), a monumental monograph of the prehistoric past of Romania, focussing especially on the Geto-Dacians. This volume enjoyed great popularity, also beyond academia, having a profound impact on Romanian culture because of the 'incontestable value of the work, but also the fascinating personality of the Magister [Pârvan]' (Lica 2006, 1020). However, the situation took a radical twist after the Second World War and the installation of the communist regime, which was interested in stressing the links with the large neighbour to the east, the USSR, and the importance of the Slavs rather than the unique national roots of the Romanians (Babeș 2008, 9). Additionally, a superficial Marxist discourse flooded the whole spectrum of archaeological writing (Dragoman 2009, 192; Matei-Popescu 2007, 288).

In 1964 there was yet another important ideological shift. That was the year when Nicolae Ceaușescu became the head of the Romanian Socialist Republic and his wish was to break away from the strict control of the Soviets. Hence, he diminished the control of the academia to a point, at least during the initial years of his rule (Dragoman and Oanță-Marghitu 2006, 62–4), and started to strongly encourage nationalist writings in all disciplines, including archaeology. This meant that priority was given to the research which, in a more direct or indirect manner, illustrated the greatness of the Romanian nation and its people. Therefore, a more radical version of the contemporary French 'archéologie nationale' (Fleury-Ilett 1996) took shape, which prompted the focussing of archaeological research in areas that had the potential to illustrate the unique character of Romania and its glorious past. For instance, important funds were given for research at the site of Sarmizegetusa Regia, the supposed capital of the Dacian kingdom located in the southwest of Transylvania, an excavation

Figure 14.1: Ceauşeuscu driving the first Dacia car produced (taken from Fonoteca Online a Comunismului Românesc, cota 169/1968).

which is running to this day. As Ceauşescu and some party members became aware of the unique potential of the Dacian ancestorhood, under their guidance, the Thracoman/ Dacoman movement was born. Its adepts considered that the Dacians were the only, or at least the most important element that lead to the ethnogenesis of the Romanians.[6] This over-enthusiasm with the Dacians can be seen even in the name of the car brand that Ceauşescu established (Figure 14.1), Dacia, which remains very popular to this day. Nonetheless, few scholars embraced the idea of the Dacians as the only ancestors. Some archaeologists also attempted to resist the party orders to stress the importance of the Dacians and retreated to a positivistic discourse, similar to what was happening in Serbia during the same period (Babić 2002). However, such an attitude only helped to sustain and naturalise the dominant discourse (Tilley 1998, 318). The result was thus a gain in importance of the many writings which did reflect the views of Ceauşescu (*e.g.* Berciu 1986; Berciu *et al.* 1980; Crişan 1977; Fruchter and Mihăilescu 1972; Gostar and Lica 1984; Mărghitan 1983; Scorpan 1972; Vulpe and Zahariade 1987).[7] The peak of the Thracoman phenomenon was reached in 1980, when celebrations were held for the 2050th anniversary of the birth of the first Romanian state – that of the Geto-Dacian king Burebista.[8]

Dacians in Archaeology

The impact of Ceauşesu's views on archaeological writing was extensive. The ideas dating from before the Second World War were not only brought to the fore, but were augmented to an unprecedented level. The Dacian ancestorhood became often clearly stated and ideas about their superiority were visible in many studies. In such works, material culture, seen as inherently holding ethnic information, became just a tool to recount the glorious deeds of the ancestors. Therefore, it was not uncommon to read that 'the result of this deep entanglement [of the Dacians and Romans] [...] was the appearance of a people who would write a glorious and grand destiny in this part of Europe [the Romanians]' (Vulpe and Zahariade 1987, 221).

After the end of the communist regime following the 1989 revolution, even though the Thracoman movement was largely abandoned by the academia, little changed in how archaeology was written. Scholars still wrote that 'The conquest of Sarmizegetusa and the death of the hero king [Decebalus]... brutally ended the rise of a wonderful civilization through its own strength [the Dacians]' (Glodariu *et al.* 1996, 43). However, most publications showed by this point a general retreat of archaeologists to the 'ivory tower' of objectivism/ positivism, in a similar manner to what happened in Asturia and Léon after the fall of Franco (Marín Suárez *et al.* 2012).

During the last ten years or so, the nationalist voice has been considerably tempered. Various scholars work now in a critical manner with their data, but the interpretations are often still stuck within the same paradigm, operating with ethnic terms and attributing ethnic labels to material culture. Working within such a theoretical framework, one can easily argue that 'The discoveries between the Balkans and the Danube... prove that the Geto-Dacians represented the main demographical and political forces in the area' (Sîrbu *et al.* 2007, 163). Such a situation is possible because of the quasi total lack of archaeological theory, which leaves the culture-historical ideas unchallenged (Anghelinu 2003, 256). Most scholars would argue that they are doing atheoretical archaeology, operating in a realm of objective data. This makes Anghelinu ask himself 'Why is there no theory in the prehistoric archaeology of Romania?'(Anghelinu 2001), a question to which he also provides an answer: because researchers are only concerned with gathering data and with having a rigorous data analysis methodology.

However, a number of scholars have started incorporating ideas coming from western European literature, which has partly eroded the link between material culture and ethnicity. Therefore some authors agree today that while 'There is no doubt that the swords... are of Celtic origin... this does not automatically mean that their owners... were Celts' (Bondoc 2008, 147). On the other hand, the divorce between artefacts and ethnicity is proving to be more problematic in the case of the Dacians, since the same author adds further down on the same page that, 'As for the curved knives of the *sica* type, in general the form and type are very common with the Thracians, Getai and Dacians'(*ibid.*, 147). Therefore, although hidden behind a positivist discourse, Romanian archaeology still retains an acute affinity for the Dacians.

Today, Romanian scholars thus find themselves in the paradox of trying to do an objective archaeology of what they consider to be their nation's ancestors. Since western European archaeological and anthropological literature is slowly becoming known to the academic world of Romania, and with it the acknowledgement of the problems of ethnic labels, scholars are trying to find ways to justify the current situation. There are little signs however of researchers renouncing the ancestral link with the Late Iron Age. Few voices have started questioning the dominant view of a united Dacian ethnicity, but the effect has been minimal and detractors are mostly ignored (Babeş 1990; Dragoman and Oanţă-Marghitu 2006; Niculescu 2004; Popa 2010; 2002; Strobel 1998a; 1998b). The large majority of researchers still fail to see that the archaeological discourse and interpretation are engulfed in a sea of nationalist loaded terms and suffocated by the constructed ancestral link. By arguing that the terms they use are 'harmless conventions'(Sîrbu 2006, 195; Vulpe 1998), coupled with the extensive use of words such as 'scientific'(Dragoman 2009), scholars are trying to maintain the illusion of objectivity, both for themselves and their readers.

Dacians for the people

The reason for the current state of archaeological writing, but at the same time its effect, lies in the huge success of what can be called the 'Dacianisation' of the Romanians. With the deliberate intervention of the state and with the help of museums and national education, the inhabitants of Romania were literally transformed in descendants of the Dacians as this quote from a fifth-form history text book shows:

> 'The Getae and the Dacians are the same people. They [...] broadly occupied the current territory of our country, which in antiquity was named Dacia. The Geto-Dacians are the ancestors of the Romanian people' (Băluţoiu and Vlad 1999, 77).

The modern Romanian citizens have entirely incorporated the Dacian ancestorhood into their identity. People are at this point very interested in hearing and reading about their ancestors. This interest stems from the heroic image of the Dacians that people get by going through the educational system and by coming in contact with cultural institutions, especially museums. The current positivist archaeology, despite operating in an intrinsic nationalist framework, cannot provide them with the knowledge they want.

This void of knowledge is now being filled by a wave of non-academic publications that enjoy a great deal of popularity. Numerous books (*e.g.* Crainicu 2009; Oltean 2007; Pănculescu 2008) and magazines (*e.g.* Dacia Magazin) have thus appeared, in which different aspects of the Dacians are discussed by authors lacking archaeological training. Most of these writers continue the discourse from the 1980s and propagate the ideas from the Ceauşescu era, leading to the creation of a mythical aura around the Dacians.

These publications are often backed up by organizations, such as Dacia Revival International Society or Dacia Nemuritoare, that have wealthy financial contributors. Some of them also hold symposiums, like the annual International Dacology Congress, where Dacian enthusiasts present their ideas. Additionally, as a more recent development, Dacian re-enactment groups have appeared, recreating the Dacian dress, crafts and especially fighting technique (Figure 14.2).

The crisis of the next step

Many Romanians seem to present an inherent need to have a straight and easy reply to questions such as, 'Who are you (as a nation)?' and 'Where did you come from?'. The answers used to this date are provided by archaeology: 'the descendants of the Dacians and

Figure 14.2: Dacian reenactment members around the andesite sun at the site near Grădiştea de Munte (Sarmizegetusa Regia) courtesy of Terra Dacica Aeterna. (A colour plate of this figure is at the back of the volume.)

the Romans', and 'we come from the Dacians and the Romans'. But since a Latin heritage is claimed by more than one nation in Europe (*e.g.* France, Italy, Spain, and Portugal), it is the Dacian component that gives a feeling of uniqueness to Romanians as a whole. While identity is also defined through shared traditions, customs and folklore, a nation cannot exist without a past (Hobsbawm 1992).Without the Dacians as ancestors, there is a fear that Romania and its people would not be able to justify both their existence as a nation and the territory that they occupy, losing also part of the country's international prestige. This 'solid' past, spreading through the millennia, appears to be a means of protection against the adjacent nations perceived as naturally aggressive (Verdery 1992).

What, if anything, can be done in a situation like this? The Romanian people want to hear about their 'glorious' ancestors. Since archaeological research is entirely funded by the state, and thus by the people, are archaeologists not ethically constrained to answer these calls, especially in a time like the present when national solidarity is dropping in the face of advancing globalism? Moreover, if the ancestors are taken out of archaeology, would it not make the writings of non-academic Dacian enthusiasts even more popular? The Dacians have become an integral part of what it means to be Romanian; Dacia has become an integral part of Romania.

Archaeologists need to become more introspective before they can decide on the next step. Researchers should enunciate the theoretical framework in which they operate and be aware of the preconceptions that they work with. Simply importing concepts from

Western scholars is, however, not the answer, since it would be naïve to think that Western archaeology is the holder of truth and objectivity.[9] Nonetheless, in order to situate oneself, it is necessary to explore the diversity of archaeological approaches (Bintliff 2011, 8) and understand how knowledge is created (Latour 1999, 24–79). Also, scholars have to be conscious of the intricate relationship between the subject and the object of research, as well as the fundamental role played by the social context of the researcher (Shanks and Tilley 1987b, 29–60). At the end of this process, archaeologists will become more aware of the role they play and thus more capable of deciding on the future direction of their research.

Acknowledgements

First of all I wish to thank the editors for giving me the possibility to publish in the current volume. I also want to thank my supervisor, Dr Simon Stoddart, for his support and input in the writing of this article. Last but not least, I am very grateful for the help of Meikel Kuijpers and Barbara Hausmair without whom the article would have not reached its current form.

Notes

1 Ethnogenesis is used as strictly referring to the birth or establishment of an ethnic group. The concept itself has been proven to be highly problematic (Geary 2002) and has recently come under heavy critique (Bowlus 2002), especially when applying it to pre-modern contexts (Brather 2004).

2 The main argument of archaeologists for identifying the Getai and Dacians as the same people is a passage from Strabo (VII,3,12) which says that the two populations had the same language. Considering that the conception of ethnicity in Romania is one in which language is a definitory element (Graves-Brown and Jones 1996, 8) there is no surprise that the existence of a unified Geto-Dacian ethnic group is considered to be proven.

3 There are of course exceptions (*e.g.* Ursachi 1995).

4 By that time B. P. Hașdeu, an important Romanian scholar, had already published *Istoria critică a Românilor* (*The critical history of Romanians*) (Hașdeu 1984[1873–1874]) in which the link between the Dacians and the Romanians was already mentioned, although the fundamental component was considered to be the Roman one.

5 The Pelasgians were an elusive population of the Greek world, first mentioned in Book 2 of Homer's *Iliad* (II, 840–5). They also appear in the *Histories* of Herodotus (I, 56–7).

6 Therefore, the Latin component of the previously presented genealogical equation was reduced to a minimum. This situation contrasts with the situation before the Second World War, when, despite a great deal of importance being given to the Dacians, the Roman heritage was considered primordial.

7 While some authors genuinely believed what they were writing, many of them were over-emphasising the grandeur and importance of the Dacians just to please certain Communist Party officials and allow their research to get published. It comes then as no surprise that after 1989 some of these scholars began to critically analyse the work that had been done in the period before, including their own (*e.g.* Lica 2006).

8 The year was fixed by the Romanian Communist Party as archaeology could not provide a fixed date. The choice of 1980 undoubtedly had to do with the fact that approximately at the same time Bulgaria was celebrating 1300 years from the settling of the Proto-Bulgarians (Bulgars) in the territory of today Bulgaria and the establishment of their first state, that of Asparuh, in 681 AD (Babeș 2008, 9).

9 Such an approach would contradict the post-processual ideas which sustain that there is no truth and that archaeology is ultimately subjective (Hamilakis 2007, 13). Additionally it would encourage a colonialist relationship between the West and Romania.

References

Anghelinu, M. (2001) De ce nu există teorie în arheologia preistorică din România? *Sargetia* 30, 39–50.

Anghelinu, M. (2003) *Evoluţia Gândirii Teoretice în Arheologia Românească: Concepte Şi Modele Aplicate în Preistorie*. Târgovişte, Cetatea de Scaun.

Babeş, M. (1979) Unitatea şi răspândirea geto-dacilor în lumina documentelor arheologice (secolele III î.e.n. – I e.n.). *Studii şi Cercetări de Istorie Veche şi Arheologie* 30(3), 327–45.

Babeş, M. (1990) Daci sau romani? Etnogeneza românească între ştiinţă şi plăsmuire. *Alternative '90* 1(7), 20–1.

Babeş, M. (1999) Staţiunea Geto-Dacă de la Cetăţeni. Descoperiri şi informaţii recuperate. *Studii şi Cercetări de Istorie Veche şi Arheologie* 50(1–2), 11–31.

Babeş, M. (2008) Arheologie, societate şi politică în România, înainte şi după 1989. *Studii şi Cercetări de Istorie Veche şi Arheologie* 59–60, 5–15.

Babić, S. (2002) Still innocent after all these years? Sketches for a social history of archaeology in Serbia. In P. F. Biehl, A. Gramsch and A. Marciniak (eds) *Archäologien Europas Geschichte, Methoden und Theorien*, 309–22. Münster, Waxmann.

Băluţoiu, V. and C. Vlad (1999) *Istorie. Manual pentru clasa a V-a*. Bucureşti, Editura All.

Berciu, D. (1986) Două milenii şi jumătate de la prima atestare a izvoarelor scrise antice privind lupta geţilor pentru apărarea libertăţii şi independenţei. *Arhivele Olteniei* 5, 48–56.

Berciu, D., Daicoviciu, H., Preda, C.,Protase, D. and Vulpe, A. (1980) Vatra dacică spaţiul neîntreruptei noastre dăinuiri. *Scînteia*, 4.

Berciu, I. and Popa, A. (1971) Cetatea dacică de la Piatra Craivii, in *Sesiunea de comunicări ştiinţifice a Muzeelor de istorie. Decembrie 1964*, vol. 1, Bucureşti, 261–84.

Bintliff, J. (2011) The death of archaeological theory? In J. Bintliff and M. Pearce (eds) *The death of archaeological theory?*, 7–22. Oxford, Oxbow.

Bondoc, D. (2008) Descoperirile de epocă La Tène de la Padea, jud. Dolj. *Studii şi Cercetări de Istorie Veche şi Arheologie* 59–60, 137–63.

Bowlus, C. R. (2002) Ethnogenesis: the tyranny of a concept. In A. Gillett (ed.) *On Barbarian identity: critical approaches to ethnicity in the early Middle Ages*, 241–56. Studies in the early Middle Ages. Turnhout, Brepols.

Brather, S. (2004) *Ethnische Interpretationen in der frühgeschichtlichen Archäologie. Geschichte, Grundlagen und Alternativen*. Berlin, W. de Gruyte.

Căpitanu, V. and Ursachi, V. (1972) Descoperiri Geto-Dacice în judeţul Bacău. *Crisia* 2, 97–114.

Ciugudean, D. and Ciugudean, H. 1993. Un Mormânt de războinic Geto-Dac de la Tărtăria (jud. Alba). *Ephemeris Napocensis* 3, 77–9.

Crainicu, F. (2009) *Legendele dacilor liberi*. Bucureşti, Dacica.

Crişan, I. H. (1977) *Burebista şi Epoca Sa*. Bucureşti, Ştiinţifică şi Enciclopedică.

Dana, D. and Matei-Popescu, F. (2006) Le recrutement des Daces dans l'armée romaine sous l'empereur Trajan : une esquisse préliminaire. *Dacia* 50, 195–506.

Densuşianu, N. (1986) *Dacia Preistorică*. Bucureşti, Editura Meridiane.

Dragoman, A. (2009) Ideology and politics in researching the (E)Neolithic in Romania. *Dacia* 53, 191–214.

Dragoman, A. and Oanţă-Marghitu, S. (2006) Archaeology in communist and post-communist Romania. *Dacia* 50, 57–76.

Fleury-Ilett, B. (1996) The identity of France: archetypes in Iron Age studies. In P. Graves-Brown, S. Jones and C. Gamble (eds) *Cultural identity and archaeology: the construction of European communities*, 196–208. London, Routledge.

Florea, G., Vaida, D. L. and Suciu, L. (2000) Fortificaţii Dacice din nord-estul Transilvaniei. *Istros* 10, 221–30.

Fruchter, E. and Mihăilescu, G. (1972) Despre necesitatea includerii unui capitol privind cultura spirituala a Dacilor în istoria filozofiei din România. *Crisia* 2, 149–54.

Geary, P. J. (2002) *The myth of nations: the medieval origins of Europe*. Princeton and Oxford, Princeton University Press.

Gheorghiu, G. (2005) *Dacii pe Cursul Mijlociu al Mureşului: (Sfârşitul sec. II a. Ch. – Începutul sec. II p. Ch.)*. Cluj-Napoca, Mega.

Glodariu, I. (1989) *Cetatea Dacică de la Căpîlna*. Bucureşti, Editura ştiinţifică şi enciclopedică.

Glodariu, I., Iaroslavschi, E., Rusu-Pescaru, A. and Stănescu, F. (1996) *Sarmizegetusa Regia, Capitala Daciei Preromane*. Deva, Muzeul Civilizaţiei Dacice şi Romane.

Gostar, N. and Lica, V. (1984) *Societatea Geto-Dacică de la Burebista la Decebal*. Bucureşti, Junimea.

Graves-Brown, P. and Jones, S. (1996) Introduction. Archaeology and cultural identity in Europe. In P. Graves-Brown, S. Jones and C. Gamble (eds) *Cultural identity and archaeology: the construction of European communities*, 1–24. London, Routledge.

Hamilakis, Y. (2007) *The nation and its ruins: antiquity, archaeology, and national imagination in Greece*. Oxford, Oxford University Press.

Haşdeu, B. P. (1984) *Istoria Critică a Românilor*. Bucureşti, Minerva.

Hitchins, K. (1992) Historiography of the countries of eastern Europe: Romania. *The American Historical Review* 97(4), 1064–83.

Hobsbawm, E. J. (1992) Ethnicity and nationalism in Europe today. *Anthropology Today* 8(1), 3–8.

Hodder, I. (1986) *Reading the past: current approaches to interpretation in archaeology*. Cambridge, Cambridge University Press.

Latour, B. (1999) *Pandora's hope: essays on the reality of science studies*. Cambridge, Mass, Harvard University Press.

Lica, V. (2006) De la Thracologie la Thracomanie. Glose marginale, in *Fontes Historiae. Studia in honorem Demetrii Protase*, Bistriţa – Cluj-Napoca, 1011–28.

Lockyear, K. (2004) The Late Iron Age background to Roman Dacia. In W. S. Hanson and I. P. Haynes (eds) *Roman Dacia. The making of a provincial society*, 33–74. Journal of Roman Archaeology. Supplementary Series. Portsmouth, Rhode Island.

Macrea, M. and Glodariu, I. (1976) *Aşezarea Dacică de la Arpaşu de Sus*. Bucureşti, Editura Academiei Republicii Socialiste România.

Măndescu, D. (2006) *Cetăţeni: Staţiunea Geto-Dacă de pe Valea Dâmboviţei Superioare*. Brăila, Editura Istros.

Mărghitan, L. (1983) Mărturii de continuitate Dacă, Daco-Romană şi timpurie Românească pe valea Mureşului mijlociu şi inferior. *Studia Antiqua et Archaeologica* 1, 103–19.

Marín Suárez, C., González Álvarez, D. and Alonso González, P. (2012) Building nations in the XXI century. Celtism, nationalism and archaeology in northern Spain: the case of Asturias and León. *Archaeological Review from Cambridge* 27(2).

Matei-Popescu, F. (2007) Imaginea Daciei romane în istoriografia românească între 1945 şi 1960. *Studii şi Cercetări de Istorie Veche şi Arheologie* 58(3–4), 265–88.

Miller, D. and Tilley, C. (eds) (1984) *Ideology, power and prehistory*. Cambridge, Cambridge University Press.

Niculescu, G. A. (2002) Nationalism and the representations of society in Romanian archaeology. *Nation and national ideology*, New Europe Collège.

Niculescu, G. A. (2004) Archaeology, nationalism and 'The History of the Romanians' (2001). *Dacia* (48–49), 99–124.

Oltean, D. (2007) *Burebista şi Sarmizegetusa*. Bucureşti, Editura Saeculum I.O.

Oltean, D. (2008) *Munţii Dacilor. Călătorii pe plaiurile regeşti ale Sarmisegetuzei*. Bucureşti, Dacica.

Pănculescu, C. (2008) *Taina Kogaiononului. Muntele sacru al dacilor*. Bucureşti, Ştefan.

Pârvan, V. (1926) *Getica: O Protoistorie a Daciei*. Bucureşti, Cultura Naţională.

Pescaru, A. and Ferencz, I. V. (eds) (2004) *Daco-Geţii: 80 de ani de Cercetări Arheologice Sistematice la Cetăţile Dacice din Munţii Orăştiei*. Deva, Muzeul Civilizaţiei Dacice şi Romane.

Petan, A. (2007) O descoperire senzationala: Scrierea dacica de la Chitila. *Formula AS* 755. Available at: http://www.formula-as.ro/2007/755/mica-enciclopedie-as-27/o-descoperire-senzationala-scrierea-dacica-de-la-chitila-7712 [Accessed 02/2012].

Popa, C. N. (2010) A new framework for approaching Dacian identity. In S. Berecki (ed.) *Iron Age communities in the Carpathian basin*, 395–423. Bibliotheca Musei Marisiensis. Seria Archaeologica. Cluj-Napoca, Mega.

Preda, C. (1986) *Geto-Dacii din Bazinul Oltului Inferior: Dava de la Sprincenata*. Bucuresti.

Scorpan, C. (1972) Continuitatea în Dobrogea şi problema unităţii culturii Geto-Dace. *Crisia* 2, 155–74.

Shanks, M. and Tilley, C. 1987a. *Re-constructing archaeology: theory and practice*. Cambridge, Cambridge University Press.

Shanks, M. and Tilley, C. 1987b. *Social theory and archaeology*. Cambridge, Polity Press.

Sîrbu, V. (1996) *Dava getică de la Grădiştea, jud. Brăila.* Brăila.

Sîrbu, V. (2006) Dacii şi Celţii din Transilvania şi Vestul României, in *Fontes Historiae. Studia in honorem Demetrii Protase*, Bistriţa – Cluj-Napoca, 199–221.

Sîrbu, V. Luca, S. A. and Roman, C. (2007) Tombs of Dacian warriors (2nd – 1st C. BC) found in Hunedoara–Grădina Castelului (Hunedoara County). *Acta Terrae Septemcastrensis* 7(1), 155–77.

Strobel, K. (1998a). Dacii. Despre Complexitatea mărimilor Etnice, Politice şi Culturale ale Istoriei Spaţiului Dunării de Jos. *Studii şi Cercetări de Istorie Veche şi Arheologie* 49(1), 61–95.

Strobel, K. (1998b) Dacii. Despre Complexitatea mărimilor Etnice, Politice şi Culturale ale Istoriei Spaţiului Dunării de Jos. *Studii şi Cercetări de Istorie Veche şi Arheologie* 49(2), 207–27.

Tilley, C. (1998) Archaeology as socio-political action in the present. In D. S. Whitley (ed.) *Reader in archaeological theory: post-processual and cognitive approaches*, 305–30. Whitley. Routledge readers in archaeology. London, Routledge.

Tocilescu, G. G. (1877) *Dacia înainte de Romani.* Bucureşti, Tipografia Academiei Romane.

Ursachi, V. (1995) *Zargidava: Cetatea Dacică de la Brad.* Bucureşti, Caro Trading.

Verdery, K. (1992) Comment: Hobsbawm in the east. *Anthropology Today* 8(1), 8–10.

Vulpe, A. (1998) Geto-dacii? *CICSA* 1–2, 2–11.

Vulpe, A. and Zahariade, M. (1987) *Geto-Dacii în Istoria Militară a Lumii Antice.* Bucureşti, Editura Militară.

15

BROKEN MIRRORS? ARCHAEOLOGICAL REFLECTIONS ON IDENTITY

Nicole Taylor

Introduction

Archaeologists studying identity from mortuary evidence are often preoccupied with the frustrating situation of being so close to the remains of past people, yet so far from them in terms of outlook. We often question whether it is possible to separate ourselves from our specific socio-political-economic contexts, and truly get to grips with how abstract ideas like identity were conceived in the past. However, it is argued here that such attempts are deflecting our energies from other, potentially more fruitful approaches to the archaeology of identity. If we are inextricably embedded in our own modern contexts, we should instead be focusing on ways to use that as a positive influence on our studies of the past. Building upon what has come before in archaeologies of death, and attempting to integrate other current social theories, could help us to gain a deeper understanding of how death and identity may have been experienced and performed in prehistory. Additionally helpful, would be discussing how our own identities and experiences impact upon our engagement with the past, and how we might usefully overcome the generally instituted 'scientific' detachment from the meaningful and emotive aspects of funerary practices. It is suggested that prehistoric mortuary evidence is actually a mirror for our concepts of identity, but that this can still reflect real and significant past meanings, as well as informing alternative understandings for modern management of death and burial.

We have never been ancient...

This paraphrasing of Latour (1993) is designed to highlight the fact that archaeology is a modern phenomenon, which owes its existence to a specific intellectual tradition and social history that enabled and placed value upon the systematic study of the past. Its current configurations are also the product of a specific disciplinary history. The logical paradox that archaeology could not exist without the very conditions that 'make it more difficult for us to comprehend [the] past' (Thomas 2004, 18) has long been recognised in the theory of our discipline.

Archaeologies of death are just one facet of research where we have sought many ways to understand the past in its own terms. Traditional archaeological approaches understood burials as religious statements which could be interpreted through the use of ideological metaphors and analogies drawn from history, ethnography, and even everyday experience (Lull 2000, 576). Processual approaches regarded mortuary remains as a literal reflection of the entire range of complexities forming social realities of the past, therefore seeking middle-range theories to complement rigorous testing of their hypotheses, often also using ethnographic analogies as a starting point (*ibid.*, 577). Postprocessual archaeologies have generally sought to understand the contextual symbolism of mortuary remains, which are not considered to be directly reflective of society or individual status; rather than being directly comparable universal patterns, funerary rites are considered as particular, symbolic historic occurrences (*ibid.*, 577–8).

Each of these perspectives has had some influence on the ways in which current archaeologists are approaching the study of identity through mortuary remains. Yet there still remains a conceptual distance between us and the past people whose burials we aim to understand and interpret. Archaeology produces inferences about the past located firmly in the present, which can restrict our potential for understanding our subject matter exactly as it was understood in the past. Härke (2002, 340) has discussed the shift from archaeological interest in 'life in the past (to be inferred from its dead remains) to death in the past'. Taking this idea further would lead to the development of what could be called 'archaeologies of death in the present-past' (*sensu* Campbell and Hansson in their response to Tarlow 2000), meaning interpretation of past death (and in the specific case of this chapter, death and identity) through our modern capacity for understanding such a concept. The present frames and conditions our understandings and representations of the past (Pluciennik 1999, 673), since they must be 'conceivable as a past' in light of what has come before (Rudebeck, commenting on *ibid.*, 670).

To be clear, this chapter is not advocating wholehearted presentism, and it is apparent that archaeologists should remain vigilant against completely misinterpreting the past and constructing that which we wish to study, as are other social sciences (see for example Kashima *et al.* 2002, vii on the dangers of test subjects appropriating academically constructed concepts of identity). As is made clear by Tarlow (2000) and those who commented on her article, past meanings will always be elusive due to our restricted potential for understanding the past. This inability to know how closely our interpretations tally with prehistoric understandings demonstrates why it makes sense to instead seek ways in which meaningful actions in the past can be interpreted in terms we are able to comprehend. As Thomas (commenting on Tarlow 2000, 739) states, '[m]y own experience of a past materiality is the only one that is available to me' and it is argued that the same is true of our potential for understanding concepts of identity. The very title of the conference which generated this volume also demonstrates how archaeology has become a highly self-reflective and reflexive field, able to see the importance of asking whether a notion such as identity is really 'our concept or theirs'. An added advantage of this present-bound and reflexive approach is that it enables archaeology to contribute in turn to those disciplines which study death and identity in modern societies. Acknowledging that archaeology researches past instances of modern understandings of identity and other similar concepts emphasises the utility and relevance of our discipline for the modern world in which we practice it, as well as highlighting how the relevance of our interpretations lies in the present for which they were constructed (Pluciennik 1999, 665).

Reaching across the distance

There is another compelling reason to insist that we must embrace our own socialisation, our inescapable modern contexts as archaeologists: it affects our work, even if we choose to ignore it. By attempting to make explicit our concepts and how we are seeking *them* and not a wholly objective 'truth' of the past, we can be more reflexive and, just as importantly, allow others to evaluate our work more fully. It seems that often in our pursuit of 'scientific rigour' we end up distancing ourselves too far from our data and interpretations, and even the experience of archaeology. As such, our subjectivity is masked and implicit, yet it still has the same effects on our research and interpretations. Therefore, even the proponents of a fully objective archaeology should recognise the necessity of making explicit any potential sources of bias that come from our inability to step outside our own contexts if they wish to counter these effects.

However, it seems that this should be done for the opposite reason, in order to incorporate more humanity into our discourses on the past. There is much to be gained by making explicit our modernity, our concepts, and the impact that our own contexts have on us as we research the past, especially when it comes to mortuary archaeology and identity studies, since death and identity are also inescapable facets of modern life.

Despite the theoretical developments made regarding subjectivity and multivocality within the postprocessual and post-modern archaeological movements, there still remains the tendency to present the past from a distanced, objective perspective. Early attempts to 'humanise' archaeological discourses through new approaches were often associated with what were seen to be radical new theoretical perspectives and therefore considered as experimental, or at the very least interesting sidelines from mainstream research. For example, Spector's (1991) use of prose and a fictional narrative style to portray her archaeological and ethno-historical understanding of Dakota society is difficult to separate from her explicitly feminist agenda: the method of data presentation and dissemination is entangled with the theoretical leanings of the author. However, while it is now accepted that the past was not peopled with unfeeling automatons reacting solely to functional and economic stimuli, we have yet to find an acceptable way to integrate our expanded interpretations into standard archaeological discourse. Despite changing theoretical and methodological approaches to the material, archaeology has remained fairly conservative in its narrative forms and ways of presenting the past (Pluciennik 1999). One example of our inability to present the past in new ways can be found in our publication conventions: reports are full of descriptive dimensions and scaled line drawings, while artefacts and burials are still routinely presented through technical drawings, which often show cross-sections that cannot be seen (or no longer exist) in real-life. Generally, archaeological texts still use the narrative style where emphasis is placed on sequence (in this case, usually chronology) in an attempt at explanation (Pluciennik 1999, 666). Continuing attempts at presenting archaeology in different ways, in terms of both our data and our interpretations, will hopefully inspire our discipline to widen its ways of understanding the past. The creation of our tangible products (such as illustrations or texts) is an embodiment of the process of how we negotiate our identity through our relationships with each other and the archaeology itself (Bateman 2006, 80); new processes of creation and different forms of end-product can play a real role in altering our perceptions and conceptions of the past. The rise of 3D models and reconstructions, in addition to the continued use of photographs and two-dimensional artistic representations, show the importance of more naturalistic interpretations in conveying a sense of the past which we understand from our data.

Modern advantages

As previously touched upon, archaeology is a product of its own disciplinary history. As such, the archaeology of death has undergone many changes, often discarding many of the approaches of previous generations of practitioners, in terms of both theory and method. When constructing methodologies for the study of death and what we understand as identification in prehistory from a present perspective, we should now consider a more integrated approach, and build on the best of what has come before. In altering our perception of the past, our question regarding identity and mortuary remains changes from 'our concept or theirs?' to 'what meaningful past material actions can be interpreted as what we currently understand as identification?'. This shift in focus is subtle, and requires similarly subtle shifts in methodology which in turn open up new potential avenues of investigation. In addition to considering what methods from the history of archaeology still hold value for current lines of investigation, this also means continuing to embrace the interdisciplinarity which has most recently been taking archaeology by storm.

There have already been efforts to carry out what could be considered to be a more 'present-past'-orientated archaeology. Researchers, such as Tarlow (2000), Murphy (2011) and others, have been focusing on emotion in archaeology, often using present examples as a gateway to understanding how we might conceptualise potential past responses and the meanings behind certain types of burials. It could be argued that in the case of historical archaeologies (such as the aforementioned examples), there is a closer connection between the modern values used as analogy and the archaeological material being interpreted, especially when the practices studied are still part of local oral tradition. However, Sørensen and Bille (2008) were able – through consideration of modern understandings of abjection, absence, and presence, as pertaining to the act of cremation – to construct a conceivable interpretation of prehistoric cremations (*sensu* Rudebeck, commenting on Pluciennik 1999, 670).

Our approach to death and identity can also be informed by insights from other social sciences. Rather than merely borrowing case studies from these disciplines as analogies, we can seek to widen our own understandings of the concepts we are studying; this will allow further insight into how to connect our concepts with the physical evidence of the past. There has been much research in social anthropology and sociology into mortuary and funerary rituals and the varying responses extant societies have to death, which can aid archaeological understandings of the range of emotions potentially recognisable in material responses to past death (Howarth 2000). Social psychology offers various insights into identity construction, (re)negotiation and maintenance (see for example Jenkins 2004; Kashima *et al.* 2002; Simon 2004) which can be used to hone the concept of identification which we aim to research. Even communication studies have contributed to the relatively new field of 'death studies', considering funerary rites as ritualised means of identity communication and on-going social relationships between the dead and the society they leave behind (Bennett and Bennett 2000; Reimers 1999). The importance of concisely defining the modern concept we are seeking in evidence of the past cannot be understated (Brubaker and Cooper 2000); this kind of transparency will further enable our research to transcend the conservatism of the vast majority of archaeological narratives through acceptance of the fact that, as Criado-Boado states, 'archaeological narrative (re)presents subjectivity' (comment on Pluciennik 1999, 668).

In addition to using modern theoretical approaches, another advantage of the current state of archaeology is that we have access to a wider range of natural science techniques than ever before. From palaeobotany to phosphate analysis, geomagnetic survey to x-ray fluorescence, and thin-sectioning to stable isotope analysis, scientific approaches have contributed greatly to the forms of evidence and analysis available to archaeologists. The potential for multidisciplinary studies of death and identity has never been greater, and it is encouraging to see how current research is taking advantage of this fact. Certain methodological approaches are in fact fast becoming standard practice: consider how many archaeologists are combining stable isotope analysis with material culture and osteological information in order to gain more holistic insights into death and identity (whether related to geographical origins, social status, diet or even ideological changes) (see for example Bentley *et al.* 2004; Budd *et al.* 2004; Carlson 1996; Evans *et al.* 2006a; Evans *et al.* 2006b; Ezzo *et al.* 1997; Montgomery 2010; Price *et al.* 2000; Richards and Schulting 2006; Turner *et al.* 2009; White *et al.* 2004; White *et al.* 1998).

Yet, as with theoretical approaches, it is important that archaeology does not just discard its own past in favour of the latest methods and fads on offer. Theory and methodology should be complimentary and tailored to the research questions at hand; however, even here archaeologists have had a tendency to overlook older methods which have since fallen out of favour. As previously mentioned regarding innovative approaches to disseminating archaeological knowledge, certain methodologies have also suffered through their close connection with specific theoretical perspectives. For example, the use of quantitative statistical analyses generally lost favour in Anglo-American archaeology as postprocessual theories gained popularity, and while typological analyses have been expanded upon and remain a backbone of German archaeological research, they have yet to completely shake off their associations with traditional culture historical approaches. Many of these seemingly out-of-fashion methodologies still have much value for archaeological research; in fact, they may have even more utility now, since they are used more critically and combined with a wider range of theories.

Examples from the author's own research

The author's own research is looking at identity through cremation cemeteries. In addition to using spatial analysis and statistical methods to test hypotheses built from recent archaeological and social psychological theories about identity construction and negotiation, the research is also considering some of the more non-discursive elements of mortuary rituals and our study of them. Even when seeking to find indications for meaningful past processes that we would now consider as identification, cremation burials present particular challenges: the alteration of the body by fire and its secondary burial generally serve to remove certain archaeologically well-established forms of identification, for example bodily orientation and adornment.

Additionally, when it comes to Late Bronze Age Urnfield cremation cemeteries, there appears at first glance to be even fewer characteristics which can be used in our investigations: often they are so-called flat burials, where no above-ground features can be noted during the excavation and there is little differentiation between burial pits. On the basis of these limitations, many archaeologists have chosen to neglect the potential for cremation cemeteries to have been used in identification processes which are just as complex as those expressed in inhumation burials. This research history is one of the factors that prompted the author's desire to discover the potential of cremations for archaeological insights into identification through mortuary practices. Hence, attempts to include a wide range of evidence, concepts and interpretations which consider less mainstream ideas within mortuary archaeology and general death studies, will contribute to the holistic and multidisciplinary nature of this research.

The first case-study site, Vollmarshausen (Kr. Kassel, Hessen, Germany), demonstrates a range of variability in mortuary practices which could be interpreted in line with the concept of identification outlined below. The working concepts are as follows: identity is a multifaceted, dynamic and complex process of negotiation between various self-aspects on the basis of context, which requires visible (and often tangible) expression in the form of identification. Identification is itself a process of categorisation which can be embodied and requires communication to be effective; it is when this communication occurs through material means that we as archaeologists are able to access it. Burial form and structural features, along with the type and location of grave goods, are considered to have been used as material expressions of the identities chosen for the deceased by the bereaved. Some of the burial features at Vollmarshausen can also be considered from a more experiential point of view, in order to try and further explore how the meanings and actions of the past could be understood in the present. Just as statistical analyses of burial features might be considered to be part of an old-fashioned processual tool-kit and critiqued for their removal of individual agents from the actions they carried out, postprocessual outlooks based on phenomenological reasoning could be considered esoteric, overly-subjective and 'unscientific'. The point is that there were useful methods and approaches being used in each stage of the development of the current discipline of archaeology and as such, it is foolhardy to continue to re-invent the wheel and to allow past prejudices to colour our views of perspectives which could offer us greater insights into our research materials. Widening our methodologies to encompass both the scientific and the experiential, objectivity and subjectivity, can surely only result in a more expansive archaeology which will offer us myriad ways to understand the past.

One example of the ways in which different approaches are combined can be seen in the investigations of the capstones present at Vollmarshausen. Capstones are flat stones which were placed over the mouths of ceramic vessels included in the burial. This usually refers to the cinerary urns used in the burial type denoted as round pit cremations with urns, where they cover the majority of the diameter of the cremation pit as well. However, capstones are also present over some accessory vessels in both the aforementioned burial type, in some round pit burials which are without cinerary urns and even in ceramic deposits (which contain no cremated remains but may still be the remains of disturbed cremation burials).

Capstones are most frequently found in relation to round pit cremations with urns from the period Hallstatt B (*c.* 1050/1020–800 BC). The correspondence analysis in Figure 15.1 shows that as a burial feature, capstones are most closely linked with another feature, namely

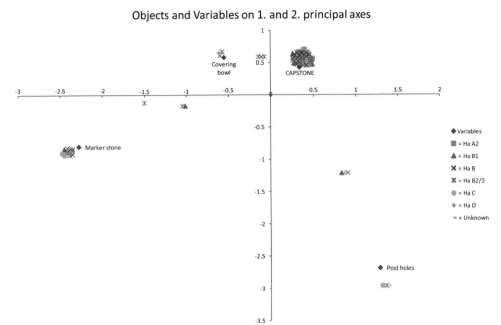

Figure 15.1: Correspondence analysis of burial features at Vollmarshausen, with capstones emphasised in uppercase.

covering bowls (covering bowls are shallow ceramic vessels which were inverted over the mouth of cinerary urns or, more rarely, other accessory vessels). These bowls are therefore considered to be lids for the urns, and their connection to capstones suggests that the latter might also have been used to similar effect. There is no evidence that capstones were more commonly used in burials according to the usual suspects among identity groups (sex or age). There is a weak (and, due to the small numbers involved, not proven to be statistically significant) pattern that only female burials have capstones in combination with either marker stones or postholes, which would create specific types of burial architecture depending on the size and location of the upright stones and posts. In addition, spatial analysis of the capstones reveals that they are most commonly found in the East I cemetery district (Figure 15.2). While this is not unexpected (this district has the highest frequency of round pit with urn burials), it is interesting to note that, despite the correspondence shown in Figure 15.1, there are no covering bowls in this district.

In addition to exploring these fairly traditional elements of the use of capstones in the cemetery, more experiential aspects have also been considered, in line with some of the other archaeologists currently working on mortuary archaeology. Inspired by Sørensen's (2010) study of modern cremation burials, work has begun to consider how the capstones might have affected the prehistoric community who saw them. If they were visible above ground how might they have altered and choreographed movement? How might they have focused attention and commemoration? And how different would they have been in the past to the stark black and white illustrations we generate of them for our purposes? If they were not

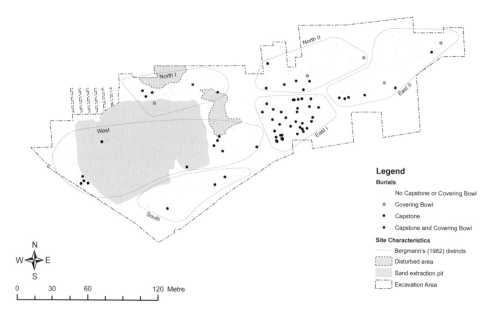

Figure 15.2: Vollmarshausen, Kr. Kassel, Hessen, Germany. Distribution of capstones and covering bowls within the cemetery.

visible above ground, what might have been the reason for their placement in the burial? How might they have confronted the bereaved when they returned to the urns (as evidenced by the holes and other disruption to the urns documented by the excavator (Bergmann 1982))?

It is an interesting general aspect of our discipline that while we are trying to understand material culture phenomena, such as grave assemblages or structures, we rarely conceptualise them in their original forms during our research processes; they are normally considered as abstract attributes in databases, as numbers in catalogues, as elements of imagined cross-sections drawn through burials in illustrations. Again, this attitude owes much to the history of archaeology: early antiquarian studies often included stylised, naturalistic watercolour depictions of sites (especially burial monuments) which although capturing a sense of place, were seen as overly romantic and non-scientific. However, when combined with more modern and objective representations, these paintings and sketches add to our understanding of archaeological sites. In fact, the popularity of reconstruction images (drawings, paintings, 3D models and so forth) in archaeological dissemination and especially public or community archaeology shows the value of such representations as 'tools to think with' and alternative interpretations. The addition of a more emotive account of how we, as researchers, engage with our material and what potential reactions we can envisage it having had on past populations given the conceptual, theoretical, and methodological approach we have adopted could surely only contribute further to discussion and pave the way for further interpretation on the basis of a wider range of information.

Conclusion

In shifting our focus of enquiry and interpretation ever so slightly, we can turn our limitations into opportunities. By considering our discipline as one grounded in the modern world, we can make greater use of other modern social and natural sciences and their approaches. For example, archaeologists have long suggested that repeated material culture patterns (in terms of form, style, combination, or use) reflect specific meanings for the past societies who perpetuated them. This is supported by social psychological studies on living people which have also shown that 'meanings are embedded in public symbols that are shared by people, and transmitted from one generation to the next' (Kashima *et al.* 2002, vii). Exploring the many facets of the modern concept of identity allows us to widen our understanding of the scope of behaviours and material responses which may be interpreted as identification, whether in present or past societies.

Additionally, archaeologists should strive to ensure that they use the most suitable techniques at their disposal for investigating the past through contemporary understandings. We are fortunate to have such a wide suite of methods at our disposal, and those we select for a specific project should be chosen solely on the basis of their own strengths, rather than on what is considered fashionable or passé at the moment. Archaeologists should also not be afraid to experiment with new or unconventional forms of dissemination and presenting their interpretations: as long as the aims and assumptions involved are made explicit, and the underlying data and methodologies are outlined, the resultant work should be able to stand on its own merit, even if it is used in combination with a theoretical outlook that might later become unpopular. It should be possible to combine the more accepted objective (re)presentations with more subjective human and creative ones without one detracting from the other; we should seek to add to our sources of data and inspiration, rather than narrowing our perspectives. Pushing the boundaries of which (re)presentations of the past are acceptable in terms of 'being conceivable as a past' (Rudebeck, commenting on Pluciennik 1999, 670) is perhaps one way in which we can attempt to broaden the understandings of the past available to us in our modern contexts. In any case, we should ensure that we do not ascribe any concepts to the past uncritically or unproblematically; even when we make use of modern perspectives on death and identification processes we need to ensure that we are still focusing on meaningful actions in the past, even if we are unlikely to ever be able to conceptualise them in the same way as the people who performed them. In doing so we might just be able to make the most of the distorted reflections of identity offered to us in archaeological burials.

Acknowledgements

The author would like to thank her supervisors and colleagues in the Forging Identities project for their inspiration and support and Dr Jutta Kneisel for her wise advice and insights.

The research leading to these results has received funding from the European Union Seventh Framework Programme (FP7/2007-2013) under grant agreement n° 212402.

References

Bateman, J. (2006) Pictures, ideas, and things: the production and currency of archaeological images. In M. Edgeworth (ed.) *Ethnographies of archaeological practice*, 68–80. Oxford, AltaMira.

Bennett, G. and Bennett, K. M. (2000) The presence of the dead: an empirical study. *Mortality* 5(2), 139–57.

Bentley, R. A., Price, T. D., and Stephan, E. (2004) Determining the 'local' Sr-87/Sr-86 range for archaeological skeletons: a case study from Neolithic Europe. *Journal of Archaeological Science* 31(4), 365–75.

Bergmann, J. (1982) *Ein Gräberfeld der jüngeren Bronze- und älteren Eisenzeit bei Vollmarshausen, Kr. Kassel : zur Struktur und Geschichte einer vorgeschichtlichen Gemeinschaft im Spiegel ihres Gräberfeldes.* 2 vols. Marburg, Elwert.

Brubaker, R. and Cooper, F. (2000) Beyond 'identity'. *Theory and Society* 29(1), 1–47.

Budd, P., Millard, A., Chenery, C., Lucy, S., and Roberts, C. (2004) Investigating population movement by stable isotope analysis: a report from Britain Investigating population movement by stable isotope analysis: a report from Britain. *Antiquity* 78 (299), 127–41.

Carlson, A. K. (1996) Lead isotope analysis of human bone for addressing cultural affinity: a case study from Rocky Mountain House, Alberta. *Journal of Archaeological Science* 23, 557–67.

Evans, J., Stoodley, N., and Chenery, C. (2006a) A strontium and oxygen isotope assessment of a possible fourth century immigrant population in a Hampshire cemetery, southern England. *Journal of Archaeological Science* 33 (2), 265–72.

Evans, J. A., Chenery, C. A., and Fitzpatrick, A. P. (2006b) Bronze Age childhood migration of individuals near Stonehenge, revealed by strontium and oxygen isotope tooth enamel analysis. *Archaeometry* 48, 309–21.

Ezzo, J. A., Johnson, C. M., and Price, T. D. (1997) Analytical perspectives on prehistoric migration: A case study from east-central Arizona. *Journal of Archaeological Science* 24(5), 447–66.

Härke, H. (2002) Interdisciplinarity and the archaeological study of death. *Mortality* 7(3), 340–1.

Howarth, G. (2000) Dismantling the boundaries between life and death. *Mortality* 5(2), 127–38.

Jenkins, R. (2004) *Social identity* 2nd edn., London and New York, Routledge.

Kashima, Y., Foddy, M., and Platow, M. J. (eds) (2002) *Self and identity: personal, social, and symbolic.* Mahwah, N. J., Erlbaum.

Latour, B. (1993) *We have never been modern.* Cambridge, Mass., Harvard University Press.

Lull, V. (2000) Death and society: a Marxist approach. *Antiquity* 74(285), 576–80.

Montgomery, J. (2010) Passports from the past: investigating human dispersals using strontium isotope analysis of tooth enamel. *Annals of Human Biology* 37(3), 325–46.

Murphy, E. M. (2011) Children's burial grounds in Ireland (Cillini) and parental emotions toward infant death. *International Journal of Historical Archaeology* 15(3), 409–28.

Pluciennik, M. (1999) Archaeological narratives and other ways of telling. *Current Anthropology* 40 (5), 653–78.

Price, T. D., Manzanilla, L., and Middleton, W. D. (2000) Immigration and the ancient city of Teotihuacan in Mexico: a study using strontium isotope ratios in human bone and teeth. *Journal of Archaeological Science* 27(10), 903–13.

Reimers, E. (1999) Death and identity: graves and funerals as cultural communication. *Mortality* 4(2), 147–66.

Richards, M. P. and Schulting, R. J. (2006) Touch not the fish: the Mesolithic–Neolithic change of diet and its significance. *Antiquity* 80 (308), 444–56.

Simon, B. (2004) *Identity in modern society: a social psychological perspective.* Oxford, Blackwell.

Sørensen, T. F. (2010) A saturated void: anticipating and preparing presence in contemporary Danish cemetery culture. In M. Bille, F. Hastrup, and T.F. Sørensen (eds) *An anthropology of absence: materializations of transcendence and loss*, 115–30. New York, Springer Science+Business Media.

Sørensen, T. F. and Bille, M. (2008) Flames of transformation: the role of fire in cremation practices. *World Archaeology* 40 (2), 253–67.

Spector, J. D. (1991) What this awl means: toward a feminist archaeology. In J. M. Gero (ed.) *Engendering archaeology: women and prehistory*, 388–406. Oxford, Blackwell.

Tarlow, S. (2000) Emotion in archaeology. *Current Anthropology* 41(5), 713–46.

Thomas, J. (2004) Archaeology's place in modernity. *Modernism-Modernity* 11(1), 17–34.

Turner, B. L., Kamenov, G.D., Kingston, J.D. and Armelagos, G.J. (2009) Insights into immigration and social class at Machu Picchu, Peru based on oxygen, strontium, and lead isotopic analysis. *Journal of Archaeological Science* 36(2), 317–32.

White, C., Longstaffe, F. J., and Law, K. R. (2004) Exploring the effects of environment, physiology and diet on oxygen isotope ratios in ancient Nubian bones and teeth. *Journal of Archaeological Science* 31(2), 233–50.

White, C. D., Spence, M. W., Stuart-Williams, H. L. Q., and Schwarcz, H .P. (1998) Oxygen isotopes and the identification of geographical origins: the Valley of Oaxaca versus the Valley of Mexico. *Journal of Archaeological Science* 25(7), 643–55.

16

CONCLUDING THOUGHTS. EXPANDING IDENTITY: ARCHAEOLOGY, THE HUMANITIES, AND THE SOCIAL SCIENCES

T. L. Thurston

Introduction

The concept of identity, once limited to mid-20th-century neo-Freudian psychological studies of personality, has in a much-altered form spread like wildfire over the last decades, through both the humanities and the social sciences. With each discipline it has penetrated, it takes on new meanings and provokes new methods of study. While authors in the Humanities, such as literary criticism, philosophy or history, frequently use the word, the way in which it is conceptualized is often based on an individual author's interpretation of how people perceive their own ethnicity, gender, or class, and by extension, the author's interpretation is extrapolated to a group, a generation, a nation. Did Shakespeare's characterization of Othello reflect the Early Modern perspective on African identity? A number of humanists have suggested this, and it equates more or less with the dictionary definition of identity: a sort of 'essential' quality that defines a person or a thing. Needless to say, the social sciences reject most types of essentialism, and also seek clearer definitions of concepts like identity. How would a social scientist go about studying not simply identity, but identity in the archaeological record?

Initially, I grew interested in this topic when listening to scholarly assertions that certain events would naturally provoke a universal response in human beings – a tacitly acknowledged notion that there are some things we can assume about human identity behaviors no matter how deep or far we dive into the past. In fact, there *are* some general behaviors that *can* be so assumed, at least as a starting place for investigation, because they are cognitive rather than cultural responses, having to do with the architecture of our brains and the structure of our limbic systems. Yet we cannot make such assumptions about just *any* set of phenomena, even if in our own minds they seem to be deeply inherent behaviors. In the following brief discussion, I hope to outline some background in areas of interest for which social science research can facilitate our envisioning, and hence investigation, of prehistories less like our own 'imaginaries', and more grounded in what actually might have happened in the past.

Identity in the social sciences

European archaeology has roots in the humanities, and is usually housed in Faculties of philosophy, religion, history, and the like, which by definition are populated by scholars who celebrate a single social entity or cultural region. Anthropology, the home discipline of American archaeology, is a cross-culturally comparative social science, partnered with sociology, economics, political science, psychology, and other disciplines that seek answers to broad questions about the human condition, not limited to a single cultural context, but nevertheless rooted in specific case studies. While the ways in which we have understood and studied identity have in the past been quite different, these various threads of archaeology have now reached a point of convergence on the general ways in which we define it.

To reiterate a common current trope for *identity*, outlined many times in previous chapters, identity operates on many levels: individual and group; impacted by ethnicity, class, status, occupation, age and gender; tied to the local, the regional, the transcontinental. Individuals participate in all of these nested scales of interaction at the same time, putting on different identity hats, or combinations thereof, as context requires or demands, or merely as the individual is moved. While individual identity is always interesting if one can find it archaeologically, getting at group identity is often our goal, and the current complex of transnational, migratory, and hybridized identities in our own time has made it possible for us to understand that past eras were rife with cosmopolitan interactions and likely to have echoed such conditions. This has, of course, complicated archaeological research a great deal.

Humanists often use the term *identity* as a general way of indicating the impact of experience on the individual, and how it affects the attitudes they hold. This approach works well in many settings, including as an overarching metaphor for an archaeological context. Archaeologists, however, in addition to framing and situating a study – and no matter what their theoretical orientation – usually also wish to identify and understand something 'real' about past human experience, even if it is admittedly very little, overly broad (or narrow), and contingent upon the next set of findings.

Yet now that scholars across the archaeological disciplines largely share the social science definition of 'identity' as a phenomenon, what do we do with it? Do we simply add it to our introductory paragraphs, describe some aspects of material culture or landscape patterning and end with a recap of what identity means? Or do we use current understanding of the behaviors attached to identity, and the issues created by identity, to frame research questions we may wish to prosecute through the archaeological record?

As a way of interpreting data in search of specific social conditions, political trajectories, and supernatural cosmologies, social science research aims for a more predictive and replicable method of studying intangibles like identity. For archaeologists, this means identifying research involving cognitive, rather than cultural behaviors, since culturally molded performances vary enough in the contemporary world to make them totally inappropriate for comparison with the past – the main critique of their use. Cognitive effects though work similarly in any person or group with whom we share a brain structure, and thus are possible to consider in the past. This means we might carefully compare the material remains of what we know are cognitive-related past 'behaviors' with the contemporary research findings of psychologists, economists, sociologists, political scientists, and the like. The interpretation of such findings is based on the archaeological understanding of a time and place, while the meaning of the inferred behaviors can be infused with insights from the present.

Social science approaches to identity

With a few notable exceptions (*e.g.* Diaz-Andreu *et al.* 2005; Jones 1997), it is most typical for archaeologists to cite other archaeologists on issues of identity, or refer to a few now-classic ethnographic contributions such as Barth (1969) or Epstein (1978). Such oldies are goodies, but have seen too much citation that simply reiterates the notion that identity cannot be classified as an innate primordial urge (Hall 1996). Furthermore, ethnography is extremely useful for identity studies, but the concept did not originate there, nor is the wealth of more recent social science research housed only there. I begin by examining a number of social science approaches to identity that are less familiar to most archaeologists, and outline the ways in which recent scholars specifically study the *behaviors* associated with identity, as they relate to what we are likely to think, feel and do in reaction to our sense of our own and others' identity.

The identification of appropriate cognitive behaviors that leave material traces or patterns is the key to approaching past thought and feeling without falling into the trap of the subjective imaginary. Early research associated with identity, as we understand it now, often originates in psychology. The figure most credited with developing the identity concept was Eriksen, whose mid-century work on developmental psychology (1993; 1991) was focused on understanding the development of children and youth, both within a given social system, and as human beings with broadly shared biology. One of Eriksen's key findings was that personal identity was often articulated with a person's implicit belief that their worldview is shared by their society: 'a sense of being and becoming' as a group (Burke 2003,1), which when threatened by discontinuity, can cause 'identity crises'. While this is an individual experience, it is group phenomenon as age, gender, kinship, or other cohorts experienced continuities and discontinuities as peers. Eriksonian concepts are directly ancestral to the contemporary work on gender identity by Streitmatter (1997; 1993), ethnicity and ethnic conflict by Horowitz (2001; 1985) and Fowler (2001; 1995) on religious identity, among many others.

The identity concept is also found in sociology, political science, and anthropology, here as a self-aware and self-interested group-held notion, used to achieve goals and objectives. The *social constructivist* notion of identity as based on a person or group's interests and goals, which can change as the goals or conditions themselves change, remains an important concept in modern identity studies. The sociologist Erving Goffman (1959), drawing on the notion of self-awareness and group membership, developed a theory of *interaction ritual*, which located identity firmly in an individual's relationships to groups. Individuals enact roles for a cultural audience of family, peers, and authorities, and he argued that they constructed themselves through the roles they play to gain each other's approval and acceptance, sometimes masking inner realities that differ drastically from expectations, a dis-integration of the self into public and private roles.

Stryker's *symbolic interactionism* (1981) continued Goffman's themes and is still an important approach to identity. Symbolic interactionism assumes that social roles are not mere descriptors or categories, but are made up of meanings, experienced somewhat differently by each person yet also generally shared by a culture. This mutual understanding enables the individual and the wider culture to create stable expectations of culturally acceptable behavior. On one level identity is defined by an individual role: kinship, occupation, and affiliation; on another level identity is rooted in social groups: nationality, ethnicity, and level of education. Finally, identity is shaped through interior personality traits that others may not know or understand: loyalty, fearfulness, self-involvement, and the like. All are coterminous, and symbolic interactionism posits that we are bound into society through a simultaneous societal, external identity assignment and our own self-labeling. Stryker finally noted that sociality is created through enactment of roles through time: negotiation, modification, and development. As with Giddens' *structuration*, identity is recursive, society shapes our identity, which we hold, use, and turn back to renew the shape of society.

In the 1960s and 70s, the *instrumentalist* ethnographer A. I. Hallowell (*e.g.* 1976; 1955) popularized the notion that symbolizing self-aware human beings could appraise themselves as members of their own groups, asking themselves if they were living up to moral and ethical responsibilities to their communities, motivated by avoidance of shame or failure. Direct inheritors of this perspective include identity and ethnicity theorist Abner Cohen (1974; 1969) and his many contemporary descendants, such as economist Edward Miguel (Miguel 2009; Miguel and Gugerty 2005), who studies the interaction of national identities with regional economies, and sociologist H. C. White (White 1992; White and Godart 2007) whose 'network' approach attempts to overthrow old *political economy* models for social movements. White argues that it is not 'persons' but groups who collectively and with self-awareness claim an 'identity', construed as a web or network of practices locked in by the pressures of the social environment.

Cognition, replication and predictability

While explorations of identity as an abstract notion, or of identity in particular societies, are helpful for characterizing the past, I will now focus on studies that are somewhat different in nature. These are usually classified as behavioral: behavioral economics, behavioral psychology, behavioral organization, and the like. They deal with generalizations made from work with sizeable groups, in an attempt to characterize broader impacts and responses. While the social and cultural parameters of the subjects under study may differ from those of prehistoric people, they are usually cross-cultural, either by design or by virtue of the large number of scholars working on the same problems, and are held constant for variables that would skew the data based on the respondent's social milieu. They are, in fact, meant to get at cognitive issues, not cultural ones. Certainly, many notions about ancient people's identity cannot be based on inferences from contemporary social science research alone, yet if they get us thinking about possibilities, or provide lines of investigation by further archaeological means, they are worth looking at.

A full exploration of all such studies that might be relevant to archaeological research could encompass an entire volume; here I will only mention one body of theory – *social identity theory* as outlined by Tajfel and Turner (1985; 1979) and refined by many authors, (*e.g.* Burke 2003; Chemers 2001; Hogg 2007; Grint 1997; Northhouse 2007). Social identity is the portion of a person's identity that lies in understanding of their membership in broader social groups. The phenomena linked to these perceptions are statistically replicable at very high levels cross-culturally, in both set experiments and in natural societal settings. The original theory deals with intergroup conflict between high-status and low-status elements, how people pass from lower to higher status groups, and under what conditions social or even violent conflict is avoided or fomented. A wealth of pre- and protohistoric cultural and regional interactions can be framed along these lines, and test implications imagined for different sorts of interactive settings.

The initial hypotheses of social identity theory were tested by examining minority groups, and/or groups with low social statuses (majority or minority) in many contexts. The theory was able to predict behaviors within and between groups, based on the way in which people understood a number of factors. The first is *legitimacy*: acceptance of a given hierarchy of statuses among groups. The second is *stability*: how predictable and lasting the hierarchy of statuses is. *Status* refers to the self-assigned and non-self-assigned prestige or standing of the group within broader society (not necessarily the same), and finally *permeability* refers to the ability of individuals to move into other, higher status groups, *i.e.* the level of acceptance for outsiders joining the ranks of the more privileged.

Using the concept of two poles bracketing a continuum, Tajfel and Turner (1979) modelled 'social mobility' versus 'social change' societies. In doing so, they postulate that in the 'social mobility' model, individuals have the possibility of mobility through 'talent, hard work, good luck, or whatever other means'(*ibid.*, 35), and thus when they become mobile they do so as individuals, taking only their kin along the path to more success (of whatever culturally-defined type they seek). The other end of the spectrum is a society where people are largely locked into a status, perhaps a slave, caste or rigid class society, or even one where mobility is theoretically possible but economic or social conditions (ethnicity, 'race', age, gender, educational deficit, or other biases) effectively prevent mobility, or cause a perception of immobility. In this type of situation, people do not expect to interact or 'rise' as individuals but expect their 'group' to deal largely with other groups. This model is called the 'social change' model, since suppressed groups see fundamental or significant social change as the only way of improving their status.

The tipping point for when a suppressed group moves from willingness to preserve the status quo to actively fomenting a social movement aimed at major change is complex – too complex to fully deal with here, but is nevertheless directly related to people's perception of 'permeability' – conditions in which there are ways to move from their low status group into any higher status group. Even in wretched conditions, the status quo may be upheld if only the false perception (or false consciousness) of such permeability is present. Additionally, the more conflicted the relationship, the more rigid and impermeable the boundaries become, and the more uniform the response of individuals in such low status groups will be toward higher status groups. Solidarity and uniformity of behavior within the 'ingroup' rises with antagonism toward the 'outgroup'. Furthermore, ingroup members come to see the outgroup as a faceless mass of antagonists as opposed to individuals.

Some of this may seem intuitive, but it is not. It is overwhelmingly statistically upheld, and only became understood as a function of institutional structures and social interactions when this research was initially conducted in the 1970s. From this, it follows that if one can identify ingroups and outgroups, and characterize the level and type of their interactions, one can hypothetically characterize the psychological and emotional nature of their interactions, plus the likelihood that the low status ingroup is willing to take steps to foment significant social change, reform, or rebellion.

Since the original research was done, much has been added to it, creating a dynamic and contemporary perspective. One major area of application could be of great interest to archaeologists: the emergence of leaders interpreted through social identity theory. A vast corpus of work (*e.g.* Hogg 2001) uses the notion of ingroup–outgroup relations as described above to understand how leadership emerges and functions in societies where the group that one belongs to (any type of group: kin, political, occupational, religious, social) is extremely important for social relations.

A number of recent studies focus on statistically replicable data that predict the reasons why people support the emergence of a leader, whether in a consensus-based society or a hierarchic setting such as a military context, where support, if not choice of a leader, is at issue. Such 'leader emergence' work uses the concepts of dominance, the ability to influence others, self-monitoring, the ability of leaders to reflect upon their relative standing among followers or potential followers, and prototypicality: the level and extent to which the potential leader embodies or exhibits behaviors, or values approved by the group at local and 'national' levels (Brodbeck *et al.* 2000; Dickson *et al.* 2006), and reflects or mirrors, in microcosm, how the group characterizes itself. Others have examined not only how the leader is held to a prototype by followers, but how followers are targeted and recruited by leaders using group prototypical traits to assess how a follower will fit in (*e.g.* Pierro *et al.* 2005; van Knippenberg *et al.* 2005).

The *perception* of whether a leader is fair and honest is a constantly significant factor in such studies, leading to so-called leadership categorization theory (*e.g.* Lord *et al.* 1984) and implicit leadership theory (*e.g.* Lord and Maher 1991). Other work focuses more specifically on the type of qualities common to leaders who gain real support from followers, such as intelligence, skill, and charismatic personality (Cha and Edmondson 2006; Dasborough and Ashkanasy 2002; Judge *et al.* 2004a; Lord and Hall 2005,). A longstanding debate has continued over whether a group's notion of good leadership qualities is a long-term stable concept, or one that rapidly fluctuates or changes. Recent cognitive models address this by examining the way in which individuals mentally represent key leadership concepts (Lord *et al.* 2001) that allow for 'both the stability of leadership concepts and their changeability over time and across contexts, based on connectionist approaches to the modeling of cognitive architecture'.

A very important and quite new concept is that of organizational 'sense-making': attempts by a leader to change the attitudes and beliefs of their followers. Ethnographic studies (*e.g.* Pratt 2000) have revealed that there is a high success rate among leaders that purposefully 'break' the sense or logic of their own follower's beliefs, in order make them 'seek' for new sensibilities or meanings, because this typically increases their solidarity with their leader's society or organization. Even more remarkable is the current research that distinguishes hierarchical, top-down sense-making leadership from bottom-up processes coming up from other echelons: lower level leaders or even ordinary people (Balogun and Johnson 2004; Maitlis 2005).

These broad areas of study purposefully include studies of cross-cultural variations in order to reduce or eliminate the likelihood that the outcomes are cultural; they appear to be largely cognitive and thus generally predicable for the present and perhaps the past (Ensari and Murphy 2003). In considering, for example, the heterarchic nature of Iron Age societies in Germanic and Celtic Europe, with their rulers, assemblies and judiciaries, the understanding of how such cross-culturally significant and ubiquitous factors work could be of great interest. Similarly, in approaching the origins of formal, structured leadership and political institutions that emerged in the course of the Holocene, the consideration of such phenomena with cognitive, and thus more likely consistent factors would be interesting.

As a final example, recent studies have been carried out on groups that specifically are immigrants into host societies: what might this tell us, for instance, about the experience of identity in the context of ancient trade diasporas, colonialism, and imperialism? Terry *et al.* (2006) sought to understand what perceptions impact the identity of 'outsiders' or foreigners who find themselves in unfamiliar lands surrounded by people of a host culture. Do they easily move into new social circles, have difficulty in doing so, or do responses vary? The answers to pre- and protohistoric questions found in such studies might in fact lead us in quite different directions and with more authority than we now have. Again using concepts and expectations of social identity theory (Tajfel and Turner 1985; 1979), Terry *et al.* (2006) first confirmed what might perhaps seem intuitive to any thoughtful researcher: the status of the visitors' national/group identities (high or low) as viewed *by the host society*, had enormous impacts on the visitor's feelings of inclusion or exclusion, and in turn on their behavior.

Yet there were other factors that are far more difficult to intuit, if possible at all. These were contingent first upon whether *they themselves* believed that the statuses they were labeled with were legitimate, and second, on whether they felt that group boundaries were permeable, permitting socialization with groups among their hosts. Generally, foreigners adjusted and performed better psychologically, socioculturally, and in terms of productivity if they understood that the host society viewed them as people of high status, and vice versa – adjusting poorly if viewed as low-status.

However, if *they themselves* accepted the legitimacy of a low-status designation, negative feelings were mitigated by any perceived ability to penetrate other groups. The ability to cross social boundaries and interact with other groups counteracted the negative feelings and resulted in good adjustment, despite awareness and acceptance of low status.

If however, they rejected the legitimacy of a low-status designation by the hosts, they did not adjust well at all. In other words, they were affected by the dissonance between their self-perception as worthy of respect and high status, and the more negative pSerception of their hosts. In this case, it did not matter if they could penetrate other groups or cross group boundaries – it had no relation to a positive adjustment. Resentment at being categorized differently than they categorized themselves led to negative perceptions and self-isolation.

What is the significance of such research for those of us concerned with pre- and protohistoric contexts? Imagine for example, the purported relations between Greeks and Celts during the founding of Masillia. It is often assumed that a primary factor in intercultural and colonial interactions was how the Greeks felt about themselves as colony-planters, as a superior or dominant faction. Through this application of social identity theory, we discover that this is not a given, and in some conditions might be unlikely. An intrusive group's self-assessment is only part, and not the biggest part of their self-image and resultant behavior.

Did the local inhabitants see the migrants as high or higher than themselves in status?

During the hegemony of the 'Hellenization' model perhaps, but this is now a discredited and discarded model. It is more likely that they were regarded as equal or lower in status. If the Greeks accepted this *and* they could interact with locals socially, they would have been successful. If they did not accept the legitimacy of the local 'label' of lower status, their ability to penetrate socially would not have mattered. They would have been ill-adjusted and perhaps less successful in the establishment of their enclave and their colonial undertakings.

A broad study of many aggregated individuals, with other variables held constant, shows that strangers in a host society who experience such cognitive dissonance in terms of status may become hostile, angry, and isolated. We could infer from this that those immigrants or inhabitants of enclaves who display material disintegration from wider circles might be experiencing such identity dissonance, have failed to socialize across boundaries, and have isolated themselves. Given the cognitive response of contemporary people, we might ask if our archaeological subjects were failing to thrive in the host society's context, despite the fact that they perceived themselves as a group worthy of respect. The archaeological data itself would need to be carefully assessed to evaluate these different possibilities, perhaps suggesting different directions for study.

A useful addition to current archaeological theory

In the past, broad proclamations about the human condition that emanated from the humanities were often harshly critiqued by social scientists (MacDonald 1994; Rojek and Turner 2000; Rosenau 1991,168) for extrapolating too broadly and often inaccurately from single case or minimal number case studies, largely with the goal of bolstering extant interpretations. Additionally, scientistic, statistical 'model-building' using decontextualized generalizations were also highly critiqued as pointless constructs of things that only exist hypothetically. These were both valid critiques in their day. Perhaps the value of such extrapolations – one inductive from the specific to the general, the other deductive from the generalized to the specific – can both benefit from comparing or contrasting case studies with broader analyses comprising larger databases. The author is not the first to suggest that topics such as identity formation, ethnicity, and other socially constructed phenomena benefit from a blended theoretical and methodological framework. There was a time when these two perspectives were seen as incompatible, but that time is largely over.

The types of identity of interest to archaeologists are many and varied; I have limited my observations to a few general principles. Yet these and many others can be used to understand the past on a number of levels. Rose has asked us (1996,133) to think about what *codes of knowledge* 'support and valorize' particular social 'traits' and anticipate production of various human personas. While especially noting that every society embraces a heterogeneous notion of what is preferable, acceptable, and tolerable, this refers to the fact that the socialization of humans within their respective groups is a complex of conscious and unconscious strategies for producing a person who will take a recognized place within society. The combination of informed insight from the humanist perspective combined with replicable deductive outcomes and/or studies of cognition, the architecture of the human brain, and how individuals and groups understand and manipulate their social milieus, may illuminate the causes, meanings and markers of identity.

References

Balogun, J. and Johnson, G. (2004) Organizational restructuring and middle manager sensemaking. *The Academy of Management Journal* 47, 523–49.

Barth, F. (1969) *Ethnic groups and boundaries. The social organization of culture difference.* Oslo, Universitetsforlaget.

Brodbeck, F. C., Frese, M., Akerblom, S., Audia, G., Bakacsi, G., Bendova, H., Bodega, D., Bodur, M., Booth, S., Brenk, K., Castel, P., Den Hartog, D., Donnelly-Cox, G., Gratchev, M. V., Holmberg, I., Jarmuz, S., Correia Jesuino, J., Jorbenadse, R., Kabasakal, H. E., Keatingm M., Kipiani, G., Konrad, E., Koopman, P., Kurc, A., Leeds, C., Lindell, M., Maczynski, J., Martin, G., O'Connell, J., Papalexandris, A., Papalexandris, N., Prieto, J. M., Rakitski, B., Reber, G., Sabadin, A., Schramm-Nielsen, J., Schultz, M., Sigfrids, C., Szabo, E., Thierry, H., Vondrysova, M., Weibler, J., Wilderom, C., Witkowski, S., and Winderer, R. (2000) Cultural variation of leadership prototypes across 22 European countries. *Journal of Occupational and Organizational Psychology* 73, 1–29.

Burke, J. P. (2003) *Advances in identity theory and research.* Springer, New York.

Cha, S. E. and Edmondson A. C. (2006) When values backfire: leadership, attribution, and disenchantment in a values-driven organization. *The Leadership Quarterly* 17, 57–78.

Chemers, M. M. (2001) Leadership effectiveness: an integrative review. In M. A. Hogg and R. S. Tindale (eds) *Blackwell handbook of social psychology: group processes*, 376–99. Oxford, Blackwell.

Cohen, A. (1969) *Custom and politics in Urban Africa: a study of Hausa Migrants in a Yoruba Town.* London, Routledge and Kegan Paul.

Cohen, A. (1974) *Two-dimensional man: An essay on power and symbolism in complex society.* London, Routledge and Kegan Paul.

Dasborough M. T and Ashkanasy N. M. (2002) Emotion and attribution of intentionality in leader member relationships. *The Leadership Quarterly* 13, 615–34.

Díaz-Andreu, M. and Lucy, S. (2005) Introduction. In M. Diaz-Andreu, S. Lucy, S. Babic and D. Edwards (eds) *The archaeology of identity*, 1–12. London, Routledge.

Dickson, M. W., Resick, C. J., and Hanges, P. J. (2006) Systematic variation in organizationally-shared cognitive prototypes of effective leadership based on organizational form. *The Leadership Quarterly* 17, 487–505.

Ensari, N. and Murphy, S. E. (2003) Cross-cultural variations in leadership perceptions and attribution of charisma to the leader. *Organizational Behavior and Human Decision Processes* 92, 52–66.

Epstein, A. L. (1978) *Ethos and identity: three studies in ethnicity.* London, Tavistock Publications.

Eriksen, T. H. (1991) The cultural contexts of ethnic differences. *Man* 26, 127–44.

Eriksen, T. H. (1993) *Ethnicity and nationalism: anthropological perspectives.* London, Pluto.

Fowler, J. W. (1995) *Stages of faith: the psychology of human development.* New York, Harper Collins.

Fowler, J. W. (2001) Faith development, theory and the postmodern challenges. *International Journal for the Psychology of Religion* 11(3), 159–72.

Goffman, E. (1959) *The presentation of self in everyday life.* New York, Doubleday.

Grint, K. (1997) *Leadership: classical, contemporary and critical approaches.* Oxford, Oxford University Press.

Hall. S. (1996) Who needs identity? In S. Hall and P. du Gay (eds) *Questions of cultural identity*, 1–17. London, Sage.

Hallowell, A. I. (1955) *Culture and experience.* Philadelphia, University of Pennsylvania Press.

Hallowell, A. I. (1976) *Contributions to anthropology: selected papers.* Chicago, University of Chicago Press.

Hogg, M. A. (2001) A social identity theory of leadership. *Personality and Social Psychology Review* 5(3), 184–200.

Hogg, M. A. (2007) Social psychology of leadership. In A. W. Kruglanski and E. T. Higgins (eds) *Social psychology: a handbook of basic principles* (2nd ed.). New York, Guilford.

Horowitz, D. L. (1985). *Ethnic groups in conflict.* Berkeley, University of California Press.

Horowitz, D. L. (2001) *The deadly ethnic riot.* Berkeley, University of California Press.

Jones, S. (1997) *The archaeology of ethnicity: constructing identities in the past and present.* London, Routledge.

Judge, T. A., Colbert, A. E. and Ilies, R. (2004) Intelligence and leadership: a quantitative review and test of theoretical propositions. *Journal of Applied Psychology* 89, 542–52.

Lord, R. and Maher, K. (1991) *Leadership and information processing: linking perceptions and processes.* Boston, Unwin & Hyman.

Lord, R. G., Brown, D. J., Harvey, J. L. and Hall, R. J. (2001) Contextual constraints on prototype generation and their multilevel consequences for leadership perceptions. *The Leadership Quarterly* 12, 311–38.

Lord, R. G., Foti, R. J. and Devader, C. L. (1984) A test of leadership categorization theory: internal structure, information-processing, and leadership perceptions. *Organizational Behavior and Human Decision Processes* 34, 343–78.

Lord, R. G. and Hall, R. J. (2005) Identity, deep structure and the development of leadership skill. *The Leadership Quarterly* 16, 591–615.

MacDonald, S. P. (1994) *Professional academic writing in the humanities and social* sciences. Illinois, Southern Illinois University Press.

Maitlis S. (2005) The social processes of organizational sensemaking. *The Academy of Management Journal* 48, 21–49.

Miguel, E. (2009) *Africa's Turn?* Boston, MIT Press.

Miguel, E. and Gugerty, M. K. (2005) Ethnic diversity, social sanctions, and public goods in Kenya. *Journal of Public Economics* 89, 2325–68.

Northhouse, P. G. (2007) *Leadership, theory and practice* (3rd ed.). California, Thousands Oaks, Sage.

Pierro, A., Cicero, L., Bonaiuto, M., van Knippenberg, D. and Kruglansk, A. W. (2005) Leader group prototypicality and leadership effectiveness: the moderating role of need for cognitive closure. *The Leadership Quarterly* 16, 503–16.

Pratt M. G. (2000) The good, the bad, and the ambivalent: managing identification among Amway distributors. *Administrative Science Quarterly* 45, 456–93.

Rojek, C. and B. Turner (2000) Decorative sociology: towards a critique of the cultural turn. *The Sociological Review* 48(4), 629–48.

Rose, N. (1996) Identity, genealogy, history. In S. Hall and P. du Gay (eds) *Questions of cultural identity*, 128–50. London, Sage.

Rosenau, P. M. (1991) *Post-modernism and the social sciences: insights, inroads, and intrusions*. Princeton, Princeton University Press.

Streitmatter, J. (1997) An exploratory study of risk-taking and attitudes in a girls-only middle school math class. *The Elementary School Journal* 98(1), 15–26.

Streitmatter, J. (1993) Gender differences in identity development: an examination of longitudinal data. *Adolescence* 28(109), 55–66.

Stryker, S. (1981) *Symbolic interactionism: a social structural version.* Menlo Park, Benjamin Cummings.

Tajfel, H. and Turner, J. C. (1979) An integrative theory of intergroup conflict. In W. G. Austin and S. Worchel (eds) *The social psychology of intergroup relations*, 33–47. California, Monterey, Brooks/Cole.

Tajfel, H. and Turner, J. C. (1985) The social identity theory of intergroup behavior. In S. Worchel (ed.) *Psychology of intergroup relations*, 7–24. University of Michigan, Nelson-Hall Publishers.

Terry, D. J. Pelly, R. N. Lalonde and J. R. Smith (2006) Predictors of cultural adjustment: intergroup status relations and boundary permeability. *Group Processes and Intergroup Relations* 9(2), 249–64.

van Knippenberg, B., van Knippenberg, D., De Cremer, D. and Hogg, M. A. (2005) Research in leadership, self, and identity: a sample of the present and a glimpse of the future. *The Leadership Quarterly* 16, 495–99.

White, H. C. (1992) *Identity and control: a Structural theory of social action*, Princeton, Princeton University Press.

White, H. C. and Godart, F. (2007) Stories from identity and control. *Sociologica* 3, 1–17.

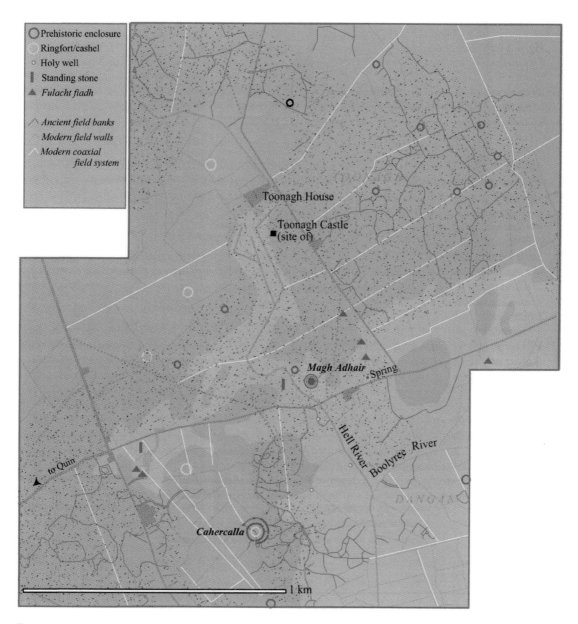

Figure 6.1: At Toonagh, southeast County Clare, the prehistoric landscape is substantially preserved and is concentrated on the thin, fertile, soils over plateaux of limestone bedrock (so-called 'rockland': stippled). An organic patchwork of small fields – defined by low earth and stone banks – with some well-defined access 'lanes' contains a reasonably evenly dispersed pattern of small domestic enclosures. Clusters of fulachta fiadh (burnt mounds) occur on the margins of wetland areas including those at 'Magh Adhair'; here a turlough (seasonal lake) remains largely dry during the late summer and early autumn, although water can be accessed by digging close to the surface. After heavy rain the turlough fills spectacularly when water gushes from the small rock cleft ('cave') on the edge of the basin. Magh Adhair appears to have been a ceremonial enclosure in late prehistory, defined by a substantial ditch and external bank, possibly with an internal mound. The area around this, on the edge of the Hell River, appears to have been artificially levelled to create a wide flat apron. In the early medieval period, Magh Adhair became associated with the Dál gCais, and later the Uí Briain kings of Thomond.

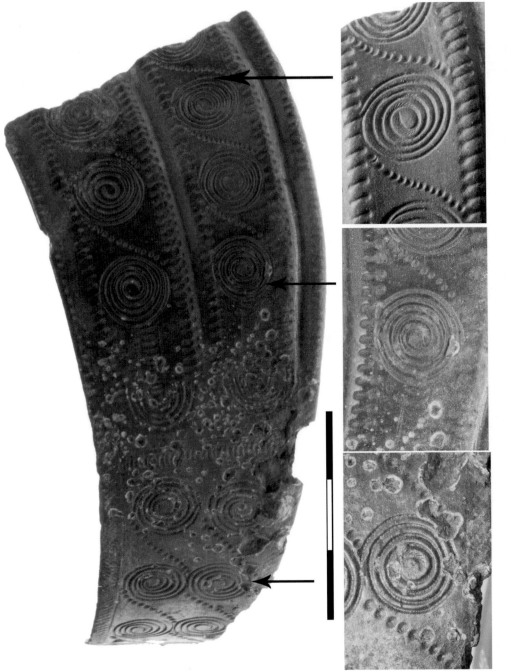

Figure 9.1: The neck collar from Weitgendorf I, Kr. Priegnitz (MM II8269) in Mecklenburg shows a recognizable sequence of crafting steps.

Figure 10.2: Aerial view of Beaghmore stone circle complex, County Tyrone (Tyr 020:004) (Courtesy of the Northern Ireland Environment Agency).

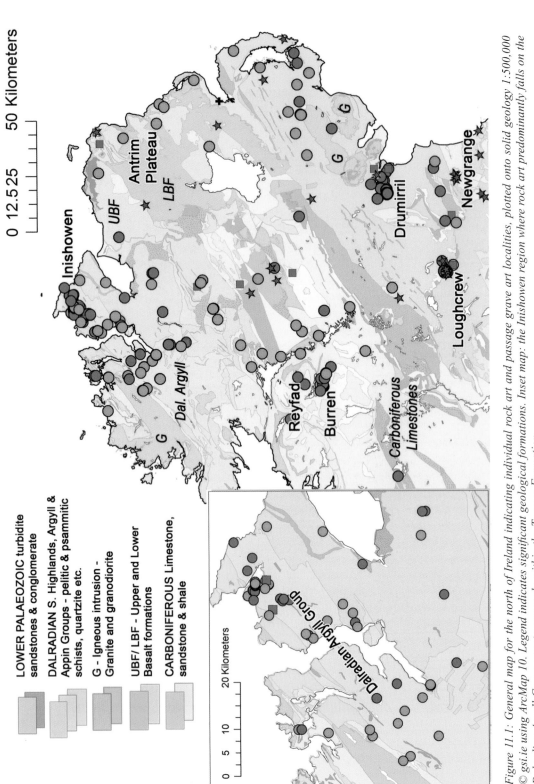

Figure 11.1: General map for the north of Ireland indicating individual rock art and passage grave art localities, plotted onto solid geology 1:500,000 © gsi.ie using ArcMap 10. Legend indicates significant geological formations. Inset map: the Inishowen region where rock art predominantly falls on the Dalradian Argyll Group, most commonly within the Termon Formation.

LOWER PALAEOZOIC turbidite sandstones & conglomerate

DALRADIAN S. Highlands, Argyll & Appin Groups - pelitic & psammitic schists, quartzite etc.

G - Igneous intrusion - Granite and granodiorite

UBF/ LBF - Upper and Lower Basalt formations

CARBONIFEROUS Limestone, sandstone & shale

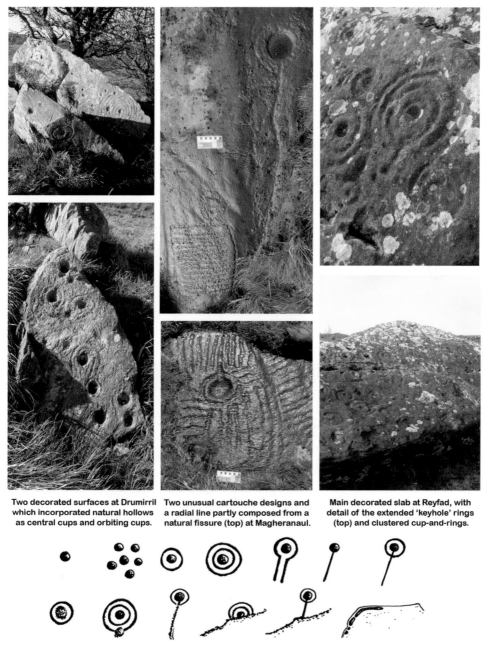

Two decorated surfaces at Drumirril which incorporated natural hollows as central cups and orbiting cups.

Two unusual cartouche designs and a radial line partly composed from a natural fissure (top) at Magheranaul.

Main decorated slab at Reyfad, with detail of the extended 'keyhole' rings (top) and clustered cup-and-rings.

Common motifs: single cup, rosette, cup-and-ring, multiple cup-and-ring, extended 'keyhole' ring, tailed cup, radial cup-and-ring.

Common uses of natural features: natural depression as central cupmark, natural depression as orbiting cupmark, fissure employed as tail, fissure truncates motif, radial motif converges with fissure, lip (edge) enhanced with cups/ gutter.

Figure 11.3: Rock art motifs encountered at the study sites of Drumirril, Magheranaul and Reyfad, and common motifs and incorporation of natural features into designs.

Figure 12.2: Photograph of elk figures of the silhouette/scooped style, which cluster together; and with other types of motif. Scooped elks are more likely to cluster than any other motif. This image is from Lillforshällan, Laxön, Nämforsen. Accompanied by a 3D reconstruction of the Lillforshällan panel.

Figure 12.4: Examples of unusual, experimental motifs at Laxön, Nämforsen. a) human-elk 'centaur' on DX, b) human-fish 'mermaid' hybrid on DX, c) boat merging into antlers of elk on F1. These motifs are often more isolated than other types of motif, though this alters across elevation.

Figure 14.2: Dacian reenactment members around the andesite sun at the site near Grădiştea de Munte (Sarmizegetusa Regia).